PREFACE

A substantial portion of the research for this monograph was carried out at the House of Lords Record Office and materials from that collection are printed with the permission of Maurice F. Bond, Clerk of the Records. He and H. S. Cobb, Assistant Clerk, have advised me on many points and made important corrections. I am grateful for their assistance and for the kindness and unfailing courtesy of F. C. R. Deacon and other members of the staff who preside over the Search Room. I have also worked with pleasure at the Library of the Inner Temple and wish to thank W. W. S. Breem, the Librarian, for his friendly help, and to express my appreciation to the Treasurer and Masters of the Bench for permission to photograph and to publish manuscripts in the Petyt collection. My thanks go to Jean Preston, Curator of Manuscripts at the Huntington Library, who greatly facilitated my work there and has authorized quotation of documents in the Ellesmere collection. For permission to use other material I am grateful to the Folger Shakespeare Library (Washington, D. C.), to the Cambridge University Library, to James M. Osborn of Yale University, to the Yale Center for Parliamentary History, and to the Trustees of the British Museum. Crown-copyright records in the Public Record Office have been quoted by permission of the Controller of H.M. Stationery Office. I have relied on Esther S. Cope in a number of ways, on Caroline Robbins, J. C. Sainty, William Huse Dunham, Jr., Sheila Lambert, Allida L. Shuman, Catherine Drinker Bowen, Edward C. K. Read and Benjamin R. Foster. Marie Burtenshaw typed many versions of the manuscript with scrupulous care.

In presenting seventeenth-century material, I have normally modernized spelling and capitalization. Roman numerals have been exchanged for arabic, and occasionally contractions expanded to clarify meaning. Punctuation has sometimes been simplified, but on the whole changed very little.

E. R. F.

Bryn Mawr College
May 1972

ABBREVIATIONS

Add.: Additional manuscripts, British Museum, London.
Berkowitz: Berkowitz, David S. "Young Mr. Selden," unpublished Ph.D. thesis, Harvard University.
Bond, "Acts of Parliament": Bond, Maurice F. 1958. "Acts of Parliament. Some Notes on the Original Acts Preserved at the House of Lords, their Use and Interpretation." *Archives* 3, 20.
Bond, "Clerks of the Parliaments": Bond, Maurice F. 1958. "Clerks of the Parliaments, 1509–1953." *English Historical Review* 73.
Bond, "Formation of the Archives": Bond, Maurice F. 1957. "The Formation of the Archives of Parliament, 1497–1691." *Journal of the Society of Archivists* 1, 6.
Braye: Manuscripts formerly in the possession of Lord Braye, now scattered.
C.J.: *Journals of the House of Commons*. 1803—(51 v., London). California.
Clarke: Clarke, M. V. 1936. *Medieval Representation and Consent* (London).
Coke, *Fourth Institute*: Coke, Sir Edward. 1681. *The Fourth Part of the Institutes of the Laws of England* (London).
Commons Debates 1621: Notestein, Wallace; F. H. Relf; Hartley Simpson, eds. 1935. *Commons Debates 1621* (7 v., New Haven).
Commons Debates 1629: Notestein, Wallace and Frances Helen Relf, eds. 1921. *Commons Debates for 1629* (Minneapolis).

Cottoni Posthuma: Howell, James, ed. 1672. *Cottoni Posthuma: Divers Choice Pieces of that renowned Antiquary Sir Robert Cotton* (London).
D'Ewes: D'Ewes, Sir Simonds. 1682. *The Journals of all the Parliaments during the reign of Queen Elizabeth* (London).
El.: Ellesmere manuscripts. Huntington Library, San Marino, California.
Elsyng, *Manner of Holding Parliaments*: Elsynge, Henry. 1768. *The Manner of Holding Parliaments in England* (London).
Exact Abridgement: *An Exact Abridgement of the Records in the Tower . . . Collected by Sir Robert Cotton*. 1657 (London).
Foster, "Procedure in the House of Lords": Foster, Elizabeth Read. 1966. "Procedure in the House of Lords During the Early Stuart Period." *Journal of British Studies* 5, 2.
Foster, *Proceedings in Parliament 1610*: Foster, Elizabeth Read. 1966. *Proceedings in Parliament 1610* (2 v., New Haven).
Gardiner, *Commons Debates 1625*: Gardiner, Samuel Rawson, ed. 1873. *Debates in the House of Commons in 1625*. Camden Society, new series, 6 (London).
Gardiner, *Debates in the House of Lords 1621*: Gardiner, Samuel Rawson, ed. 1870. *Notes of the Debates in the House of Lords Officially taken by Henry Elsing, Clerk of the Parliaments, A.D. 1621*. Camden Society, first series, 103 (London).

Gardiner, *Debates in the House of Lords 1624:* Gardiner, Samuel Rawson, ed. 1879. *Notes of the Debates in the House of Lords Officially Taken by Henry Elsing, Clerk of the Parliaments, A.D. 1624 and 1626.* Camden Society, new series, **24** (London).

Gardiner, *History of England:* Gardiner, Samuel Rawson. 1899. *History of England from the Accession of James I to the Outbreak of the Civil War 1603–1642* (10 v., London).

Hakewill, *Manner of Passing Bills:* Hakewil, W. 1659. *The Manner How Statutes Are enacted in Parliament by Passing of Bills* (London).

Hale, *The Jurisdiction of the Lords House, or Parliament:* Hargrave, Francis, ed. 1796. *The Jurisdiction of the Lords House, or Parliament considered according to Ancient Records by Lord Chief Justice Hale* (London).

Harl.: Harleian manuscripts, British Museum, London.

Harl. Misc.: The Harleian Miscellany. 1810 (12 v., London).

The Hastings Journal: de Villiers, Lady, ed. 1953. *The Hastings Journal of the Parliament of 1621.* Camden Society, third series, **20** (London).

H.L.R.O.: House of Lords Record Office.

H.M.C. Buccleuch: Historical Manuscripts Commission. *Report on the Manuscripts of the Duke of Buccleuch & Queensberry.* 1926. **3**, **6** (London).

H.M.C. Fourth Report: Historical Manuscripts Commission. *Fourth Report of the Royal Commission on Historical Manuscripts. Part I.* 1874 (London).

H.M.C. Hastings: Historical Manuscripts Commission. **78**. *Report on the Manuscripts of the late Reginald Rawdon Hastings, Esq.* 1947. **4** (London).

H.M.C. Third Report: Historical Manuscripts Commission. *Third Report of the Royal Commission on Historical Manuscripts.* 1872 (London).

Hobart, *Reports:* Hobart, Sir Henry. 1671. *The Reports of the Reverend and Learned Judge, the Right Honorable Sr Henry Hobart* . . . (3rd edition, London).

Hooker: Vowell, John, *alias* Hooker. 1575 [?]. *The Order and Usage of the Keeping of a Parliament in England* . . . [Exeter ?]. All references are to the British Museum copy, said to have been printed in 1575.

Lapsley: Lapsley, Gaillard T. 1951. *Crown, Community and Parliament in the Later Middle Ages* (Oxford).

L.J.: *Journals of the House of Lords.* 1767– . (61 v., London).

Manuscripts of the House of Lords, **10**: Bond, M. F., ed. 1953. *Manuscripts of the House of Lords. 1712–1714.* **10**, new series (London).

Manuscripts of the House of Lords, **11**: Bond, M. F., ed. 1962. *The Manuscripts of the House of Lords. Addenda 1514–1714.* **11**, new series (London).

Neale, *Elizabeth I and Her Parliaments 1584–1601:* Neale, J. E. 1957. *Elizabeth I and Her Parliaments 1584–1601* (London).

Neale, "Proceedings in Parliament relative to . . . Mary Queen of Scots": Neale, J. E. 1920. "Proceedings in Parliament relative to the Sentence on Mary Queen of Scots." *English Historical Review* **35**.

Parchment Coll.: Parchment Collection, House of Lords Record Office.

Pettus: Pettus, Sir John. 1680. *The Constitution of Parliaments in England* (London).

Petyt: The Petyt Collection. Library of the Honourable Society of the Inner Temple, London.

Pike: Pike, Luke Owen. 1894. *A Constitutional History of the House of Lords* (London).

Pollard, "The Clerical Organization of Parliament": Pollard, A. F. 1942. "The Clerical Organization of Parliament." *English Historical Review* **57**.

Pollard, "The Clerk of the Crown": Pollard, A. F. 1942. "The Clerk of the Crown." *English Historical Review* **57**.

Powell and Wallis, *House of Lords in the Middle Ages:* Powell, J. Enoch and Keith Wallis. 1968. *The House of Lords in the Middle Ages* (London).

P.R.O.: Public Record Office.

Relf, *Debates in the House of Lords 1621:* Relf, Frances Helen, ed. 1929. *Notes of the Debates in the House of Lords Officially taken by Robert Bowyer and Henry Elsing, Clerks of the Parliaments, A.D. 1621, 1625, 1628.* Camden Society, third series, **42** (London).

Richardson and Sayles, "The Early Records of the English Parliament": Richardson, H. G., and George Sayles. 1929. "The Early Records of the English Parliament." *Bulletin of the Institute of Historical Research* **6**.

Richardson and Sayles, "The Early Statutes": Richardson, H. G. and George Sayles. 1934. "The Early Statutes." *Law Quarterly Review* **50**.

Richardson and Sayles, *Rotuli Parliamentorum Anglie Hactenus Inediti:* Richardson, H. G. and George Sayles, eds. 1935. *Rotuli Parliamentorum Anglie Hactenus Inediti MCCLXXIX–MCCCLXXIII.* Camden Society, third series, **51** (London).

Rot. Parl.: Rotuli Parliamentorum ut et Petitiones, et Placita in Parliamento. n.d n.p.

Scobell: Scobell, Henry. 1689. *Remembrances of Methods, Orders, and Proceedings . . . in the House of Lords* (London).

Selden, *Of Judicature:* Selden, John. 1681. *Of the Judicature in Parliaments, A Posthumous Treatise: Wherein, The Controversies and Precedents belonging to that Title, are Methodically Handled* (London).

Sims, *Expedicio:* Sims, Catherine Strateman, ed. 1954. *Expedicio Billarum Antiquitus An Unpublished Chapter of the Second Book of The Manner of Holding Parliaments in England by Henry Elsynge, Clerk of the Parliaments. Studies presented to the International Commission for the History of Representative and Parliamentary Institutions.* **16** (Louvain).

Spedding, *Letters and Life:* Spedding, James, Robert Leslie Ellis, Douglas Denton Heath, eds. 1861–1876. *The Works of Francis Bacon. The Letters and Life* (14 v., London).

Statutes of the Realm: The Statutes of the Realm. 1810–1828. (11 v., London).

Taylor, *The Jewel Tower:* Taylor, A. J. 1965. *The Jewel Tower* (London).

Wilkinson: Wilkinson, Bertie. 1931. "The Protest of the Earls of Arundel and Surrey in the Crisis of 1341." *English Historical Review* **46**.

Willson, *Bowyer:* Willson, David H. 1931. *The Parliamentary Diary of Robert Bowyer 1606–1607* (Minnesota).

THE PAINFUL LABOUR OF MR. ELSYNG

Elizabeth Read Foster

CONTENTS

	PAGE
Introduction	5
Mr. Elsyng and his work	7
Mr. Elsyng, clerk of the parliaments	9
The Journal of the House of Lords	21
The Parliament Roll	29
Mr. Elsyng's *Modus Tenendi Parliamentum apud Anglos*, Book Two, "of the matters handled in the Parliament"	35
War and peace	36
Subsidies	38
Judicature	42
Mr. Elsyng and the uses of antiquity	45
Advice to the Earl of Danby	46
Conclusion	50
Appendix	50
Mr. Elsyng's drafts for Book Two	50
Memorandum for the Earl of Danby	60
Index	65

INTRODUCTION

Henry Elsyng was clerk of the parliaments, 1621–1635, and author of an historical treatise, *The Manner of Holding Parliaments in England*, which he sometimes also designated by its Latin title, *Modus Tenendi Parliamentum apud Anglos*. In an age devoted to precedent, Elsyng brought to his office the skills and training of an archivist and antiquarian; and through the clerkship, he made a significant contribution to the development of parliament. Each of the constituent elements of this institution redefined its own particular function in the early seventeenth century: crown, Lords, and Commons. As clerk, Elsyng served all three, but his immediate relationship was with the House of Lords.

The upper house played an interesting role during the years of Elsyng's clerkship. Concerned for privilege, procedure, and the nature of the record, the Lords established standing orders, a clear statement of their privileges as peers, and a permanent archive of parliament.[1] No law could pass without the Lords' approval and they weighed legislation carefully. Under the pressure of general public discontent, they greatly expanded their judicial activities. They served as judges when charges were formally brought by the Commons against royal officials—against little men at first, later against the lord chancellor himself, presiding officer of the upper house, and even against a royal favorite, the Duke of Buckingham. The Lords also investigated complaints brought by individuals, sometimes deciding the matter at issue, sometimes referring it to other courts. Though not as aggressive politically as the lower House, in 1624 the Lords embarked on a major debate of foreign policy. In 1628 they joined with the Commons in presenting the Petition of Right, which "humbly" showed the king that subjects should not be taxed save by parliament, nor imprisoned without cause certified. Faced by the concerted action of both houses, King Charles grudgingly gave assent.

The study which follows is an essay on Elsyng's work, his "painful labour," to borrow the phrase of his fellow antiquarian Sir Robert Cotton.[2] My research began unexpectedly when, at the Library of the Inner Temple, I came upon unpublished pages which seemed to belong to the second book of Elsyng's treatise. The story became more insistent when a reference in a report of the Historical Manuscripts Commission suggested that the essay "Of the Judicature of Parliaments" (usually attributed to the seventeenth-century scholar John Selden) was in fact another chapter written by Elsyng. Further investigation supported this hypothesis. Then, in pursuit of another project, I read Elsyng's parliament rolls, the ultimate record of a session, and found myself deep in this book.

There follow the few biographical details which will be useful to understand the training and qualifications which Elsyng brought to his work. In later sections I shall explore his activities as keeper of the records and as clerk, his writings on parliament, and finally the political advice which at the end of a long career he tentatively offered to the crown.

Elsyng was born in 1577, the son of a citizen and merchant taylor of London, and baptized at St. Dunstan's in the West. When he was five, his father died. Shortly thereafter his mother married Henry Knyvett, a half-brother of Robert Bowyer, known to parliamentary historians for his diary of the House of Commons (1606–1607) and his notes of the House of Lords (1610–1621). Educated at St. Albans School, Elsyng in 1595 became a "pensioner" at Caius College, Cambridge. Two years later without attaining a degree, he left Cambridge and entered the Middle Temple, where like many gentlemen of the time, he read law.[3]

---

[1] Bond, "Formation of the Archives," pp. 153–156.

[2] *Cottoni Posthuma*, p. 34.

[3] I am indebted to Mr. J. C. Sainty for information concerning Elsyng and his family and for most of the biographical references which follow. Edw. Alex Fry, ed., *Inquistiones Post Mortem of the Tudor Period for the City of London*. The British Record Society, **36**, 3 (London, 1908): pp. 64–65; *Collectanea Topographica et Genealogica* (London, 1837) **4**: p. 103; Joseph Lemuel Chester and George J. Armytage, eds., *The Parish Registers of St. Antholin, Budge*

The connection with Robert Bowyer was of signal importance to Elsyng's career. The two men shared chambers at the Temple and in 1600 Elsyng married Bowyer's beloved niece for his first wife. As Bowyer progressed in public life through the influence of his patron Lord Buckhurst (later Earl of Dorset), he generously shared his advancement with his nephew.[4] In 1604 Bowyer and Elsyng became joint keepers of the records in the Tower. Later, when Bowyer became clerk of the parliaments, Elsyng assisted him in the House of Lords and apparently took notes of proceedings there in 1614, before succeeding to the clerkship himself in March of 1621.[5] When Bowyer died, he left property to the sons of Elsyng's first marriage. To the elder son, Bowyer gave books and manuscripts, with the provision that no copies should be made of those which concerned records in the Tower or "any the journal books of parliament remaining in the office of the clerk of the parliament" save for family use. To Elsyng himself, Bowyer bequeathed

all my plate which was given unto me by . . . my noble friend Robert Earl of Dorset . . . as a small token of my love unto him who by his friendly respect towards myself in the whole course of our conversation and his entire affection and extraordinary kindness towards Blanche his late wife . . . hath deserved more of me than I can return to him.[6]

Uncle and nephew had remained close friends all their lives, colleagues in the law, at the Tower, and in parliament.

The two men were members of a wider group, a remarkable family of clerks and record keepers. Thomas Knyvett, who assisted in the House and held a grant in reversion of the clerkship, was Elsyng's half-brother. John Throckmorton, who married Elsyng's sister-in-law, worked with him as deputy clerk of the parliaments, and later assisted John Browne, also a member of the same family, who became clerk in 1638.[7]

Elsyng's eldest son, Henry, helped his father in the House of Lords. His father had, he said later, "been at great charge" to send him to Oxford and "to train him up in the knowledge and execution" of the clerical office. To this education, the young man added several years of foreign travel "to better his knowledge and to gain languages." He is reputed to have known Latin, French, and Italian. When young Henry returned from abroad, his father was dead and the clerkship for which he had hoped had been granted to another. He became instead, perhaps through the assistance of Archbishop Laud, underclerk or clerk of the House of Commons in 1639, a post in which he served with distinction.

At length, when he saw that the greater part of the house were imprisoned and secluded; and that the remainder would bring the king to a trial for his life, he desired to quit his place . . . by reason, as he alleged of his indisposition; but most men understood the reason to be, because he would have no hand in the business against the king.

His loyalties, like his father's, lay with the crown. In 1660, the monarchy restored, king and parliament made provision for his children.[8]

These men learned from each other. Like families who long practiced the same craft or were musicians from generation to generation, this group of clerks and record keepers shared and improved their skills. William Bowyer, who had kept the records in the Tower, trained his son, Robert.[9] Robert trained Elsyng senior; Elsyng trained young Henry. All must have been conscious of a strong tradition of devotion to the record and to the institution of parliament.

By virtue of his position in society, his education and training, his industry and devotion, Elsyng set his stamp upon the clerical office and thus upon parliament. Respected by scholars in his own day, he moved easily among gentlemen and on one occasion at least among peers. A clerk, that is a clerk like Elsyng, could be of considerable importance in determining agenda and forwarding the business of the House. The political, legislative, and judicial activities of the Lords in the period 1621–1629 were firmly based on orderly procedure which Elsyng registered in the roll of standing orders, and an efficient parliament office which Elsyng maintained. He may have intended that his work, *The Manner of Holding Parliaments in England*, should replace the medieval *Modus Tenendi Parliamentum*, which, whatever modern historians may think of it, had long been considered an authoritative

---

Row, London (Harleian Society Publications, Registers, **8**, London, 1883): p. 30; John and J. A. Venn, *Alumni Cantabrigienses*, Part I (Cambridge, 1922) **2**: p. 100; Charles Henry Hopwood, ed., *Middle Temple Records* (London, 1904–1905) **1**: p. 372, **2**: p. 453. A pedigree of the Elsyng family is in W. Bruce Bannerman, ed., *Miscellanea Genealogica et Heraldica*, fourth series, **5**: p. 142.

[4] Willson, *Bowyer*, pp. ix–x; Bond, "Formation of the Archives," p. 153; J. G. Taylor, *Our Lady of Battersea* (London, 1925), p. 212; will of Robert Bowyer (P.R.O., PROB 11, PCC. 93 Savile).

[5] Elsyng, *Manner of Holding Parliaments*, p. 97; Relf, *Debates in the House of Lords 1621*, p. vi. Elsyng signed for supplies delivered to the clerk in 1614 (Braye 112, #40, Osborn Collection, Yale University).

[6] Will of Robert Bowyer (P.R.O., PROB 11, PCC.93 Savile).

[7] Bond, "Formation of the Archives," pp. 153–154; Bond, "Clerks of the Parliaments," pp. 83–84). Once more I am indebted to Mr. Sainty, who worked out the relationship between Elsyng and Throckmorton in an unpublished memorandum which he shared with me. Throckmorton's will refers to Browne as his kinsman. Miss Edmond's notes and her genealogy of Browne are on deposit at the House of Lords Record Office.

[8] P.R.O., SP 16/DXXXVI/94, fol. 277. Anthony à Wood, *Athenae Oxoniensis* (London, 1721), p. 177. See also Sheila Lambert, "The Clerks and Records of the House of Commons, 1600–1640," *Bulletin of the Institute of Historical Research*, **43** (1970): pp. 218–220.

[9] Bond, "Formation of the Archives," pp. 152–153.

guide to the past.[10] Elsyng's treatise, his notes, the papers he assembled, the formal record he compiled, and his brief essay of political advice, brilliantly reveal both the parliaments he served and the painful labour of "that most industrious and able gentleman." [11]

MR. ELSYNG AND HIS WORK

The Tower guarded London on the east. Here the king stored records of his chancery, and among them, some of the earliest records of his parliaments. To the west, up the river, past the City and hard by the Abbey, sprawled the royal palace of Westminster, long abandoned as a residence. The king's courts and his parliaments met in the buildings of the palace: the Lords in the White Chamber, the Commons in St. Stephen's Chapel. Henry Elsyng began his public career in 1604 as keeper of the records in the Tower, a position held jointly with his uncle Robert Bowyer, and lived nearby in a house on Tower Hill. Sometime around 1615 he moved to Westminster, probably to help Bowyer who was then clerk of the parliaments. By 1621 Elsyng assumed the clerkship himself and held it until a few months before his death in 1635 or 1636. As clerk he served on the floor of the House of Lords, wrote the record of the king's highest court, and established in the ancient Jewel Tower of the palace yet another repository for the king's records, the archive of parliament.[1]

In Elsyng's day, many men searched the records in the Tower of London, paying fees to the keepers, who helped them find what was needed and supplied fair copies for a price. Elsyng and Bowyer were rightly jealous of their skills and defended the privilege which provided their livelihood. They lodged a protest when Ferdinando Pulton, who proposed to make an edition of the statutes at large, applied for access to the Tower without fee and, since he was an old man of almost eighty, requested that the keepers each day deliver a roll of parliament to his house. As keepers they could not in all conscience, they said, remove a record from the Tower. Moreover, Pulton could not read what was written without their help, "both for want of exercise and skill in that kind." Nor were all the acts which he needed to be found in parliament rolls, "but . . . in rolls of other natures as occasion then required, so as Mr. Pulton nor any other knoweth how or where to find the same except the officers. . . ."

Not only were the rolls difficult to read—the crabbed medieval hand, the abbreviated Latin and law French which faded as men wound and rewound the clumsy parchment. Words must also be understood in context. Research pushed too far by unskilled persons might prove unsettling to the law and dangerous to the crown. Bowyer and Elsyng knew that much that was accepted as statute law did not in fact appear as statutes in any record. Some "acts of parliament" were proclamations, some ordinances.

Very many there be of like quality which if in the new print [of Pulton's proposed edition] shall be affirmed as statutes to agree with the record, the world shall be abused, if the secret be opened; then the dealing of our predecessors will be disputed and a question perhaps arise what the king may do by proclamation, and how the subject may be bound thereby.

They continued, "Great advice and discretion is to be used." [2]

Events had recently shown, they recalled, what damage could be done by indiscriminate use of the parliament rolls,

the inconvenience of general searches and free access to the records though allowed heretofore to none but sincere and honest persons and upon warrant, did notwithstanding appear in the last session of parliament, when of notes long before taken, other use was made than was expected or liked.

Moreover, Bowyer continued, the keepers had long had their own project for publishing the statutes. Five volumes covering most of the reigns of Edward III and Edward IV had already been prepared by Heneage, Bowyer's predecessor as keeper. Bowyer himself "at great charge" had added more.[3]

Much of what the keepers wrote was of course special pleading to protect their own prerogatives; but their protest gives a fair picture of their responsibilities and activities. They saw themselves as more than custodians. Bowyer's father, William, when keeper, had begun the collection later published under the name of the antiquarian, Sir Robert Cotton, as *An Exact*

---

[10] *Ibid.*, p. 155.
[11] Hakewill, *Manner of Passing Bills*, preface.
[1] For a reference to Elsyng's house on Tower Hill, see Braye 112, #37 (Osborn Collection, Yale University). Bowyer also had property there. Elsyng bequeathed three hundred pounds to his son, Robert, on condition that Robert release to his brother Henry the two tenements on Tower Hill inherited from Bowyer (will of Henry Elsyng, P.R.O., PROB 11, PCC., 28 Pile). Elsyng's daughter, Mary, was baptized at St. Margaret's, Westminster, in 1615 (Arthur M. Burke and H. Hensley Hensa, eds., *Memorials of St. Margaret's Church, Westminster: the parish registers, 1539–1660,* London, 1914), p. 90. Elsyng wrote personal letters from Westminster in 1616 and 1617 (British Museum, Egerton 2715, fols. 201, 206). Sims, p. xvii. Bond, "Clerks of the Parliaments," p. 83. The date of Elsyng's death is unknown. His will was proved in 1636. Bond, "Formation of the Archives," p. 156.

[2] British Museum, Titus B.V., fols. 279–282ᵛ. Cf. Henry Elsyng, "*Expedicio Billarum Antiquitus*" (Sims, *Expedicio,* pp. 85–87), where Elsyng also discussed statutes and public ordinances, or "acts of parliament" which were not drawn into statutes. An undated letter from Pulton to Ellesmere, indicating that he and Bowyer had settled their differences, asked for a reward for them both (El. 1964). Pulton died in 1618 at the age of eighty-two.
[3] British Museum, Titus B.V., fol. 282. The reference is to the debates in 1610. For Pulton's project and the council's license for him to proceed, see *Statutes of the Realm* 1: pp. xxvii–xxviii.

Abridgement of the Records in the Tower.[4] Robert Bowyer, the son, used the records in a variety of ways, compiling precedents under different heads to illuminate his investigations of procedure,[5] and may have drafted the modern version of the *Modus Tenendi Parliamentum* which Elsyng later completed.[6] Thus there was an antiquarian tradition behind Elsyng when he began to study the records in his charge. He inherited and used the collections made by Heneage and by the Bowyers. He also worked his own way through the creaking parchment rolls to understand for himself the history of the king's parliament.[7]

Henry Elsyng's work as keeper of the records in the Tower was a natural apprenticeship for his duties as clerk. He would find the clerkship congenial—making and preserving the records of parliaments which he served as he had kept those committed to him from the past. He lived in times as exciting as those of which he had read in the medieval rolls. When he assumed his full responsibilities as clerk in March, 1621, the lower House had already launched a sweeping investigation of grievances and of the state of the kingdom, which lead to charges against Mompesson and Michell, who held royal grants, against Bennett and Yelverton, officers of the king, and finally to the impeachment of the lord chancellor, Francis Bacon, presiding officer of the upper House. The parliament of 1624 continued the program begun in 1621. The drive against royal grants culminated in a statute against monopolies and complaint of grievances found partial satisfaction in the impeachment of the lord treasurer, Lionel Cranfield, Earl of Middlesex. Both houses plunged into a debate of foreign policy under the leadership of Prince Charles and the Duke of Buckingham, newly returned from an unsuccessful attempt to negotiate a marriage alliance with Spain. The establishment of a commission to receive and disburse revenues raised by the subsidy (or property tax) involved parliament in supplying a war.[8] An attempt to sacrifice a great lord, the Earl of Bristol, as a scapegoat for the mistakes of the Spanish escapade raised serious questions of privilege in the upper house. When the king imprisoned the Earl of Arundel in 1626 for a matter "personal to his Majesty," the Lords "struck" and refused to carry on the business of parliament until Arundel had been seated. Parliament continued to debate foreign affairs and war throughout the sessions of 1625, 1626, 1628–1629, and was occupied also with charges against the king's favorite, Buckingham. Impeachment proceedings were temporarily set aside as both houses debated arbitrary imprisonment and other issues later incorporated in the Petition of Right.

There was much to record and many papers to preserve. During Elsyng's term as clerk, and doubtless with his encouragement, the Lords established their first permanent archive in the Jewel Tower, where Elsyng also set up his office.[9] The house held Elsyng responsible for its papers. When a committee of lords, investigating charges against the Earl of Bristol in 1626, "called the clerk for the letter, which was read here . . . ," he "answered, that the Duke of Buckingham, who delivered that letter to be read, did presently take the same from him again." This, the committee said, was "contrary to order; for, being the house was once possessed thereof, it ought not to have been taken out of the house, nor delivered, without leave of the house."[10]

The investigations, hearings and impeachment proceedings which occupied the house brought a variety of papers to Elsyng's care. He kept documents, account books, and similar material offered as evidence.[11] He held the patent for making gold and silver thread, which had been granted to Mompesson.[12] He was in charge of a "rich cabinet" said to have been offered as a bribe to Bacon, which must have been as awkward to store as the gravestones presented as evidence several centuries later and now in the custody of the clerk of the records in the Victoria Tower.[13] Peers who attended conferences with the Commons and reported back to the upper house filed speeches and notes with Elsyng. In this way all the records cited concerning arbitrary imprisonment came to Elsyng's care, which he was ordered to keep, releasing only copies. Lords who spoke for committees of the house deposited their reports with the clerk. In 1628 the Earl of Devonshire left notes concerning the Muscovy Company at the parliament office, where they were docketed "My lord of Devonshire's notes which are to be safely kept."[14]

---

[4] Richardson and Sayles, *Rotuli Parliamentorum Anglie Hactenus Inediti*, pp. xxii, 231.

[5] For some of Robert Bowyer's collections, see my *Proceedings in Parliament 1610* 1: pp. xxii–xxiii; Petyt 538/11, fols. 1–112ᵛ, 308–327; Petyt 538/12, fols. 341–387ᵛ.

[6] D'Ewes said that he used "a manuscript treatise which I had by me entitled *Modus Tenendi Parliamentum apud Anglos*, compiled especially as I conceive by Robert Bowyer Esquire, and afterwards enlarged by Henry Elsyng Esquire." D'Ewes's description of the contents of the manuscript identifies it as Elsyng's Book One (D'Ewes, preface). See Petyt 538/12, fols. 1–77ᵛ, which a later hand has ascribed to "R. C. Bowyer."

[7] Sims, *Expedicio*, pp. 35–36; below, pp. 37–42.

[8] See H.L.R.O., Main Papers, H.L., June, 1624–March, 1625/6, for warrants for payments.

[9] Bond, "Formation of the Archives," p. 156; Taylor, *The Jewel Tower*, pp. 16, 33. Elsyng referred to "my office in the old palace at Westminster" (H.L.R.O., Main Papers, H.L., 4 June, 1621).

[10] L.J. 3: p. 574.

[11] See below, p. 18. For other examples, see H.L.R.O., Braye 1, the material concerning Mainwaring and Bristol.

[12] H.L.R.O., Main Papers, H.L., 8 November, 1626. See also the letters patent for a license for salting, drying and packing fish, endorsed in Elsyng's hand "delivered in open court *pr. Comite* Montgomery to be cancelled. . . ." (H.L.R.O., Main Papers, H.L., 5 August, 1619), and L.J., 3: p. 329.

[13] L.J., 3: pp. 119, 156.

[14] H.L.R.O., Main Papers, H.L., 9 April, 1628, and Relf, *Debates in the House of Lords 1621*, p. 85. For other papers

In a different category, but equally Elsyng's responsibility, were messages and letters from the king, official versions of royal speeches or those of the lord keeper speaking for the king, all ultimately to be entered in the journal.[15] Formal messages from parliament to the king, "propositions" or petitions were, like bills, also in Elsyng's care: the messages sent by both houses in 1624 urging James to break treaties with Spain, the messages concerning the commission for levying money by impositions (or additional customs duties), and the suppression of the offending books of Dr. Mainwaring, a high church divine, the petition against foreign nobility and one concerning a grant to the Earl of Oxford.[16] Most famous of all was the Petition of Right and the king's several answers to it: the answer of June 2, delivered to the clerk "by the king himself in parliament before the Commons came," the answer of June 7 sent to the clerk "to the end it mought be recorded in the upper house."[17] Elsyng was also responsible for material sent up from the lower house. Thus the "Commons' Declaration and Impeachment against the Duke of Buckingham," the schedule of grants and gifts made to him together with the Duke's replies, all engrossed in parchment, were filed among the Lords' papers.[18] There was plenty for an archivist to do.

The ability to read ancient records which Elsyng had developed as keeper also served his purposes as clerk. The House of Lords did not like to think of itself as innovating. Trained to search the rolls of parliament, Elsyng could supply precedents to reassure the house when it embarked on an unfamiliar course. In 1626, when the House of Commons summoned the Duke of Buckingham to answer charges, the Lords turned for guidance to the past. "The question is whether the duke may answer the Commons' demand herein or no"—the surviving report is entirely in Elsyng's hand —"The precedents are these. . . ." Two years later, when the upper house was debating how to proceed on a petition against popish recusants, Lord Saye suggested that it would be useful "to have the clerk see what was done in the like case before." Similarly, Bowyer, as clerk, had been directed to look for precedents for the censure of Dr. Cowell, and in 1621, Thomas Knyvett, Elsyng's half-brother, was employed by the house to seek earlier records of impeachment.[19] In law and in government, men of the seventeenth century considered precedent the safest guide. The upper house was fortunate. In carrying out a policy to stand firm in what it thought had been the ways of its ancestors, it had the assistance of clerks who had the attributes and appetites of antiquarians.[20]

The "painful labour of Mr. Elsyng," as keeper and clerk, was all directed to one end: the preservation of the king's records, particularly the record of parliament. As clerk, he compiled a significant portion of that record himself, the journal of the House of Lords and the roll of parliament, which continued for the years 1621–1629 the story he had cherished from the past. Elsyng's labors did not end with the session, but continued during vacations when he retired to his manor of "Cornewall," near Chipping Norton, in Oxfordshire. Probably it was at "Cornewall" that he wrote most of *The Manner of Holding Parliaments in England*, which described first the "form" of parliament, and then "matters handled."[21] Based on notes he had taken in the Tower and on his own observations in the house, Elsyng's book was the sum of his experience on Tower Hill and in Westminster.

MR. ELSYNG, CLERK OF THE PARLIAMENTS

Henry Elsyng was admitted as deputy clerk of the parliaments on March 12, 1621, when Robert Bowyer became too ill to carry out his duties. On March 21, Elsyng took the clerk's oath and served until 1635. Though he had been granted the reversion to the clerkship several years before[1] and had long been associated with Bowyer and with parliament, apparently Elsyng's promotion did not proceed smoothly. The Earl of Oxford was said to have claimed the right to make the appointment. On March 19, Elsyng begged Sir Robert Cotton to "move my noble lord the Earl of Arundel . . . to move the Lords that I may be sworn" without prejudice to Oxford's claim. Elsyng explained that he was too preoccupied with the work of parliament to wait upon Arundel himself. Undoubtedly Elsyng was a busy man and his new duties lay heavy upon him. Probably he was also counting on Cotton's reputation as an antiquarian and his intimacy with the Howards to achieve his purpose.[2] Nothing further

---

concerning conferences, see H.L.R.O., Main Papers, H.L., 29 March, 14, 19, 20, 23 May, 18 June, 1628. For Devonshire, see H.L.R.O., Main Papers, H.L., 19 June, 1628. For other committee material, see H.L.R.O., Main Papers, H.L., 2 April, 1628, 9 February, 1628/9.

[15] For the king, see H.L.R.O., Braye 68, 72, 81; H.L.R.O., Main Papers, H.L., 25 May, 1626, 7 April, 12 May, 29 May, 6 June, 18 June, 20 June, 1628. For the lord keeper, see H.L.R.O., Braye 71; H.L.R.O., Main Papers, H.L., 2 June, 1628.

[16] H.L.R.O., Braye 68; Braye 95, #14 (Osborn Collection); H.L.R.O., Main Papers, H.L., 16 June, 1628; 14, 19 February, 1628/9.

[17] H.L.R.O., Main Papers, H.L., 2 and 7 June, 1628.

[18] H.L.R.O., Parchment Coll., H.L., 15 May, 8 June, 1626.

[19] H.L.R.O., Main Papers, H.L., 3 March, 1625/6; L.J., 3: p. 514; Relf, *Debates in the House of Lords 1621*, p. 66, n.; Foster, *Proceedings in Parliament 1610* 1: pp. 27, 186; H.L.R.O., Main Papers, H.L., 30 March, 1621.

[20] As Bacon had said in 1610, when he was a member of the lower House: "*State super vias antiquas, sed videte quaenam sit via recta, et ambulate in ea*" (Jeremiah 6:16. Spedding, *Letters and Life* 4: p. 183).

[21] For Cornewall, see Elsyng's will (P.R.O., PROB 11, PCC. 28 Pile); Sims, *Expedicio*, p. 143; *H.M.C. Fourth Report*, appendix, p. 369.

[1] Bond, "Clerks of the Parliaments," p. 83. H.L.R.O., Draft Journals, Braye 11 (12 and 21 March, 1620/1).

[2] On March 12, Oxford had introduced a motion that the

was heard of Oxford's claim. Lord North "and other lords" moved that Elsyng be sworn as clerk and the ceremony took place in the house itself.[3] Elsyng copied out the oath and entered it in the Lords journal.[4] The reference in the oath to Oxford's claim which Elsyng had suggested was apparently dropped.[5]

The position upon which Elsyng thus entered was important and he filled it well. In the sixteenth century, and later in the eighteenth, the clerkship was a sinecure, its duties farmed out to subordinates.[6] Not so with Henry Elsyng. All the significant business of the upper house was transacted before his eyes and recorded with his pen. Most of the papers which came to the house, he docketed himself. He drafted and signed the orders and saw to their execution. In April, 1621, Elsyng apologized for sending a footman to the Earl of Bridgewater instead of coming himself. He explained that he had to "attend my lord chief justice with an order for the lieutenant of the Tower . . . and it may be I must go to the Tower."[7] He was clerk, communication center, administrative officer, and dispatcher. He even distributed alms for the house.[8] The duties of the clerk had not yet been differentiated. Looking back, it is not difficult to recognize that Elsyng was responsible for and carried out functions later assigned to the clerk of the parliaments, the reading clerk, the clerk of the journals, the clerk of ingrossments and enrollments, of committees, and of private and public bills.[9]

As clerk, Elsyng received payment of £40 each year and may also have had the use of a house.[10] His major source of income was not his salary but the fees and emoluments customarily attached to his office. The clerk like many officials in the seventeenth century collected the major part of his income in bits and pieces. John Browne, clerk of the parliaments in 1649, was said to have received £500 in fees and similar payments.[11] Probably Elsyng did not realize as much, but his receipts may well have been substantial. The schedule of these fees was apparently set by the Lords and probably revised periodically.[12] A few months after he took office, Elsyng asked the subcommittee charged with the oversight of the journal "to consider of my fees."[13] A list shows what he actually received in 1621.[14] Each lord when he first entered parliament paid the clerk a fee according to his rank: a marquis £6 13s. 4d., an earl £4 10s., a baron £2 10s. The archbishops were charged at the same rate as the marquises. The great bishops, of London, Durham, and Winchester, owed £3 6s. 8d. each. Other bishops paid £2 10s. All paid 20s. for proxies.[15] For certifying private acts, which were not included in the parliament roll, the clerk received 33s. 4d. for the first skin and 6s. 8d. for every other skin.[16] He charged 10s. for an order "unless the same be long," for copies (probably of bills, speeches, and other parliamentary papers) 2s. "after the sheet." He received £5 at the first reading of every private bill, and 5 marks upon the release of a prisoner.[17]

In 1626 the house voted that each earl should give the clerk 40s., each viscount 30s., and each bishop and baron 20s., "for his pains in this and former parliaments."[18] It was not always easy to collect what was due.[19] Apparently this unpleasant duty fell to the

---

king "be moved not to grant any more reversions of the said office hereafter until the House be first moved therein" (L.J., 3: p. 42; Bond, "Clerks of the Parliaments," p. 78, n. 2). For Elsyng's letter to Cotton, see British Museum, Julius C. III, fol. 170. The letter is undated, but the reference to the subsidies suggests March 19.

[3] L.J., 3: pp. 59–60. For the oath and its significance, see "The Oath of the Clerk of the Parliaments," H.L.R.O. Memorandum. Elsyng paid the clerk of the crown who read the oath 20s. (Relf, *Debates in the House of Lords 1621*, p. 30).

[4] H.L.R.O., Draft Journals, Braye 11, 21 March, 1620/1; L.J., 3: pp. 59–60.

[5] British Museum, Julius C. III, fol. 170.

[6] Bond, "Clerks of the Parliaments," pp. 78–80.

[7] El. 7931.

[8] Relf, *Debates in the House of Lords 1621*, p. 53.

[9] See "Clerks in the Parliament Office 1600–1900," H.L.R.O. Memorandum No. 22, for a list of clerks, which also shows how the clerical office was subdivided in the course of time.

[10] Bond, "Clerks of the Parliaments," p. 80; Pollard, "The Clerk of the Crown," p. 312. Hooker wrote, "He hath for his allowance an ordinary fee for term of life" (Hooker, p. [27]). I have used the British Museum copy of Hooker's book; the same text is available in Holinshed's *Chronicles*, as Sheila Lambert has pointed out (*Bills and Acts*, Cambridge, 1971, p. 29). For the clerk's house, see Hakewill, *Manner of Passing Bills*, preface. Elsyng's will refers to his house in Westminster, but makes no disposition of it (P.R.O., PROB 11, PCC. 28 Pile); Taylor, *The Jewel Tower*, p. 17.

[11] Bond, "Clerks of the Parliaments," p. 80.

[12] For fees in 1597, see L.J., 2: p. 225. Hooker said the clerk received £3 for every private bill enacted. When he made copies of bills, he "hath for every ten lines a penny according to the custom" (Hooker, p. [27]). For fees in 1628, see L.J., 3: p. 878. The subcommittee was to see what fees were due all officers and report at the next session.

[13] H.L.R.O., Main Papers, H.L., 2 June, 1621.

[14] Braye 112, #86 (Osborn Collection).

[15] In 1601 Viscount Montagu had paid £4 10s. "for his first coming and entrance unto the parliament according as my lord taketh place with the earls," and he paid 30s. for his proxy (Braye 112, #36, Osborn Collection). The Earl of Dover also paid £4 10s. in 1628 (Relf, *Debates in the House of Lords 1621*, p. 67).

[16] For a list of fees received for certificates in 1619 by Robert Bowyer as clerk, see Braye 112, #91 (Osborn Collection).

[17] Braye 112, #86 (Osborn Collection).

[18] Gardiner, *Debates in the House of Lords 1624*, p. 231; L.J., 3: p. 682. A schedule of fees drawn up later, after Elsyng's time, is more detailed and probably reflects the experience of his years as clerk (Braye 111, #5, Osborn Collection).

[19] H.L.R.O., Minute Book #5, fol. 3, lists the lords who owe entrance fees, a number from previous parliaments. Some names have been crossed off and marked "pd." See also "A Catalogue of the Nobility of England made the 12th day of March 1627 according to their several creations," where "pd." has been marked opposite some names, "x" opposite others (H.L.R.O., Main Papers, H.L., 12 March, 1627/8). For difficulties in collecting fees due for the apprehension of men on

clerk's "man" or assistant, who seems to have been paid by the clerk himself and who also received fees.[20]

The clerk of the crown, always attendant upon the lord chancellor, continued to serve in parliament in Elsyng's time as he had done from medieval days.[21] John Hooker, writing in Elizabeth's reign, spoke of two clerks, one the clerk of the parliament, and "the other named the clerk of the crown." "The clerk of the crown," he said, "is to supply the place and room of the clerk of the parliament in his absence: and hath in all things the like charges and profits as the clerk ought to have." The clerk of the crown was, according to Hooker, deputy clerk of the parliament.[22]

It was natural that the clerk of the crown or his deputy should assist the clerk of the parliaments on certain occasions. The two men sat together on the nether woolsack, facing the throne.[23] When Elsyng was occupied with other business for the Lords, Benbow, then deputy clerk of the crown, took notes of proceedings.[24] But the office of clerk of the crown, which had its own history in parliament, and its own duties, remained distinct from that of clerk of the parliaments.[25] Thus the clerk of the crown in Elsyng's day, Sir Thomas Edmondes, received the returns of writs issued from the office of the pettybag, and the warrant to issue a new writ on the occasion of the death of the Earl of Hertford.[26] Edmondes read the oath when Elsyng was sworn in as clerk of the parliaments.[27] In March, 1621, a document received from the lower house was committed to his keeping.[28] In the same month, his deputy took notice of an order of the house concerning the lands of Sir Giles Mompesson, and later received the money collected for distribution to the poor.[29] The clerk of the crown continued also to participate in the ceremony at the close of a session. "These two clerks at the end of the parliament ought," as Hooker said, "to be present in the house, and within the lower Bar at a board before them, their faces towards the king, and there the one [the clerk of the crown] must read the bills which are passed both houses, and the other must read the consent or disagreement of the king."[30] Clerk of the crown and clerk of the parliaments continued to play their separate roles during the early seventeenth century. One might help the other, but for daily assistance Elsyng had to look elsewhere.

Robert Bowyer, Elsyng's predecessor, had apparently appointed his own deputy clerk. He made a specific agreement with Owen Reynolds that Reynolds should serve as "underclerk" or "otherwise his deputy." Bowyer agreed to pay Reynolds £10 per year and also allowed him one third "of all such money as shall be received for all such copies" as he should write. "For engrossing private acts, transcripting of them into the chancery, writing of proxies and orders of the house" and similar work Reynolds was to "receive such due fees as have been allowed him for his pains in like cases" during the clerkship of Sir Thomas Smith (1597–1609).[31] Both Reynolds and Bowyer appear to have signed the list of acts for 1610 in the "Long Calendar."[32] Unfortunately no similar agreement has survived from Elsyng's time. But as the business of parliament increased and proliferated in the early years of the seventeenth century, a number of "assistants" apparently helped the clerk. Some appear briefly, as Thomas Knyvett and others, who were collecting precedents in 1621.[33] Others worked more regularly.

In 1621 a committee of lords devised an oath to be taken by assistant clerks. "Such clerks as the clerk of the upper house employed either in the office" or who

---

order of the House, see H.L.R.O., Main Papers, H.L., 3 April, 1628, and L.J., 3: p. 710: "The humble petition of James Maxwell, Henry Elsyng and Humfrey Leigh Esqrs."

[20] Braye 112, #37 (Osborn Collection).

[21] Elsyng lists the clerk of the crown as an officer of the house (Cambridge University Library, Mm.6.62). Among the manuscripts formerly at Crowcombe Court was a paper "On the Duties of the Clerk of the Crown" (*H.M.C. Fourth Report*, appendix, p. 373).

[22] Hooker, pp. [27–27ᵛ]. He went on to say of the clerk of the crown: "He must give his attendance to the higher house from time to time and do what shalbe enjoined him. All such acts as be not imprinted, if any man will have them exemplified under the broad seal: he must exemplify them, and have for the same his ordinary fees." Hooker also described the duties of "the chancellor" or "principal clerk of the higher house." The term "clerk of the parliament," rather than "clerk of the parliaments," was frequently used in this period (Bond, "Clerks of the Parliaments," p. 81).

[23] Pollard, "The Clerk of the Crown," pp. 313; Elsyng, *Manner of Holding Parliaments*, p. 112.

[24] Petyt 538/7, fol. 296.

[25] Pollard, "The Clerk of the Crown," pp. 312–333. See Pettus, pp. 382–383, for a seventeenth-century description of the duties of the clerk of the crown.

[26] For Edmondes, see "Officers of the House of Lords, 1485 to 1971," H.L.R.O. Memorandum No. 45. For Benbow, see Petyt 538/7, fol. 268, and L.J., 3: p. 61, where Benbow is called "deputy clerk of the crown"; British Museum, Tib. D. 1, fol. 2, where he is said to be "clerk unto Sir George Coppin, clerk of the crown" (1609/10). Pettus, p. 383. L.J., 3: p. 90.

[27] Relf, *Debates in the House of Lords 1621*, p. 30.

[28] *Ibid.*, p. 24.

[29] Petyt 538/7, fol. 268; L.J., 3: p. 698.

[30] Hooker, p. [27ᵛ]; Pettus, p. 383. The subsidy was not not read in this way, but was presented by the speaker of the house of commons and received by the clerk of the crown. See Pollard, "The Clerk of the Crown," p. 331.

[31] Braye 112, #37 (Osborn Collection).

[32] Preserved at the H.L.R.O. See the reference to "a calendar made by Robt. Bowyer ... of the several acts in the office with the assistance of his servant Owen Reynolds" quoted by Willson, *Bowyer*, p. xii, n. (from British Museum, Lansdowne 496, fol. 2). Bowyer also referred to his calendar of acts (Petyt 537/6, fol. 168).

[33] H.L.R.O., Main Papers, H.L., 30 March, 1621. The gentlemen who had searched the records were to be paid (L.J., 3: p. 74).

served him in parliament were to take the Oath of Supremacy, the Oath of Allegiance, and also

> this oath following . . . You shall swear, that with faithfulness and secrecy you shall serve in the place wherein you are employed under the clerk of the higher house of parliament, neither shall you discover or report to any person or persons (not a member of that house) anything that you shall hear in that house, or read in the journal book.[34]

Notes refer to "the clerk's man," "the clerk of the upper house his man."[35] In 1621 Elsyng wrote of "my clerks," and in 1625 of two underclerks.[36] He spoke of Will Harrison as his clerk in 1621; and it was Harrison who drew up the book of petitions in 1626.[37] John Throckmorton was apparently receiving the same fees as the "clerk's man" in 1624 and signed himself D.C.P., or deputy clerk of the parliaments, on the final manuscript of the Lords journal for 1629.[38] Richard Crane was signing for Elsyng in 1624 and was probably assisting him in 1621.[39] Elsyng's son, Henry, kept a "scribbled book" in 1628.[40]

Clearly, the position of "clerk's man" or assistant clerk was well recognized with a schedule of fees and an oath of its own. During Elsyng's tenure, a number of men functioned in this capacity. The powers, responsibilities, and duties, probably well understood at the time, can now only be surmised. Whether the assistants did what needed to be done, day by day, or whether specific responsibilities were assigned to each, is difficult to determine. Their work, and possibly that of others who remain nameless, can be traced in minute books, proxy books, committee books, books and catalogues of petitions and bills, drafts for the Lords journal and the final version of the journal itself.[41] As demands upon the parliament office increased, these services multiplied. The hand of the assistants is also to be seen in the parliamentary papers and speeches supplied for individual lords. The assistants' lists of copies to be made and fees due indicate that this was a lucrative business for them. Surviving manuscripts in muniment rooms and public repositories show that interest in parliamentary affairs ran high.[42]

As clerk, Elsyng had basically two major responsibilities. The first was to record the business of parliament, and of the upper house. This responsibility meant preserving the papers, bills, orders, petitions, and statutes which constituted the archive, preparing the journal of the House of Lords, and certifying the acts of parliament in the parliament roll. Elsyng's work in this area is discussed above and in chapters which follow. The second responsibility of the clerk, the subject of this chapter, was to organize and expedite the business of parliament, particularly of the upper house, and to transmit its orders.

The care of the parliament house did not fall within the concerns of the clerk but, as part of the palace of

---

[34] The lords subcommittees "for the orders and customs of the house and the privileges of the peers" had been ordered to devise an oath, and apparently sought the assistance of Hakewill and Selden (L.J., 3: p. 42; Bodleian Library, Carte 78, fol. 450ᵛ). The subcommittee drafted the oath quoted, but it was never administered (H.L.R.O., Main Papers, H.L., 21 March, 1620/21). Among Lord Huntingdon's papers, there is another version of the oath (possibly an earlier draft) "for such clerks as the clerk of the upper house of parliament shall employ in his service, either in the house, or in the office, where the records of parliament are kept." First the Oath of Supremacy was to be administered, then the Oath of Allegiance, and last the following: "You shall swear that with faithfulness and secrecy you shall serve in the place wherein you are employed as an underclerk to the clerk of the higher house of parliament, neither shall you discover or report to any person or persons (not a member of that house) any thing that you shall hear in that house, or read in the journal book." The same oath with appropriate modifications was to be given to all other officers of the house. Order was also to be taken that none should "harken at the doors," and that the retiring rooms were to be kept clear for lords and their committees (*H. M. C. Hastings* 4: pp. 289–290).

[35] Braye 112, #86 (Osborn Collection); Relf, *Debates in the House of Lords 1621*, p. 85.

[36] El. 7931; Elsyng, *Manner of Holding Parliaments*, p. 112. See also L.J., 3: p. 682. A list of officers of the upper house refers to the "clerk's chief clerk," and to the "underclerk" (Braye 111, #5, Osborn Collection).

[37] H.L.R.O., Main Papers, H.L., 20 June, 1621; 6 February, 1625/6.

[38] Braye 112, #86 (Osborn Collection); H.L.R.O., Manuscript Journal, Vol. 14, 4 *Car.* I, 20 January, 1628/9—10 March, 1628/9, p. 61.

[39] H.L.R.O., Main Papers, H.L., 4 May, 1624; 4 April, 1628, fees due to "Mr. Crane"; Relf, *Debates in the House of Lords 1621*, p. 53. See also H.L.R.O., Main Papers, H.L., Book of Proceedings of Committees, 17 March, 1627/8—24 June, 1628.

[40] Add. 40,091.

[41] H.L.R.O., Minute Books #1–5; H.L.R.O., Proxy Books, #1, #2; H.L.R.O., Committee Books [Appointments], H.L. 1621, 1624, 1625. For some catalogues of bills and petitions, see H.L.R.O., Main Papers, H.L., 12 December, 1621, 23 February, 1625/6, 28 February, 1625/6; H.L.R.O., Braye 76, "The State of the Bills *A°* 3 and 4 *Car. Regis*, dd. to Mr. Attor. 16 Jan. 1628/9." For a book of bills, see H.L.R.O., Main Papers, H.L., 6 February, 1625/6. This is partly in the hand of a clerk, partly in that of Elsyng. The main body of the draft journals was prepared by Elsyng and is in his hand. He has, however, left blanks to be filled in by his assistants as directed. See H.L.R.O., Braye 11, Draft Journal, 12 March, 1620/1, fols. 2–2ᵛ; 16 March 1620/1, fol. 34; 20 March 1620/1, fol. 61. H.L.R.O., Braye 12, Draft Journal, 24 April, 27 April, 30 April, 2 May, 1621 [the material here looks very much like the hand of Mr. Benbow, *cf.* Petyt 538/7, fol. 296ᵛ]; H.L.R.O., Braye 13, Draft Journal, 27, 28, 29 May, 1624, 16 February, 15 March, 1624/5. The same pattern is followed in the draft journals for 1628/9 (H.L.R.O., Braye 14 & 15). For a discussion of the draft journals, see below, pp. 25–28, where the preparation of the final version of the Lords journal is discussed in detail.

[42] For the schedule of fees due for copies, see Braye 112, #86 (Osborn Collection); Braye 111, #5 (Osborn Collection). For copies made for specific lords, see H.L.R.O., Minute Book #1, fol. 1; H.L.R.O., Minute Book #2, fols. 59ᵛ–60ᵛ; H.L.R.O., Minute Book #3, fol. 127ᵛ. In Minute Book #1, there is also a folio of memoranda under the date of 27 March, 1620/1 of copies to be made. Several of these items have been checked off, as if the work were completed.

Westminster, was under the general supervision of the lord chamberlain.[43] Thus hay sometimes used for stuffing the woolsacks and cloth for covering them were charged to the wardrobe accounts.[44] The clerk does seem to have been responsible for ordering from the king's printer the supplies necessary for the parliament office. In 1604 Barker delivered to Sir Thomas Smith, then clerk, two sets of the statutes at large, one in nine volumes, the other in two; Pulton's and Rastell's Abridgements; "two books of computation of years"; one Book of Common Prayer "of the largest volume with prayers for the parliament inserted"; and "one fair Bible in folio." Barker also supplied paper, almanacs, "a large bag of turkey leather with silk strings, for the parliament bills," and "two boxes covered with leather, with locks and keys to them, to lock in the bills."[45] Another list of supplies, probably a memorandum rather than a receipt, also includes the statutes, abridgments, almanacs, and books of computation. This time the Book of Common Prayer must include the prayers proper for parliament and also "those touching the powder treason." The clerk will need "four realms of fine paper and the like of the coarse sort and more from time to time as there shalbe cause," "two fair journal books, two or three dozen skins of the best sort of parchment and more as occasion shall serve," "one hundred farrells of vellum parchment," "a fair standish," and "two fair inkhorns furnished."[46]

In 1614, Barker delivered paper and parchment for the upper house (£4 16s. 8d.), and for the lower house (£2 16s. 8d.). He brought a standish and inkhorn, and another bag of turkey leather, somewhat more costly than it had been in 1604. He delivered yet another Book of Common Prayer and two testaments of the largest size; the statutes at large in "divers volumes" (at a cost of £6), and another copy at the same price "for the parliament house," a book of statutes of 1 Elizabeth and 3 James, another of 1 Elizabeth, 3 and 7 James, Pulton's and Rastell's Abridgments ("fair bound"); Speed's Chronology of England (also "fair bound"); one large Bible ("fair bound and gilt"); one Holinshed's Chronicles ("two volumes, fair bound"); one copy of Foxe's Book of Martyrs; four Bibles for the king and queen "whereof three very fair bound and gilt all over" (at a cost of £20); and a Book of the King's Bounty at 3d. There is no mention of the books Smith had acquired. The clerk was apparently setting up a new reference library in his office as well as providing volumes for use in the house. The selection was interesting, the duplication of copies puzzling. Certain proclamations were also supplied: six copies of a proclamation concerning recusants, six hundred of that concerning recusants in Ireland, and fifteen hundred of the proclamation for dyeing and dressing cloth.[47] The clerk's office apparently served as a distribution center.

One of Elsyng's duties as clerk was to maintain an accurate list of members of the House of Lords. This duty the Lords themselves held to be of the greatest importance. The order of the clerk's list of peers helped to establish precedence. In 1597 the lord treasurer had moved in the house that

for as much as the journal books kept heretofore, by the clerks of the parliament, seemed to have some error in them, in misplacing the lords, . . . that the said books . . . may be viewed and perused every parliament, by certain lords of the house to be appointed for the purpose; and the list of the lords in their order to be subscribed by them; taking unto them for their better information the king at arms.[48]

Bowyer's preparation of the initial list for 1621 shows some of the steps by which the work was done. In December, 1620, he had a list of peers created since November, 1610.[49] In January, the lord chancellor requested that Weston and Drake furnish Bowyer with the names of bishops consecrated since June, 1614, "as now they stand in order of precedence," "forasmuch as the daily presence of all their lordships is to be entered in the journal book according to their precedence."[50] In February, another note asking for the list of bishops is on file with the list itself annexed.[51] In the same month Bowyer received from "Mr. Cammell," a clerk of the pettybag, a list of barons "to whom writs of summons" had been issued[52]; and in February he had garter's roll of lords, which he observed was more accurate than his own.[53] In 1624, 1625, and 1628–1629, the list of writs of summons of the nobility which had

---

[43] "One part which his lordship is to act . . . is to take care, that all things be provided in the House of Lords that may suit with the grandeur and conveniencies of the persons who are there to be employ'd" (Pettus, p. 86). Pollard, "The Clerical Organization of Parliament," pp. 31–32. Pettus, p. 386.

[44] Warrant Book of the Great Wardrobe, 25 Eliz., p. 97 (P.R.O., LC. 5/36); Declared Accounts of John Fortescue, Esq., keeper of the wardrobe, 1589/90, p. 5 (P.R.O., LC. 9/80). I am grateful to John Nevinson for drawing this point to my attention and for supplying the references. Red "say" had been used as covering since the early sixteenth century (J. M. Davies, "Red and Green," *The Table* 27, (1968): p. 35).

[45] Braye 112, #41 (Osborn Collection).

[46] *Ibid.*, #90.

[47] *Ibid.*, #40. In 1625, 400 copies of a proclamation "were sent down by my lo. chamberlain for the members of the Commons house" (Gardiner, *Commons Debates in 1625*, p. 28. I owe this reference to Esther Cope).

[48] Quoted by Bond, "Formation of the Archives," p. 154; L.J., 2: p. 195.

[49] H.L.R.O., Main Papers, H.L., 9 December, 1620.

[50] H.L.R.O., Main Papers, H.L., January, 1620/1.

[51] H.L.R.O., Main Papers, H.L., 3 February, 1620/1.

[52] Braye 112, #42 (Osborn Collection). The clerks of the pettybag at the end of a parliament enrolled the writs issued. This roll was known as the parliament pawn. See Pettus, pp. 21ff.; *Guide to the Contents of the Public Record Office* (London, 1963) 1: pp. 16, 40.

[53] H.L.R.O., Main Papers, H.L., 4 February, 1620/1. For a reproduction of such a roll, see Powell and Wallis, *House of Lords in the Middle Ages*, pl. XIX.

been delivered to the clerk was entered in the assistant's book of notes.[54]

Once established, the list had to be kept up to date. In May, 1621, Henry, Earl of Northumberland, petitioned the house that his writ of summons be sent to him. Elsyng endorsed the petition with the order of the house and signed it as clerk of the parliaments: "that the writ be made accordingly for that the lord chamberlain hath signified his majesty's gracious pleasure therein."[55] Lords entering parliament for the first time presented their writs.[56] Lords whose titles changed also took care that their positions should be recorded. The clerk's list had acquired significance as proof both of title and of precedence.[57]

The clerk used this list, roll, or book when he called the house and when he administered the Oath of Allegiance. Each lord stood uncovered as his name was read and knelt when he took the Oath.[58] Lords summoned were expected to attend; but those properly excused by the king might appoint proxies. This privilege created problems for the clerk, for proxies were apparently filed at any time during a session. Elsyng kept a list of proxies for 1624 and 1626 in the front of his "scribbled books," the notebooks he had with him in the house. The "scribbled book" for 1628 contains a list of proxies with the dates on which they were received.[59] Proxies were also listed in special books kept by assistants to the clerk. Two have survived from Elsyng's time.[60] A schedule of fees mentions "the clerk's chief clerk who enters the proxies upon the record and into a book that is used upon all votes in the house."[61]

When members of the house were seated and sworn, the next concern was for the order of business. Control of agenda in the house changed from session to session as patterns of power shifted; but the clerk probably assisted in the planning for each day. "The Lord Chancellor Ellesmere," Elsyng wrote in 1625 or 1626,

did use every morning at his coming to the parliament to pass over the end of the house and so go through the lord treasurer's room into his own chamber. And there the clerk met him with ink and paper, and shewed his lordship what was appointed to be done that day and take his lordship's directions what bills or other matters he should first read. His lordship used to stay there, until he saw it time to go to prayers, and then came into the house at the upper end by the State and presently commanded the house to be cleared, and prayers to be said. Then immediately his lordship propounded such business as was first to be begun with.

Elsyng crossed out his earlier version of this sentence: that the chancellor "commanded the clerk to begin." "And when all the bills were read," Elsyng continued,

if no other business was propounded, his lordship would demand of the house if they would direct anything else to be done. If nothing were moved, his lordship propounded the adjournment of the house. So that oftentimes the house did not sit half an hour, and yet as long as they had any business to do, and no longer. This prevented all disrespect and preserved the dignity of the court.

Elsyng started to add "which hath been," and then thought better of it and scratched these words out. "In the parliament a° 18 *Jacobi*," he went on,

an order was made that the clerk enter no order, until the lord keeper first demand the assent of the house. This order was renewed in the parliament a° 21 *Jac*. And I humbly desire your lordship that it may be continued; and that your lordship will be pleased to prevent any other motion, until the order upon the first be agreed on, and read.[62]

The procedure of a chamber dominated by such experienced men as Robert Cecil, Earl of Salisbury, as lord treasurer, and Thomas Egerton, Lord Ellesmere, as chancellor, which Elsyng remembered from 1610 when he first assisted Bowyer, was undoubtedly more orderly than a house divided under the influence of the

---

[54] H.L.R.O., Minute Book #2, fol. 56; see also Minute Books #4 and #5.

[55] L.J., 3: pp. 128–129; H.L.R.O., Main Papers, H.L., 18 May, 1621.

[56] "he should have given his writ and not his patent" (Add. 40,086, fol. 10, Elsyng's "scribbled book" for 20 November, 1621). Elsyng, *Manner of Holding Parliaments*, pp. 95–98. See my *Proceedings in Parliament 1610*, 1: pp. 3, 94–95.

[57] See my "Procedure in the House of Lords," pp. 64–65. Bedford moved in 1628, "That though Clifford be placed now above the barons in the clerk's book, which is notwithstanding controverted by some lords . . . that his so placing at this time be not prejudicial to any other" (Relf, *Debates in the House of Lords 1621*, p. 63).

[58] For the oath, see Elsyng's "scribbled book," 20 November, 1621, Add. 40,086, fol. 11; H.L.R.O., Braye 74, the clerk's roll of peers, 17 March, 1628/9, with a note in Elsyng's hand of the date on which each was sworn. See also Elsyng's "scribbled book" for 1628 (Petyt 538/7, p. 14) for a list of those who took the oath. Names have been checked. For the call of the house, see L.J., 3: p. 214; H.L.R.O., Main Papers, H.L., [1626], a list (in the hand of an assistant) of lords absent at a call of the house with a note of the reasons for their absence and an indication of whether they had appointed proxies. In 1624 Elsyng was caught without his list when suddenly asked to call the house. He borrowed a list from the earl marshal which led him to call the house in the wrong order (Elsyng, *Manner of Holding Parliaments*, pp. 91–92). It was customary to begin with the least baron; but Elsyng started instead with the prince, as Bowyer also seems to have done (L.J., 3: p. 14). In 1628, an entry in the journal says that the house was "called by the clerk's book" (L.J., 3: p. 695).

[59] See, for example, H.L.R.O., Minute Book #2, fols. 7, 8, 11, where the clerk's assistant entered proxies as they were given him each day. Add. 40,087 and 40,089; Petyt 538/7, fols. 2–3.

[60] H.L.R.O., Proxy Book #1, 1625, and #2, March, 1627/8. The vellum cover of Proxy Book #1 has been dated in Elsyng's hand. He may also have made some corrections. Proxy Book #2 seems to be entirely in the hand of an assistant. For a list in Elsyng's hand of lords who sent no proxies, see H.L.R.O., Main Papers, H.L., 18 March, 1625/6.

[61] Braye 111, #5 (Osborn Collection).

[62] H.L.R.O., Main Papers, H.L., December, 1626.

Duke of Buckingham with John Williams or Sir Thomas Coventry presiding as lord keeper. The wider implications of Elsyng's statement are not of immediate concern here, but rather the suggestion of the clerk's role in determining agenda. Every parliament day in Ellesmere's time, Bowyer as clerk had met the lord chancellor "with ink and paper, and shewed his lordship what was appointed to be done that day and take his lordship's directions what bills or other matters he should first read."

Elsyng's words suddenly illuminate many stray sheets in the Main Papers at the House of Lords Record Office from his own term as clerk. The first, in Elsyng's hand, is dated *Lunae 27 Feb. 1625.* Then follows a heading, "Bills committed," under which four bills are listed. Under another heading, "Bills read once," two are listed. West and others, Elsyng wrote, are to appear today to answer their contempt for the arrest of Lady Purbeck.[63] It was the business for the day. There is a similar sheet for the following day, also in Elsyng's hand.[64] On the sheet for March 4 Elsyng wrote:

This morning is appointed for the great cause touching the earldom of Oxford etc. And a message to the Commons for a conference touching the Duke of Buckingham's business. May it please your lordship to move that this message be first sent. It will expedite the business, if the cause of the conference be expressed, and that they come with authority to reply. During the Commons' debate amongst themselves for this, the Lord Willoughby's counsel may be heard . . . And during the conference a bill may be read.

A second sheet for March 4 (which was Saturday) lists bills, in different stages, as before. Opposite some Elsyng has jotted dates—possibly the dates for future readings or the days for committees. Finally he has re-marked the schedule for Monday.[65] Elsyng's sheet for Tuesday, March 7, began: "This morning the committee for munitions and defense of the sea etc. are appointed to meet," then proceeded to "Bills once read." First on the list was the Earl of Nottingham's bill, which had originally been scheduled for March 4. It was, Elsyng reminded the lord keeper on March 7, "appointed to be read today." Then followed "the silk throwsters' bill," "May it please your lordship to move it may be committed." The next category was "Bills engrossed and ready for a third reading," and finally "Bills committed." As before dates and sometimes the time and place of committee meetings have been added.[66] On March 8, Elsyng again suggested that the lord keeper move the commitment of the silk throwsters' bill. However, the bill was rejected as a monopoly, as he has noted in the margin.[67] So the sheets continue. On March 13, Elsyng began with "the state of bills," then wrote:

George Gardiner an attorney and George Buttrice are to be here this morning to answer their contempt for forging the hand and seal of the Earl of Huntingdon. . . .The Lady Purbeck hath sent the names of such witnesses as will prove upon oath Stukley's procuring her coach horses to be attached *vzt*. Robert Maddox and George Gillett and one Abraham Watts, prisoner in the Fleet, who cannot come without a writ.[68]

On March 16, he provided a list of bills to be reported, noted that the committee for defense of the land had been scheduled to meet the day before, and also that he, as clerk, had received the "Bishop of Lincoln's answer sealed up and directed to the Lords." In the margin, he added that Lincoln's answer had been sent to committee and, at the bottom of the page, he jotted the agenda for the following day: "the committees for petitions are to make report of the Bishop of Lincoln's answer touching the aspersion laid upon the subcommittee and what relief Pinckney shall have etc." [69] Elsyng's schedule for March 23 included a report from the committee for defense of the kingdom concerning projects for making gunpowder, bills from the Commons "not yet read," and other bills to be sent to the lower house after their final reading in the Lords.[70] On March 28, an assistant listed bills once read, bills committed, and bills engrossed. Elsyng added the date and other matters to be considered. "The judges," he noted at the head of the sheet, "are to deliver their opinions touching the office of great chamberlain." At the foot of the page he wrote,

The grand committee for privileges etc. met yesterday upon the petition of the Earl of Bristol referred unto them and are to report the same this day to the House. The committee for defense of the kingdom etc. appointed to meet, and to name triers of Mr. Russell's project to make artificial saltpeter and to agree what recompense shalbe given him, if their lordships shall not accept of his project, notwithstanding it appear to be feasible.[71]

No other sheets of this sort seem to have survived. In 1626 at least, and probably earlier since the practice apparently dates from Bowyer's time, Elsyng was each day preparing the agenda for the house, and going over it with the lord keeper, the presiding officer, possibly leaving a fair copy with him as a guide. The sheets at the House of Lords Record Office are those which Elsyng kept for himself and on which he made notes

---

[63] H.L.R.O., Main Papers, H.L., 27 February, 1625/6. *Cf.* L.J., 3: p. 508.
[64] H.L.R.O., Main Papers, H.L., 28 February, 1625/6. *Cf.* L.J., 3: pp. 508–509.
[65] H.L.R.O., Main Papers, H.L., 4 March, 1625/6. *Cf.* L.J., 3: pp. 515–517.
[66] H.L.R.O., Main Papers, H.L., 7 March, 1625/6. *Cf.* L.J., 3: pp. 518–519, 522.
[67] H.L.R.O., Main Papers, H.L., 8 March, 1625/6, and L.J., 3: p. 522.
[68] H.L.R.O., Main Papers, H.L., 13 March, 1625/6. *Cf.* L.J., 3: pp. 525, 528. See below, p. 21, n. 38.
[69] H.L.R.O., Main Papers, H.L., 16 March, 1625/6. *Cf.* L.J., 3: pp. 529–531.
[70] H.L.R.O., Main Papers, H.L., 23 March, 1625/6. *Cf.* L.J., 3: pp. 538–539.
[71] H.L.R.O., Main Papers, H.L., 28 March, 1626. *Cf.* L.J., 3: pp. 540–541.

as business progressed. Sometimes the agenda prepared is a summary of the state of bills. Sometimes the clerk went further and recommended a motion for commitment. At either point, he might well have been persuaded to forward legislation of interest to individuals. The assistant clerk had a note in his book to notify "Mr. John Bunbury, clerk of the Grocers" "if a bill for the Apothecaries come in, he lieth at Grocers Hall in the Poultry," [72] and similar reminders for those interested in other business of the house. In Elsyng's "scribbled book" for 1621 there is a memorandom to inform Sir Charles Caesar of petitions or bills which might affect his family.[73] Elsyng carried the Earl of Nottingham's bill on the agenda for several days before it was read and specifically suggested the commitment of the silk throwsters' bill.

By 1626 he was sufficiently self-assured to jog the lord keeper about a message to the Commons and even to propose its content. "During the Commons' debate amongst themselves . . . ," he suggested, Willoughby's counsel could be heard and while some of the lords were busy with a conference, a bill could be read. It would be interesting to know whether Elsyng would have gone so far in 1621, when he was new at the job, or if Bacon, an old parliament man with experience in both houses, had continued as presiding officer. Bacon withdrew from the house in March, 1621. Ley, as chief justice, presided until Williams was appointed lord keeper. Coventry succeeded Williams in November, 1625. He was still relatively inexperienced. By 1626 Elsyng had seen many parliaments, and had gained both confidence and respect which may have made him bold to extend the clerical function.

Other clerks had also done so. Among the papers of Sir Christopher Hatton there is a memorandom: "Mr. Mason his advice to me of my manner of proceeding in parliament," which probably dates from 1587, when Hatton first became lord chancellor. Mason, then clerk of the parliaments, sketched a brief outline of Hatton's responsibilities as presiding officer in the House of Lords, adding "As for other things, the daily experience will thoroughly inform your lordship." [74] At certain times, the clerk, continuing in office from parliament to parliament, could guide a new chief through "daily experience" in the house, and serve as a connecting link from session to session, supplying advice or even direction.[75]

Elsyng's agenda sheets give a clear picture of his responsibility for expediting the business of parliament, particularly that of the upper house. Bills (with some exceptions) might begin their lives in either house and were originally drawn in paper. Each bill which the Lords considered and every proviso or amendment was read aloud by the clerk. In an age when parliamentary material did not circulate in print, reading was of great importance and apparently required a special skill. Parliament men in Elizabeth's time had complained that a chancery clerk who brought a record to the house "read it not *ut clericus*" and ordered the clerk of the parliaments to take his place.[76] Reading also required stamina. The clerk must stand and read at length, not only bills, but standing orders, examinations, commissions, precedents—all that the house desired for its information. "I have this day," Elysng wrote to Sir Robert Cotton in March, 1621, "read the Subsidy of the Temporalty and the Subsidy of the Clergy twice, which makes me faint and weary." [77]

Ordinarily after bills had passed two readings, they were sent to a committee, named by the house, to meet at a time and place also appointed. It was the responsibility of the clerk to deliver the bill to the chairman (or "first committee") with a list of members (or "committees"), and a copy of the mandate.[78] Bowyer

---

acquaint himself with them beforehand" (Hatfield MSS., quoted in Pollard, "The Clerical Organization of Parliament," p. 52, n.).

[76] H.L.R.O., "Precedents in Parliament," p. 73 (35 Eliz., from a journal kept by a member of parliament). One of the objections to Bowyer's appointment as clerk had been "a great imperfection he hath in his speech" (Bond, "Formation of the Archives," p. 153). On the importance of this function of the clerk, see Pollard, "The Clerical Organization of Parliament," pp. 39–40.

[77] British Museum, Julius C. III, fol. 170. For the reading of a commission, see H.L.R.O., Braye 13, Draft Journal, 2 November, 1624. For the reading of depositions and examinations of witnesses, see Add. 40,088, fol. 57, and the account of the Floyd case in the parliament roll (P.R.O. C65/185); L.J., 3: pp. 345–349, 352–361, 365–367, 369–370, 373–376. The clerk also read the heads of the charges against Cranfield (P.R.O. C65/188), and the articles of the Earl of Bristol (L.J., 3: pp. 576–578). For the reading of a roll of parliament concerning the trial of a peer, see L.J., 3: p. 581. For the reading of the Petition of Right, see P.R.O. C65/190 and L.J., 3: p. 843. In 1628, the clerk read an act of 31 H. VIII and the additions to the petition concerning recusants (Relf, *Debates in the House of Lords 1621*, pp. 67, 69). For standing orders, *ibid.*, pp. 155, 196. The standing orders were also read on the first day of a session, Scobell, p. 8; *Manuscripts of the House of Lords* 10: p. xliii).

[78] "The Method of Passing Bills," *Harl. Misc.*, 9: pp. 114–115, where there is also an interesting decription of the way the committee was named (*cf.* Add 36, 102, fol. 35ᵛ, the additions by John Walker to Scobell's "Remembrances on Procedure"). Elsyng's entry in his "scribbled book" for 30 April, 1621, also indicates how a committee was named. He wrote "6 of a bench," then entered the names in three columns, one for each bench. There were twelve lords named (Add. 40,085, fol. 80). When the committee was complete, the clerk read the names of members and also the time and place of meeting. "I gave the

---

[72] H.L.R.O., Minute Book #2, fly-leaf.

[73] Gardiner, *Debates in the House of Lords 1621*, p. 93, n. For an indication of the potential influence of the clerk of the House of Commons on the scheduling of bills, see my *Proceedings in Parliament 1610* 2: pp. 148–149, n. For Bowyer's influence as clerk of the parliaments, see Willson, *Bowyer*, p. xii.

[74] Folger Shakespeare Library, V.b. 303, pp. 145–146.

[75] In 1597, Egerton wrote to Cecil: "Here is like to be new lord-keeper, new speaker, new clerk, and all of us newly to learn our duties." The clerk, he said, was "to receive into his charge the rolls and records appertaining to the place, and to

had drawn up committee sheets of this kind and apparently Elsyng continued the same procedure.[79] He kept track of committees in a "committee book," a practice also inherited from Bowyer.[80] These books have survived for the years 1621, 1624, and 1625.[81] Handwriting indicates that they were compiled by Elsyng's assistants. The title of each bill is entered on a separate page, and with it the date of the second reading, the list of the committee members in order of precedence, attendants (such as judges or other advisers) assigned, and the original place of meeting appointed. To this information copied out by his clerk, Elsyng added dates of additional meetings and other information [82]: attendants will not be required on a given day; a subcommittee is to report to the grand committee.[83] He kept the roster of committee members up to date, "the absent lords to be left out, these to be added," and noted any further instructions ordered by the house.[84] Elsyng drew up schedules of bills committed.[85] In February, 1625/6, he had a Book of Bills, listing forty-one bills with dates of reading and commitment, sometimes in an assistant's hand, often in his own.[86] From these compilations and his committee books, he followed the progress of a bill, doubtless consulting with committee chairmen who might be ready to report as he planned each day's agenda.

When the first of a committee reported a bill, other members of the committee stood, uncovered. If a proviso to the bill was brought in, it was read by the clerk, explained by the presiding officer of the house, and read again by the clerk. If the committee report was favorable and, with any proviso, was approved by the house, the bill was then ready to be engrossed, and scheduled for its last reading.[87] Engrossment the clerk delegated to assistants, whom he paid himself. On private bills, the assistant could collect a fee, but public bills were engrossed at the clerk's own charge.[88] The clerk scheduled the final reading of a bill, in consultation with the presiding officer. When a vote was taken, the clerk made the tally as each lord declared his opinion, beginning with the least baron; but in doubtful cases, two lords were appointed as tellers.[89] When a bill passed, the clerk endorsed it, and, if it had originated above, sent it below.[90] Possibly the turkey leather bags carried bills from one house to another, or from the parliament office to the house. The two leather boxes were for temporary storage.[91]

At the end of a session, Elsyng waited upon the king to learn his pleasure concerning bills. At this meeting in 1624, he was charged with the additional duty of certifying to James the judges' opinion on the bill for sheriffs' accounts.[92] On the closing day, the clerk of the crown read the titles of bills, and Elsyng, as clerk of the parliaments, the king's replies.[93] These he inscribed on the acts themselves.[94] He then sent public acts to the king's printer,[95] received them again, and certified them

---

bill to the Earl of Lincoln 13 *Martii* 1623. I rec. it again 15 *Martii* of his lordship" (H.L.R.O., Committee Books [Appointments], H.L., 1624, fol. 8ᵛ).

[79] For 1610, see my *Proceedings in Parliament 1610* 1: p. xxviii. For 1621, see H.L.R.O., Main Papers, H.L., 5 February, 1620/1. For sheets from Elsyng's time, see H.L.R.O., Main Papers, H.L., 11 August, 1625, a sheet prepared by an assistant, with additions by Elsyng; H.L.R.O., Main Papers, H.L., 28 February, 1625/6, signed by Elsyng. In his "scribbled book" for 1621, Elsyng has noted that he gave a copy of the house's order concerning the subcommittee for privileges to the Earl of Huntingdon (Add. 40,085, fol. 125). For other committee sheets, see H.L.R.O., Main Papers, H.L., 5 April, 1626, and 29 May, 1628 (this last is entirely in Elsyng's hand). In the list of fees paid to the clerk's man (1621), there is an item "every committee," 3s. Later the fee seems to be 1s., "the clerk himself to have 2s. 6d. a piece" (Braye 112, #86, Osborn Collection). A schedule of fees for the "clerk of the parliaments' clerk" in 1640 indicates that he should be paid 10s. for "making up the committee fixed to a private bill, and attending at the commitment and reading the same there." He received 2s. 6d. for "a copy of a committee delivered to a private person" (Braye 111, #5, Osborn Collection. For a similar schedule dated 1640, see El. Vol. 34/A/2, p. 5).

[80] For Bowyer's book of committees, see H.L.R.O., Braye 62, and my *Proceedings in Parliament 1610* 1: p. xxviii.

[81] H.L.R.O., Committee Books [Appointments], 1621; 23 February, 1623/4—22 March, 1623/4 and 23 February, 1623/4—26 May, 1624; 23 June, 1625—10 August, 1625. In the "scribbled book" for 1624, there is a note referring to "the old committee book" (Add. 40,087, fol. 91ᵛ).

[82] For notes of additional meetings, see H.L.R.O., Committee Books [Appointments], H.L., 1621, fols. 1, 5, 6, 9, 11, 14, 23.

[83] H.L.R.O., Committee Books [Appointments], H.L., 1621, fols. 2, 3.

[84] H.L.R.O., Committee Books [Appointments], H.L., 1621, fols. 1, 2, 9, 11, 21, 23, 27, 31.

[85] H.L.R.O., Main Papers, H.L., 15 March, 1625/6.

[86] H.L.R.O., Main Papers, H.L., 6 February, 1625/6.

[87] Bond, "Acts of Parliament," pp. 209–210; "The Method of Passing Bills," *Harl. Misc.* **9**: pp. 116–118. Huntingdon observed in 1621: "Note that where my [lord] chancellor had wont to read those amendments to save his trouble and pains the clerk of the house now reads them" (*H.M.C., Hastings* 4: p. 288, n.).

[88] Braye 112, #86 (Osborn Collection): in 1621, the "clerk's man" was to have 3s. 4d. "upon every skin engrossing." In the agreement between Bowyer and Reynolds, Bowyer agreed that Reynolds should continue to collect the usual fees "for engrossing private acts, transcripting of them into the chancery" (Braye 112, #37, Osborn Collection). "The engrossment of all public bills the underclerk doth at his own charge" (Braye 111, #5, Osborn Collection).

[89] "The Method of Passing Bills," *Harl. Misc.* **9**: p. 118. For a count by Bowyer, see my *Proceedings in Parliament 1610* 1: p. 196, n.; for one by Elsyng, see Add. 40,086, fol. 73.

[90] For the endorsement, see Bond, "Acts of Parliament," p. 208, n. 26.

[91] See above p. 13.

[92] L.J., 3: pp. 422–423.

[93] Scobell, p. 35.

[94] In the case of the Petition of Right, the clerk did this at once. Five days after the king's first answer had been given, the clerk had to cut it from the Petition and inscribe the second (L.J., 3: p. 843). The original document can be seen in the House of Lords Library.

[95] For the printing of acts, see Bond, "Acts of Parliament," p. 215; Petyt 538/12, fol. 359.

into chancery in the parliament roll. Private acts might also be certified on request but in a different way.[96] He entered the titles of acts in what is now known as the "Long Calendar," and then stored the acts themselves. Subsidies were filed separately "in the great square trunk" or "square black trunk," probably because of their size. But all were safe in the archive of parliament. Thus at every stage, it was Elsyng's responsibility to attend to bills, schedule and produce them for reading, transmit them to committee chairmen, receive them again, see to their engrossment, arrange for yet another reading, send them to the House of Commons if necessary, present them to the crown, and if successful to the printer, storing the original in the archive of parliament. Old bills, on which action had not been completed, he filed for reconsideration.[97]

The main business of Elsyng's parliaments was not embodied in legislation, but was directed to the investigation of grievances, both public and private. When he assumed office in March, 1621, the House of Commons had already presented to the Lords charges against Sir Giles Mompesson concerning his patent to license inns and alehouses, his patent to manufacture gold and silver thread, and the patent for concealments. The progress of Mompesson's case through the house involved the clerk at every stage, and may serve to illustrate the responsibilities which such activities placed upon him.

The deputy clerk of the crown and the clerk of the parliaments with others searched the houses of Mompesson and Michell, who worked with him, and impounded their books and papers. These were kept by the clerk of the parliaments, on request they were delivered to the lower house, and finally returned to the House of Lords (presumably again in the custody of the clerk).[98] Papers and written proofs were not enough. The Lords wished also to examine witnesses and delinquents upon oath. The number of witnesses multiplied so rapidly that the Lords decided to delegate to three separate committees (one for each of Mompesson's patents) the task of selecting and examining those whose testimony seemed most important. The power of summoning witnesses and of giving the required oath could not be delegated but remained in the house itself.[99] Day after day witnesses were sworn by the clerk,[1] who then forwarded the names to appropriate committees.[2] Some witnesses presented depositions which the clerk apparently read aloud, and which deponents then averred to be true.[3] When delinquents involved in the case were committed to the Fleet, Elsyng prepared the warrant. When they were to appear in the house, Elsyng drew the necessary orders; and when these offenders were bailed, Elsyng received the money for their surety.[4]

The charges against Mompesson were drawn up from the "collections" of the three committees.[5] After charges had been voted, the Commons were summoned, and on March 26 Elsyng was busily "writing fair the sentence" which the lord chief justice, then presiding in the upper house, pronounced that afternoon.[6] On the following day, the Lords ordered that the judgments of the house should be "enrolled and kept in parchment," also the clerk's responsibility.[7]

In the same parliament, 1621, charges were brought against other men, among them Sir Francis Michell, Sir Henry Yelverton, Sir John Bennett, and Sir Francis Bacon, lord chancellor. In these and other hearings in the house it was always the clerk who summoned and swore in witnesses, received depositions and other documents, issued orders to imprison or bail delinquents.[8] In desperation, Elsyng asked for help in sorting depositions in Michell's case, "for they are so confused, that I cannot perfect the charge . . . and the process thereof."[9] Elsyng had also to prepare for Yelverton's use a copy of the charges against him, to read aloud the examinations of witnesses, and finally in a dramatic scene to read the submission of the lord chancellor to the house.[10] On May 28, Elsyng certified into chancery the fines assessed against him and other offenders.[11]

Many grievances, during Elsyng's tenure as clerk, came before parliament in individual petitions. A

---

[96] For Bowyer's account of the certification of acts, see British Museum, Titus B.V., fol. 281.

[97] H.L.R.O., Long Calendar, Vol. I. On the subsidy rolls, see Bond, "Acts of Parliament," pp. 204–205. L.J., **3**: p. 35.

[98] L.J., **3**: pp. 36, 38, 42; H.L.R.O., Main Papers, H.L., 6 April, 1616—29 September, 1620, *passim*.

[99] L.J., **3**: p. 47.

[1] For the oath, see L.J., **3**: p. 60; H.L.R.O., Main Papers, H.L., 21 March, 1620/1. For the swearing of witnesses, see L.J., **3**: pp. 48–49, 56, 67; Petyt 538/7, fols. 244–245A.

[2] Relf, *Debates in the House of Lords 1621*, p. 27.

[3] For depositions, see L.J., **3**: p. 50.

[4] H.L.R.O., Main Papers, H.L., 22 March, 1620/1; L.J., **3**: pp. 65, 72, 76. A note, signed by Richard Dike, entreated Elsyng "to leave a note in writing at my house" "whensoever it shall please the Lords to call me" (Add. 40,086, fol. 3).

[5] L.J., **3**: p. 70.

[6] L.J., **3**: p. 72; Petyt 538/7, fol. 296.

[7] L.J., **3**: p. 74. See below, pp. 30–33.

[8] Elsyng made a note in his "scribbled book" that Sir John Bennett came "before the setting of the court," and asked him to take notice that he was there and would appear "according to his bail" (Add. 40,086, fol. 3). For a certificate from Elsyng that Bennett had attended the house from day to day as required, see H.L.R.O., Main Papers, H.L., 21 December, 1621, and L.J., **3**: p. 151. For examples from later parliaments of orders for the appearance of witnesses, see H.L.R.O., Main Papers, H.L., 26 March, 4 April, 17 April, 16 May, 1628; 19 February, 1628/9. The clerk also summoned those who had offended in cases of privilege (H.L.R.O., Main Papers, H.L., 2 May, 1621, 31 March, 1626; L.J., **3**: p. 546).

[9] H.L.R.O., Main Papers, H.L., 18 April, 1621.

[10] L.J., **3**: pp. 78, 80, 85. In May, 1624, the Lords ordered that in trials in the house, defendants were to have copies of depositions "both *pro* and *contra*" (*ibid.*, p. 418).

[11] H.L.R.O., Main Papers, H.L., 28 May, 1621; L.J., **3**: p. 142. For similar documents in the case of Dr. Mainwaring (1628), see H.L.R.O., Braye 1.

large number have survived at the House of Lords Record Office. Elsyng's endorsements show how they progressed through parliament, and how, at each stage, a petition, like a bill, was his responsibility. He docketed petitions as they were received, scheduled them for reading, noted the date and the reference to a committee if this had occurred. Often there was a hearing, interested parties were notified, counsel assigned, and witnesses summoned.[12] The committee then reported to the house, and the subsequent order, if an order was voted, was issued by the clerk, who might also arrange for or oversee its execution.

In 1621, for example, Sir James Cunningham prayed the Lords to assist him in collecting payment from the Muscovy Company. The king, he said, on suit from the company, had revoked a grant of fishing rights off Greenland formerly made to Cunningham, but had provided that a settlement should recompense any losses. Cunningham claimed that the company refused to pay the sum recommended by the lords of the council. Elsyng's endorsement shows that Cunningham's petition was read on May 25 and referred to a committee. Representatives of the Muscovy Company were called.[13] On June 4 the committee reported that it had several times heard Cunningham, Alderman Hamersly (governor of the company), and Benjamin Dewe, company agent. The committee found that some of the money claimed by Cunningham was "due unto certain poor men."[14] The house ordered that the men should be paid and the rest of the claim deferred until the next meeting of the house.

Elsyng drafted the order himself, and also made a fair copy. On June 9 he added a postscript to the original, written at the behest of the Earl of Warwick, chairman of the committee: "Mr. Alderman Hamersly, I am required to receive this money and to pay the same unto the poor men . . . I pray send it to my office in the old palace at Westminster."[15] Notes on June 14, 16, and 20 concern the payment. George Fenton wrote that the company had no money. He would have to pay the men himself. Alderman Hamersly affirmed that he would make payment. "I certified this to George Fenton," Elsyng wrote, "who liked not of it." On June 16, Hamersly wrote Elsyng that he thought all had been paid.[16] Three years later, Elsyng was still involved with Cunningham's petition.[17] Similarly, in response to petitions from other creditors of the Muscovy Company, provision was made that "the monies . . . be paid in to the clerk of the parliament, who shall have a chest left with him by the company, with two several locks and two several keys to each of them," one set of keys to be kept by Elsyng, the other by those to whom money was due.[18]

During Elsyng's tenure as clerk, the consideration of petitions was delegated to a special committee. Apparently structured on the model of the house itself, the work of the Committee on Petitions, under the chairmanship of the Earl of Bridgewater, expanded rapidly during the sessions of 1621 and 1624, and must have absorbed much of Elsyng's time and energy.[19] By 1626, he had assigned an assistant to serve as clerk for the committee (probably Will Harrison). Catalogues and lists of petitions were prepared [20] (like those for bills prepared for the house), sometimes rudimentary agenda sheets: "This is all the business your lordships have appointed for this present Tuesday. . . ."[21] Occasionally there are minutes. Several pages of notes have survived concerning decisions in May, 1624;[22] and what purports to be a book of orders for 1628 contains running notes of proceedings from April 10 through June 24.[23] By 1626, the committee had two "books," one "wherein are entered all the petitions which the Lords Committees for Petitions do receive and deliver to me." Harrison allowed a page for each petition. Possibly his zeal faltered as time went on, or the committee failed to act. In some cases the Lords' order has been entered with the date. On others, only the name of the petitioner appears.[24] Elsyng endorsed the second "book," "Answers for Petitions." The first seven pages are in his hand. The rest, written by an assistant, have his notes, emendations, and marginalia.[25]

Petitions flooded in. In June, 1621, Elsyng wrote to Bridgewater on behalf of one Mathew Nevill who had submitted a petition earlier in the spring, "and yet it was never read, though I importuned often a reading for that and other petitions." "Time not permitting their lordships to answer them all," the com-

---

[12] Elsyng notified those who should attend (H.L.R.O., Main Papers, H.L., 2 May, 1621), and also summoned witnesses and defendants and assigned counsel (H.L.R.O., Main Papers, H.L., 26 and 31 March, 8 April, 1 and 27 May, 1628; 5 February, 1628/9).
[13] H.L.R.O., Main Papers, H.L., 25 May, 1621; L.J., 3: pp. 131–132.
[14] L.J., 3: p. 156.
[15] H.L.R.O., Main Papers, H.L., 4 June, 1621, fols. 18–21.
[16] H.L.R.O., Main Papers, H.L., 16 and 20 June, 1621.
[17] H.L.R.O., Main Papers, H.L., 16 and 23 April, 1624.

[18] L.J., 3: p. 865; H.L.R.O., Main Papers, H.L., 19 June, 1628.
[19] For a general discussion, see Relf, *Debates in the House of Lords 1621*, pp. xii-xxxii.
[20] El. 6921, Calendar of Petitions 1621. H.L.R.O., Main Papers, H.L., 12 December, 1621, catalogue of petitions endorsed for the Earl of Bridgewater. *Ibid.*, 26 May, 1624, "minutes" of committee decisions on 25 petitions. *Ibid.*, 23 February, 1625/6, catalogue of petitions received, February-March. For catalogues of petitions received on specific days, see *ibid.*, 28 February, 1625/6; 9 March, 1625/6; 18 April, 1626; 20 April, 1626; 2, 4, 16 May, 13 June, 1626. *Ibid.*, 1626, two lists: "Orders upon Petitions," "Petitions rejected."
[21] H.L.R.O., Main Papers, H.L., 23 May, 1626.
[22] H.L.R.O., Main Papers, H.L., 26 May, 1624.
[23] For notes of proceedings taken by the Earl of Bridgewater, first committee, see El. 7937 and 7938.
[24] H.L.R.O., Main Papers, H.L., 6 February, 1625/6.
[25] H.L.R.O., Main Papers, H.L., 6 February, 1625/6.

mittee authorized Elsyng, as clerk, to make preliminary disposition of some himself. He was to inform petitioners that parliament would not reverse decrees without hearing counsel on both sides, a lengthy process, and difficult to schedule. Suits in other courts, he should say, would not be stayed "upon pretence of petition exhibited in parliament and unanswered." Elsyng could also recommend that petitions be referred to appropriate courts. Thus in Nevill's case, Elsyng asked Bridgewater "which of the three answers (prescribed unto me), I may fit unto this petition." Elsyng himself thought it should be reviewed in chancery, "but," he went on to remind the earl, "it will do the poor man little good, for that he is not able to wage law, unless the petition be especially commended by your lordship to the master of the rolls." [26] Many petitioners to parliament were doubtless hoping for a cheap and expeditious remedy; but for most the remedy may not have been expeditious at all. The Committee on Petitions, taking over functions formerly exercised by the receivers of petitions, had become thoroughly clogged. In earlier times, from the fourteenth century until 1540, the clerks of the parliaments had served with the receivers as "junior members." Did Elsyng realize that he, like the committee itself, was continuing an ancient role? It would have delighted his antiquarian heart.[27]

Petitions remained in Elsyng's custody until their final disposition by the house. In 1624, Sir Richard Weston, lord chief baron of the exchequer, was ordered to copy those which had been presented against him; "the Lords," Elsyng wrote, "have commanded me not to let the original petitions to go out of my hands." [28] Earlier, in 1621, the house ordered that petitions which concerned cases pending in other courts should

> be kept by the clerk of the parliament and he to attend the judges of the courts, as the petition shall be called for, and to resume the petition from the judges to be kept, with the judges' resolution thereupon signified, and to present the petitions again to the house at the next meeting.[29]

It must have taken time. Petitions which the house dismissed or ordered to other courts were signed by the clerk and redelivered to petitioners.[30] Others were retained as part of the record. Now on file at the House of Lords Record Office, many have been endorsed and annotated by Elsyng himself. His brief record best tells the story of how much work each one had brought to the clerical office.[31]

Petitions, hearings, investigations and similar activities of parliament involved the clerk in drafting and issuing a great variety of orders. In 1621, for instance, in the case of Stafford v. Stafford, on order of the house, Elsyng drafted a warrant for a *scire facias*. Doubtless he was inexperienced. He made several emendations in the text, directing the warrant first to the deputy clerk of the crown, then crossing this off and redirecting it to William Ravenscroft, "one of the clerks of the pettybag."

As Elsyng became more accustomed to his work, the drafting of such simple orders may have been relegated to assistants. But he continued to handle a fair number himself.[32] In 1626 Elsyng drew orders concerning the earldom of Oxford,[33] and the claims of Sir Thomas Munson against the Earl of Middlesex. To the last, he added a note: "Thus I conceive the order was 14 *Martii* and if I do err herein, I desire the lords of that committee to rectify the same. H.E." The committee found no fault with his work. Elsyng's next endorsement ran, "Read and allowed. 18 *Martii*." [34] He drafted the order providing punishment for George Gardiner who had bought and sold counterfeit protections. These papers identified servants of peers who in time of parliament were free from arrest. The market value of protection was high, and forgery profitable.[35] The order of the house for the precedency of the barony of Clifford presented difficulties, reflected

---

[26] El. 6473; L.J., 3: p. 157.

[27] A. F. Pollard, "Receivers of Petitions and Clerks of Parliament," *English Historical Review* 57 (1942): pp. 202, 220; Relf, *Debates in the House of Lords 1621*, p. xxi. Elsyng observed that the clerk of the parliament was appointed a receiver of petitions in 6 E. III (Elsyng, *Manner of Holding Parliaments*, p. 270).

[28] H.L.R.O., Main Papers, H.L., 4 May, 1624.

[29] El. 7938; L.J., 3: p. 157.

[30] See L.J., 3: pp. 415-17; H.L.R.O., Main Papers, H.L., 6 February, 1625/6.

[31] For petitions with endorsements, orders, or other notations in Elsyng's hand, see H.L.R.O., Main Papers, H.L., 15 March, 1620/1; 2, 8, 18, 25, 28 May; 2, 4 June; 8 December, 1621; 8, 13 March, 1623/4; 9, 23, 30 April; 14, 28 May, 1624; 25, 28, 30 June; 1, 6, 11 July; 5 August, 1625; 23, 28 February; 1, 2, 13, 14, 15, 16, 18, 20, 21, 23, 24 March, 1625/6; 28, 29, 30, 31 March; 1, 4 April; 1, 4, 6, 24 May; 13 June, 1626; 26, 27, 31 March; 1, 3, 4, 9, 23 April; 1, 3, 7, 13, 16, 20, 22, 23, 27, 28, 30 May; 11, 14, 17, 18, 19 21, 23, 25, 26 June, 1628; 22, 24, 26, 29, 31 January; 2, 3, 5, 7, 12, 14, 19, 21, 23 February, 1628/9.

[32] For orders drafted, corrected, or written in Henry Elsyng's hand, see H.L.R.O., Main Papers, H.L., 26 May, 4 June, 1621; 28, 29 May, 1624; 8, 9, 11 July, 5, 6, 11 August, 1625; 25 February, 2, 11, 14, 16, 18 March, 1625/6; 28 March, 4, 5 April, 1626; 22 March, 1627/8; 26, 31 March; 1, 3, 4, 8, 19 April; 1, 3, 6, 7, 8, 10, 14, 16, 22, 27 May; 12, 14, 17, 18, 19 June, 1628; 31 January; 5, 16, 21 February 1628/9.

[33] H.L.R.O., Main Papers, H.L., 11 March, 1625/6; L.J., 3: p. 524.

[34] H.L.R.O., Main Papers, H.L., 14 March, 1625/6; L.J., 3: p. 527.

[35] H.L.R.O., Main Papers, H.L., 4 April, 1626; L.J., 3: p. 550. For Elsyng's order for the arrest of John Mayne who had counterfeited a protection, see H.L.R.O., Main Papers, H.L., 3 April, 1628; L.J., 3: p. 709. There were other cases (H.L.R.O., Main Papers, H.L., November, 1621, 3 December, 1621, 13 March, 1625/6; L.J., 3: pp. 170, 179, 525). For a sample letter of protection, see my *Proceedings in Parliament 1610* 2: p. 6, n. For Elsyng's comment on protections, see Petyt 538/12, fol. 176 v.

in the numerous corrections Elsyng made in his draft,[36] and he must have worked hard and long over the complex order concerning the manors of Sir Francis Coningsby.[37]

Elsyng drew orders for arrest, orders for discharge of prisoners, orders scheduling hearings, assigning counsel, for the attendance of witnesses and delinquents.[38] A sign of the times was his order in April, 1628, summoning witnesses of a riot involving soldiers and inhabitants of Whittam in Essex.[39] Elsyng must have taken pleasure in drafting a second order requiring the dean and chapter of York to pay fees due to the officers of the house.[40] He drafted the sentence of the house on Reynde for "ignominious speeches" against Lord Saye and Sele.[41] He drafted the order for a commission concerning the lands of a free grammar school, crossing off half of what he had written.[42]

So it went. With some orders Elsyng had the help of legal assistants attached to the house, or even of petitioners' counsel.[43] Other orders became standardized, and were doubtless left to assistants. But throughout his years as clerk, Elsyng continued to draft a large variety of orders himself. There were two reasons for this. First must have been the heavy schedule in the house. Elsyng did not have sufficient help. But more important was the fact that revival of impeachment and the activities of the Committee on Petitions posed fresh problems for Elsyng to solve. His many drafts of orders show how carefully he worked to find appropriate ways in which to implement the decisions of the Lords.

THE JOURNAL OF THE HOUSE OF LORDS

When parliament was in session, a major portion of Elsyng's time was devoted to collecting materials for the journal. In compiling this record, he relied on notes made in the house: his own notes and those of his assistants. He also used the written reports, petitions, and speeches which had become part of the archive. From all of these papers, Elsyng compiled a draft journal and finally the official journal of the House of Lords.

Robert Bowyer, Elsyng's friend and predecessor, had kept a full, running account of proceedings and debate in the upper House. Out of these "scribbled books," of which only one is known to have survived, Bowyer wrote his finished journal for the Lords.[1] Though Bowyer relied on his rough notes, he did not think of them as part of the official record, but written for his own "remembrance and instruction." "My scribbled book," he wrote, ". . . for my own private instruction hath as much as I could observe."[2] Bowyer well knew that his notes went far beyond what the clerk needed for the journal. Elsyng continued Bowyer's custom and in March, 1621, took over the practice of keeping "scribbled books." Notes, in his own hand, have survived for March, April, May, November, and December in 1621, and a few days of February, 1622; for February–May, 1624, for February–June, 1626, and for March–May, 1628. Other "scribbled" notes made by the clerk himself have been lost.[3]

Like Bowyer, Elsyng sometimes had difficulty in hearing or understanding what lords said. The room was large and members may have moved about or talked during the session. Elsyng several times missed remarks of Lord Paget.[4] When he could not hear

---

[36] H.L.R.O., Main Papers, H. L., 22 March, 1628; L.J., 3: p. 695.

[37] H.L.R.O., Main Papers, H.L., 31 May, 1628; L.J., 3: p. 833. See also H.L.R.O., Main Papers, H.L., 14 June, 1628 and L.J., 3: p. 855. For the significance of this case, see Relf, *Debates in the House of Lords 1621,* p. xxx.

[38] H.L.R.O., Main Papers, H.L., 8 July, 1625; L.J., 3: p. 461; H.L.R.O., Main Papers, H.L., 31 March; 1, 3, 6, 7, 8, 10, 14 May; 17, 18, 19 June, 1628, 5 February, 1628/9; L.J., 3: p. 867. Among Elsyng's papers is a list of "witnesses" and "delinquents," possibly a memorandum for orders and summons (H.L.R.O., Main Papers, H.L., [1628]).

[39] H.L.R.O., Main Papers, H.L., 4 April, 1628; L.J., 3: p. 711.

[40] H.L.R.O., Main Papers, H.L., 3, 19 April, 1628; L.J., 3: pp. 710, 753.

[41] H.L.R.O., Main Papers, H.L., 12, 14 June, 1628; L.J., 3: p. 851.

[42] H.L.R.O., Main Papers, H.L., 31 January, 1628/9; L.J., 4: p. 18.

[43] Notes for the order for the creditors of the Muscovy Company, signed by the Duke of Devonshire, were endorsed "voted and ordered but to be drawn into form by Mr. Sgt. Davenport" (H.L.R.O., Main Papers, H.L., 19 June, 1628). This bundle of papers also contains a fair copy of the order as printed in L.J., 3: p. 864, endorsed by Elsyng, Devonshire's notes, Devonshire's report on the petition, numerous earlier orders on petitions in the same matter, some docketed by Elsyng. For counsel, see the order concerning Coningsby, L.J., 3: p. 855.

[1] Foster, *Proceedings in Parliament 1610* 1: p. xxvi. See Petyt 538/7, fols. 193-224, for the way he continued this practice in 1621.

[2] Foster, *Proceedings in Parliament 1610* 1: p. 247. See also pp. xxviii–xxix, 177n., 242-243.

[3] The following "scribbled books" are in Elsyng's hand, and were kept by him while the house was in session: 1621, 12 March—29 March, Petyt 538/7 (printed in Relf, *Debates in the House of Lords 1621*); 17 April—18 May, Add. 40,085 (printed in Gardiner, *Debates in the House of Lords 1621*); 14 November—8 February, 1621/2, Add. 40,086 (printed in Gardiner, *Debates in the House of Lords 1621*). 1624: 12 February—25 March, 1 April—29 May, Add. 40,087, 40,088 (both printed in Gardiner, *Debates in the House of Lords 1624*). 1626: 6 February—29 April, 1 May—15 June, Add. 40,089, Add. 40,090 (both printed in Gardiner, *Debates in the House of Lords 1624*). 1628: 17 March—30 April, Petyt 538/7; 1 May—31 May, Bodleian Library, Rawl. A 106 (both printed in Relf, *Debates in the House of Lords 1621*). Relf prints more than Gardiner, but both have omitted sections of the "scribbled books," so that, for this and other reasons, it is useful to refer back to the manuscripts. Elsyng's notes for August 4, 1625, are in Braye 95, #12 (Osborn Collection).

[4] For Bowyer, see my *Proceedings in Parliament 1610* 1: p. xxv. Gardiner, *Debates in the House of Lords 1621*, pp. 16, 56. The Lords chamber was between sixty and seventy feet in length; see the plan of the queen's chamber in R. Allen Brown,

Lord Mandeville, he requested that his lordship read over and correct what he had managed to take. He could not hear or understand Arundel.[5] He could not hear Lord Saye and Sele and made a memorandum to ask him for a copy of an order.[6] He could not hear Buckingham, and Pembroke "spake so fast I could not follow with my pen."[7] Elsyng did not always understand what was meant. He found Bridgewater's report confusing when he spoke for the Committee on Petitions in 1624.[8] In 1626 when counsel for rival claimants to the earldom of Oxford were heard, Elsyng made a note, "perfect this pedigree, for I did not well understand it." Opposite a remark by Pembroke, he wrote, "I could not conceive this."[9] When suggestions for action were offered rapidly, it was difficult to record what each speaker said. Thus in 1628, the clerk caught a few phrases, crossed them off, and finally marked "*Quaere*" in the margin.[10]

Elsyng was frequently interrupted in his note-taking. He must rise to read bills and other material for the information of the house. "I read all and so could write no more." At such times, his assistants might take over the "scribbled book."[11] In 1621, when Elsyng was asked on short notice to copy out the sentence against Sir Giles Mompesson, the deputy clerk of the crown filled his place by taking down a report. Later Elsyng was suddenly required to draft the charge against Sir Henry Yelverton. This duty must also have interrupted his regular entries in the "scribbled book."[12] He may have been out of the house during the afternoon of May 27, 1624, for the notes seem to be in a different hand.[13] In 1626 Elsyng was called from his table to attend the lord treasurer, and half a page has been left blank. He was absent on May 24, 1628, and relied on his son to record proceedings.[14]

As Bowyer had done, Elsyng took down more than he actually needed for the construction of the final journal. On several occasions he recorded votes or named those who dissented,[15] though this information was not considered suitable for the record.[16] Elsyng also took notes when the lords adjourned the house *ad libitum* and sat as a committee of the whole. Possibly he continued his account for the information of the lords themselves. In March, 1621, shortly after he had been sworn as deputy clerk, Elsyng wrote that the Earl of Warwick "admonished" him "to take notes of this committee of the whole house by itself, which I have done and it is annexed."[17] Possibly he did it to help himself in his work or on order from the house. In a number of instances an account of the informal discussion in committee has been incorporated in the journal,[18] though such proceedings were not normally included; and on even more occasions, Elsyng busily recorded what was said in his "scribbled book."[19]

He always observed points of procedure. When the king came to the house, "the prince and lords were bare-headed all." "All the committees stood during the report" of a conference with the lower house, "and the attendant stood also."[20] When the house went into committee, "the lord chancellor removed to his seat as as a peer."[21] "When a petition is rejected no order is to be made upon it, as I conceive."[22] "It is the ancient order," he observed, when Lord Clare moved that those who came late should "pay to the poor box."[23] He carefully described how a committee brought in a bill.[24] He remarked that, when a lord was introduced into the house, he should have "given his writ and not his patent."[25] When the Bishop of Norwich answered a complaint brought by the House of Commons in 1624, he "stood in his place."[26] At the opening of parliament in 1626, "the lords and judges stood until

---

H. M. Colvin, A. J. Taylor, *History of the King's Works* (London, 1963), plan III.

[5] Gardiner, *Debates in the House of Lords 1621*, pp. 54, 60; Relf, *Debates in the House of Lords 1621*, p. 16.

[6] Add. 40,085, fol. 159ᵛ.

[7] Gardiner, *Debates in the House of Lords 1621*, pp. 58–59.

[8] "q. de hoc for I did not understand it" (Add. 40,088, fol. 139); cf. L.J., **3**: pp. 415–417.

[9] Add. 40,089, fol. 47ᵛ; cf. L.J., **3**: p. 517. Gardiner, *Debates in the House of Lords 1621*, p. 32.

[10] Relf, *Debates in the House of Lords 1621*, p. 134. His assistant was more successful (p. 134, n.). See also, p. 165: "Agreed (as I conceived) to be the sense of the house."

[11] *Ibid.*, p. 91. See above, pp. 11–12.

[12] Petyt 538/7, fol. 296; Gardiner, *Debates in the House of Lords 1621*, p. 6. See H.L.R.O., Main Papers, H.L., 2 June, 1621, fol. 10, where Elsyng also speaks of drawing part of the judgment against Yelverton, though this duty was probably not performed while the house was sitting.

[13] Add. 40,088, fols. 135ᵛ–138, top.

[14] Add. 40,089, fol. 105. The clerk had also to attend the courts and search for records in the Tower (above, pp. 10, 20). For 1628, see Relf, *Debates in the House of Lords 1621*, p. 99.

[15] The names of dissenting lords have been obliterated, but Elsyng's count is in the margin (Add. 40,086, fol. 73); Gardiner, *Debates in the House of Lords 1624*, p. 140; Relf, *Debates in the House of Lords 1621*, p. 165.

[16] Foster, "Procedure in the House of Lords," p. 64.

[17] Relf, *Debates in the House of Lords 1621*, p. 21. Bowyer had sometimes been ordered to withdraw when the house was in committee; sometimes he remained and took notes (Foster, "Procedure in the House of Lords," p. 68).

[18] For examples, see L.J., **3**: pp. 46, 63, 71–72, 289.

[19] For some examples of notes taken by Elsyng at committees of the whole house in 1621, see Relf, *Debates in the House of Lords 1621*, pp. 21, 24–25, 33–35, 38–39, 42–46, 48–49; in 1624 and 1626, see Gardiner, *Debates in the House of Lords 1624*, pp. 7–9, 11–12, 17–18, 52–57, 73–76, 77–84, 84–87, 88–90, 99–100, 114–115, 156, 168–171, 185–187, 195–196, 218–219; in 1628, see Relf, *Debates in the House of Lords 1621*, pp. 84–85, 95–98, 111–112, 118, 121–123, 125–134, 144–147, 148–149, 161–164, 166–169, 175–178, 200–204. For votes in a committee of the whole, see Relf, *Debates in the House of Lords 1621*, p. 39.

[20] Gardiner, *Debates in the House of Lords 1621*, p. 11.

[21] Relf, *Debates in the House of Lords 1621*, pp. 24–25. See also, L.J., **3**: p. 43.

[22] Relf, *Debates in the House of Lords 1621*, p. 71.

[23] *Ibid.*, p. 84.

[24] Gardiner, *Debates in the House of Lords 1621*, p. 76.

[25] Add. 40,086, fol. 10.

[26] Add. 40,088, fol. 109; see also L.J., **3**: p. 388.

the king bade them sit down, but none were covered." [27] Some descriptions of procedure were incorporated in the journal, some later in the roll of parliament, and the most important in the roll of standing orders which dates from Elsyng's own time as clerk.[28]

In addition to keeping an account of proceedings, Elsyng used his "scribbled book," as was natural, for a variety of memoranda. He recorded business assigned to him and subsequently carried through. In 1621 prisoners were released by the House of Commons for examination by the Lords. "Memorandum," Elsyng wrote, "that I delivered the catalogue of these names, and of their oath subscribed with my name unto the said lords committees." [29] When he was ordered to summon witnesses and arrange for their examination, he jotted in the margin, "They were sent for," and "He was examined by Mr. Attorney." [30] He noted the payment of fees due from lords and also those due for private bills.[31] He made a memorandum, "the clerk to remember this on Monday morning." [32] Elsyng also used his "scribbled book" for notes on the archive of parliament. He entered documents loaned out (a bill to Serjeant Bird) or received (examinations of witnesses, a bill from Mr. Attorney).[33] He kept a record of documents returned. "Memorandum . . . the clerk delivered the complaint itself unto the said Richard Crawley," who had brought it in the first place. Crawley's initials are scrawled beneath. The "scribbled book" thus served as a receipt.[34] The pages recording the examination of Sir Francis Michell bear Michell's signature, doubtless attesting to the accuracy of what had been written.[35] The bails for Sir John Bennett and for the warden of the Fleet, signed by Lord Chief Justice Ley, are sewed into the fourth book for 1621.[36] When John Selden borrowed material concerning Mompesson, he too left a signed receipt in Elsyng's book.[37]

By 1621, when Elsyng took office, the "scribbled books" kept by the clerk had ceased to be his private memoranda and come to have official status. They were regularly checked by a committee of lords. Probably this custom began in Elsyng's time. In 1597 Lord Burghley had moved that a committee be appointed to check the journal each parliament; but there is no record that Burghley's committee was actually appointed or that his proposal was carried out in subsequent years.[38] The subcommittee (of the Committee of Privileges) appointed for the journal in 1621 had a broader charge:

the said lords subcommittees shall and may daily or as often as their Lordships shall think fit peruse the journal book of this house and the entrances therein made or to be made to the end they may be duly entered by the clerk according to the resolution of the house and if they shall find any defect therein to see it amended and acquaint the house with what they do which was by the house voted accordingly.[39]

So it was that a committee of lords turned its attention to the "scribbled books" of the clerk and the draft journals which he compiled from them. Probably with Bowyer, an experienced clerk who served the last two months of his term in 1621, the committee checked only the draft journal. But when Elsyng took over Bowyer's duties in March, the lords checked each stage of his work, and read his "scribbled book" week by week.[40] On May 8, 1621, Elsyng observed: ". . . one of the lords had my book . . . so I took a loose paper to set down that which follows which I have sewed in." [41] Doubtless it was the committee which raised some of the questions in the margin of the books, suggested some of the corrections and ordered some of the deletions. Notes concerning a quarrel between the Earl of Arundel and Lord Spencer were heavily inked out, and six folios on the same matter were cut from the book.[42] Some corrections may have been suggested by

---

[27] Gardiner, *Debates in the House of Lords 1624*, p. 107.

[28] *Cf.* L.J., 3: p. 63: "the lord chief justice removed from the lord chancellor's seat to his place of assistance. . . ." See below, pp. 26, 30–32. For the standing orders see *Manuscripts of the House of Lords* 10: pp. xxxix–xlvi, 1–11.

[29] Relf, *Debates in the House of Lords 1621*, pp. 26–27.

[30] *Ibid.*, pp. 29–30. "I did write this day accordingly . . ." has been written opposite "the clerk to write to H. Starkey" (Add. 40,089, fol. 24^v).

[31] Relf, *Debates in the House of Lords 1621*, p. 67; Add. 40,087, fol. 91.

[32] Gardiner, *Debates in the House of Lords 1624*, p. 38. I think the entry on 19 March, 1620/1, P.M., is a similar memorandum. Relf transcribed "Pembroke," but "Remember" seems to me a better reading (Relf, *Debates in the House of Lords 1621*, p. 27, and Petyt 538/7, fol. 252).

[33] Gardiner, *Debates in the House of Lords 1621*, pp. 10–11. "I gave the bill to Sir W. Bird" (Add. 40,085, fol. 149^v). Elsyng borrowed and returned notes concerning Yelverton's speech (Gardiner, *Debates in the House of Lords 1621*, p. 72). See Add. 40,086, cover, for a note concerning a bill given to Serjeant Hitcham. For other notations concerning the receipt or delivery of bills and other documents, see Petyt 538/7, fols. 255–256^v; Add. 40,087, fols. 65, 67^v, 81, 84^v, 85, 94^v; Add. 40,088, fols. 5, 21, 121. Elsyng wrote concerning the order for the mitigation of fines, "Earl marshall had this away from me, it being written all with his lordship's hand" (Gardiner, *Debates in the House of Lords 1624*, p. 48).

[34] Add. 40,085, fol. 50.

[35] *Ibid.*, fols. 74^v – 75.

[36] Add. 40,086, fols 5^v–7. *Cf.* a similar practice by the clerk of the House of Commons in 1610, in my *Proceedings in Parliament 1610* 1: pp. xxxv–xxxvi, n. 4.

[37] Petyt 538/7, fol. 36.

[38] L. J., 2: p. 195. Probably the motion was voted and ordered, or it would not have been recorded in the journal. No order was, however, entered, nor were any committee names listed.

[39] Endorsed in Henry Elsyng's hand: "3 *Martii* 1620/as I take it, it is to be/v^e 17 Febr./" (H.L.R.O., Main Papers, H.L., 17 February, 1620/1). The charge for the committee in the Lords journal is less detailed (L.J., 3: p. 21).

[40] Gardiner, *Debates in the House of Lords 1621*, pp. 10, 24; Add. 40,085, fol. 79.

[41] Add. 40,085, fol. 130. Similarly he wrote notes for August 4, 1625, on a loose sheet (see above, p. 21, n. 3).

[42] *Ibid.*, fol. 150^v and the folios following. *Cf.* Gardiner,

the committee.[43] Others may have been made on Elsyng's own initiative.[44] Certain changes were made by king's counsel. On a number of occasions Elsyng made memoranda in the "scribbled book" which may have been questions which he intended to raise with the committee or problems which occurred to him as he wrote and which he planned to settle later on.[45] Often they involved debates of the greatest delicacy. On May 16, 1626, when the Duke of Buckingham spoke in his own defense, Elsyng asked, "how far I shall enter these protestations and the occasion thereof."[46] The next day Elsyng was also puzzled what to do, "q. how to enter this that follows."[47] He made numerous memoranda in his books where to get additional material needed for the next stage of his work, the draft journal.[48]

Elsyng's "scribbled books" differ from the book left by Robert Bowyer for 1610. Elsyng wrote more clearly, spaced his notes more generously on a page, and probably did not record debate in as great detail. He must always have been aware that the lords would read what he had written, that his notes were not, as Bowyer's apparently had been, only for himself. As the years went on, Elsyng's "scribbled books" reflect his growing assurance as clerk, and his increasing sense of what was needed and appropriate for the journal. After 1621, the work of the Lords' committee is not so evident in the "scribbled book." Elsyng no longer recorded the fact that they read his notes, though there are other indications that this was probably the case.[49] By 1626 and 1628, Elsyng relied more heavily on his assistants than he had earlier to fill in what was needed to complete his account. His "scribbled book" is sketchy in many places. He knew what he needed to record and let much of the rest go.

Elsyng's assistants also took notes in the house. For several parliaments, the assistants' notes run concurrently with the notes of the clerk himself: in 1621, March, April, May; in 1624, February–May; in 1628, March–May, when there are three accounts, one Elsyng's own, one kept by his son, and one by an assistant clerk. For 1625, the book kept by an assistant is the one set of running notes which has survived.[50] Only in the matter of registering attendance is there any clear division of labor between the clerk and his assistants. The House of Lords, unlike the House of Commons, kept a daily record of members present. Bowyer wrote some notes concerning attendance in his "scribbled book."[51] When Elsyng took his uncle's place, he continued to record excuses offered for absent lords and some proxies, but delegated the rest of the job to his assistants as Bowyer had probably done.[52] The assistants apparently entered the names as lords arrived—the names are not in order of precedence—[53] and recorded proxies as they were presented day by day.[54] The attendance list must have been corrected and completed later before it was realigned in order of precedence and entered in the manuscript journal for the day. Names have been marked "*Entr.*," "*exped.*," or "entered," probably as they were transferred. Possibly there was another master list against which names were checked, but the evidence is not now known.[55]

---

[50] Minute books or notes taken by assistant clerks or others: 22 March, 1620/1—18 May, 1621 (H.L.R.O., Minute Book #1, the notes for 22 March—26 March are printed in Gardiner, *Debates in the House of Lords 1621,* appendix); 12 February, 1623/4—25 March, 1624 (H.L.R.O., Minute Book #2); 1 April, 1624—15 May, 1625 (H.L.R.O., Minute Book #3). 17 May, 1625—12 August, 1625 (H.L.R.O., Minute Book #4, printed in Relf, *Debates in the House of Lords 1621*). 17 March, 1627/8—20 October, 1628 (H.L.R.O., Minute Book #5, excerpts are printed in Relf, *Debates in the House of Lords 1621,* as B, see p. 63). 17 March, 1627/8—26 June, 1628 (Add. 40,091, excerpts are printed in Relf, *Debates in the House of Lords 1621,* as A, see p. 63).

[51] For Bowyer's notes on attendance in 1610 which are limited to excuses given, see H.L.R.O., Braye 61. For his notes in 1621, see Petyt 538/7, fols. 192^v, 197^v, 201, 201^v.

[52] There are two lists of proxies in Elsyng's "scribbled books" (Add. 40,087, fols. 3—3^v; Add. 80,089, in the front) and some lists of lords excused (Add. 40,085, fol. 3; Add. 40,089 fol. 140). See above, p. 14.

[53] For example, on 21 February, 1623/4, the Earl of Warwick is listed between Lord St. John of Basingstoke and Lord Willoughby of Ersby. The Earl of Oxford is listed between Lord Brooke and Viscount Mansfield. On 23 February, the Earl of Warwick is listed between Lord Haughton and the Earl of Carlisle (H.L.R.O., Minute Book #2). This seems to indicate that the list was compiled as the lords entered, unless they did not sit in order of precedence, which seems unlikely.

[54] For examples, see H.L.R.O., Minute Book #2, fols. 7, 11.

[55] For examples of incomplete attendance lists, see H.L.R.O., Minute Book #1, March 23 and April 17, 1621; H.L.R.O., Minute Book #4, fols. 3^v, 4. For renumbering of lists in order of precedence, see H.L.R.O., Minute Book #4, fol. 3. For lists in the assistants' books marked "*entratur*," or "*exped.*," see H.L.R.O., Minute Books #1, #2. Robert Bowyer, in his transcript of the Lords journal for 17 November, 1558, remarked that "no mention is made who were present or not present." A full list of lords was given, which he had copied "so at least the number of the Lords temporal which were at this time might appear together with the place of precedency of the Prior of Saint Johns Jerusalem had amongst the said

---

Debates in the House of Lords 1621, pp. 73–74, 91–92. For other deletions, see Add. 40,085, fols. 19–19^v, fols. 120^v — 121; Add. 40,086, fols. 51^v — 52; Add. 40,090, fol. 124.

[43] Add. 40,085, fols. 67–67^v, 68, 68^v, 69, 69^v, 70^v, 74, 89.

[44] "Enter the Heads out of Mr. Sergeant's brief and the proofs" (*ibid.,* fol. 52). See fols. 124, 125^v, 128, 147^v, where queries are indicated and corrections have been made. See also Add. 40,087, fols. 102, 103, 104^v; Add. 40,088, fols. 40, 140.

[45] Add. 40,090, fols. 40, 42, 48, 56^v, 60, 61. In 1621, Crewe and Coventry read the "scribbled book" and perfected it in places which Elsyng marked (Gardiner, *Debates in the House of Lords 1621,* p. 52).

[46] Add. 40,090, fol. 63.

[47] *Ibid.,* fol. 69^v.

[48] See Relf, *Debates in the House of Lords 1621*, pp. 16–17; Add. 40,085, fols. 47^v, 52, 115^v, 117; Add. 40,086, fols. 25, 60; Add. 40,087, fols. 108^v, 118; Add. 40,088, fols. 31, 113, 139, 140; Add. 40,089, fol. 75; Add. 40,090, fols. 61, 67^v.

[49] See above, note 40; Add. 40,088, fols. 94^v, 140, 141.

In general the books kept by the clerk's assistants lack the appearance of haste which marks the "scribbled book" of the clerk himself. Though sometimes incomplete, they often contain material concerning proceedings in the house which is not found in the clerk's book.[56] In the front of their notebooks, assistants kept lists of speeches and documents to be copied for lords, as well as memoranda of various payments, jottings which give a vivid picture of the business which came to them in the house.[57] But these books do not seem to have acquired an official status comparable to that of the clerk's book. There is no evidence that they were perused by the committee for the journal. They seem rather to be independent accounts made at the same time as the clerk's "scribbled book" to assist him and his men in compiling the draft and ultimately the finished journal.[58]

The second stage of the clerk's record was the draft journal, compiled from the "scribbled" notes which he and his assistants took in the house and from additional papers which came to the clerk's table through his own efforts or as part of the archive of parliament. The draft journals which have survived for the period 1621–1629 were all the work of Henry Elsyng.[59] Sometimes he needed to correct or amplify what he had taken in the house. It was not easy to reconstruct a speech from hasty notes. In 1614 both Bowyer and Elsyng, who was then assisting his uncle, took notes of the king's speech, "but," wrote Bowyer, "in the journal book the particulars are not fit to be set down neither can any man without notes delivered from [?] the party set down perfectly a long speech of moment much less will any one treat of a king's speech." The clerk much preferred a copy of the speech itself (if it had been written out ahead of time) or at least an outline.[60]

Memoranda in Elsyng's draft journals show his efforts to obtain such texts of speeches, reports, orders, and petitions. Often he left a space to enter material as it was received. In March, 1621, he wrote, "Here leave 6 lines for this report, which the E. of Arundel hath promised to give me himself."[61] Unfortunately Arundel did not produce the report. Elsyng was still trying to perfect his account the following fall.[62] Again in 1621, Elsyng wrote in the draft journal that he hoped to "confer the scribbled book with my lord treasurer's notes." Later he observed, "I moved my lord treasurer in it and he bids me perfect it by my own scribbled book."[63] Vainly he tried to take down precedents as they were cited on March 23; later he asked the Earl of Warwick for them, and finally decided not to enter them in detail.[64]

He attempted to get a report of the conference concerning informers: "Speak to his lordship for this report. Mr. Attorney hath it. Leave 3 lines for this and speak to Mr. Attorney." Elsyng's last entry in the margin of the draft journal read: "Mr. Attorney says it is needless to be entered."[65] Elsyng began an account of Lord Chancellor Bacon's submission. Then he wrote, "insert the submission at large"; *"vd. schedulam"* is added in another hand, and then the complete text of the submission was copied by an assistant with Elsyng's original account as introduction.[66] Elsyng tried to get the report concerning Sir John Bennett and wrote in the margin of his draft journal, "speak to Sir Ed. Sackville for the charge against Sir John Bennett and enter the heads of that, and the request of the Commons that they might send up more against him." Then has been added in another hand, "Sir Ed. Sackville hath it not." So Elsyng had to manage with what he had. He crossed off the six "heads" he had begun and wrote the summary which now appears in the printed *Journal*.[67] Elsyng asked the Archbishop of Canterbury and the Bishop of Norwich for help with a report in May, 1624, and this time was more successful.[68]

In composing the draft journal, Elsyng made use of the archive of the house. Thus in his "scribbled

---

barons. And as touching the not expressing of what lords were this day present by the clerk of the upper house, it is very probable that having written the whole catalogue of names overnight and purposing to have noted such as were present this morning he was prevented by the early and seasonable death of Queen Mary . . ." ("Journals of Parliament 1553–1558," Osborn Collection). On other days, he said, the names of the lords were marked "pr." if they were present (Petyt 537/6, fol. 67). Compare the observations by D'Ewes concerning the record of attendance in the Elizabethan journals (D'Ewes, pp. 9–10, 62, 96, 111–113, 384, 422).

[56] For examples, see the excerpts from the "scribbled book" of Elsyng's son and of the "second assistant clerk" for 1628 printed by Relf in the footnotes to *Debates in the House of Lords 1621*, pp. 63ff., as A and B.

[57] See above, p. 12, n. 42.

[58] I find it useful to think of these accounts as additional "scribbled books" rather than to differentiate them as "minute books." For an analysis of the two accounts for 1541/2, see M.A.R. Graves, "The Two Lords' Journals of 1542," *Bulletin of the Institute of Historical Research* 43, 108(1970): pp. 182–189.

[59] The surviving draft journals are H.L.R.O., Braye 11 (12 March, 1620/1—27 March, 1621); H.L.R.O., Braye 12 (17 April—18 May, 1621); H.L.R.O., Braye 13 (19 May, 1624—27 March, 1625); H.L.R.O., Braye 14 (17 March, 1627/8—30 April, 1628); H.L.R.O., Braye 15 (1 May—26 June, 1628). See the cover of Elsyng's draft journal for 1621 (H.L.R.O., Braye 12) which he has endorsed, "The first draught out of the second scribbled book of the parliament *de a° 18mo RR/ Jacobi per* H.E."

[60] Braye 112, #83 (Osborn Collection). It was not considered appropriate to speak from notes, see my "Procedure in the House of Lords," p. 70. For copies of official speeches in the clerk's papers, see H.L.R.O., Braye 68, Braye 71, Braye 72.

[61] H.L.R.O., Braye 11, 12 March, 1620/1.

[62] Relf, *Debates in the House of Lords 1621*, pp. 16–17, n.

[63] H.L.R.O., Braye 11, 20 March, 1620/1.

[64] H.L.R.O., Braye 11, fol. 105. *Cf.* L.J., 3: p. 67.

[65] H.L.R.O., Braye 12, 24 April, 1621.

[66] *Ibid.*

[67] H.L.R.O., Braye 12, 21 April, 1621; L.J., 3: p. 87.

[68] H.L.R.O., Braye 13, 19 May, 1624.

book" he made a note "*vd.* the message." The original was laid in, ready to be copied for the next stage of the journal.[69] Elsyng followed the same procedure with the judgment against an offender named Blount.[70] He took pains to complete his account and assure its accuracy. "Look for the names and insert them here," he wrote in the margin of the draft journal. The words have been scratched through and the names entered.[71] Several times he left a note for himself or his assistant, "perfect this hereafter."[72] He also wrote, "Examine this with the original" and in this spirit checked the "very words" of sermons in 1628 and made the necessary corrections in his earlier draft.[73]

Some entries were made on order of the subcommittee for the journal or the house itself. Thus in March, 1621, Elsyng wrote in the margin of his draft, "I am ordered to move my lord chancellor for his notes as this report may be entered at large." Then he noted, "I took it briefly in my scribbled book and so made it up, for I could not get any notes from the lord chancellor."[74] The memorandum concerning the appointment of Sir James Ley as speaker *pro tem.* of the House of Lords, and probably also the royal commission to this effect, were entered on command of the Earl of Huntingdon. The earl was a member of the subcommittee for the journal, with special interest in the procedure of the house.[75]

The draft journal was probably begun promptly. Bowyer apparently started his draft for 1621 early in the session and seems to have finished the first section before he withdrew from parliament in March.[76] Elsyng wrote Sir Robert Cotton that he had no time "to see you, as I desire to do, for I must make up my journal book every day."[77] It was a long job, however, to complete a draft and this stage of the journal was sometimes not finished until after a session had ended. In the draft journal for 1624, Elsyng left certain leaves blank with a note that they were intended for "the business concerning the lord treasurer, *vizt.* 7 *Maii* 10 *et* 11 *Maii* which is now finished but not perused . . . and the 12 *et* 13 of May which are not perfected as yet." He added in 1625, "but now are."[78] The sections which Elsyng worked over so long were sections which dealt with Cranfield's impeachment—a detailed account of charges, examinations, Cranfield's petition, the lords' visit with him, the censure and judgment voted.[79] It is not surprising that completion was delayed. Impeachment and other judicial proceedings in the upper house posed difficult problems for the clerk. Few precedents of how to present the material came to hand and Elsyng had to devise his own formulation. The cause was important and he must be sure of the accuracy of his statements.

Often Elsyng wrote several drafts. Notes in his hand for March 11, 1624, may have been originally intended for the journal but were subsequently discarded.[80] Drafts of proceedings concerning Sir John Bourchier's petition have survived.[81] There is also a draft of the "memorial" for the bill of Monopolies, copied in a scribe's hand, which seems to have been corrected by Elsyng. The draft is much like the final version in the *Journal,* but there are minor differences.[82] Elsyng tried two accounts of the prorogation of November 2, 1624, one in English and one in Latin.[83]

He had not only to satisfy himself, but also the subcommittee of lords which read the draft journals as faithfully as they read the "scribbled books." He sketched out the proceedings of March 12, when first he took his uncle's place. "My first draught," he observed, "which I shewed to the Lords Subcommittees etc. and was ordered by them to make a new draught, reciting the particulars more at large, which I did."[84] On March 13, Elsyng received a memorandum from Huntingdon and other members of the subcommittee. This document, probably the notes for a report delivered to the Committee of Privileges, was in effect a review of the draft journal, now lost, composed by Robert Bowyer. "The lords subcommittees have viewed from the beginning of this present session of

---

[69] Add. 40,085, fol. 115ᵛ.

[70] The judgment is on a separate sheet in another hand, dated and endorsed by Elsyng "to be written in text" (Add. 40,086, fol. 25).

[71] H.L.R.O., Braye 11, 16 March, 1620/1.

[72] H.L.R.O., Braye 11, fols. 76, 77, 81, 83, 85.

[73] H.L.R.O., Braye 11, fols. 52-52ᵛ, 94-96; Braye 15, 13 June, 1628. *Cf.* H.L.R.O., Braye 1, #1, extracts from Mainwaring's sermons.

[74] H.L.R.O., Braye 11, 12 March, 1620/1. The summary in the draft journal was the best he could do and has been reproduced in the journal of the House of Lords (L.J., 3: p. 42).

[75] H.L.R.O., Braye 11, 19 March, 1620/1. *Cf.* the note in Elsyng's "scribbled book": "*Ex iussu Comit.* Huntingdon a memorandum to be entered that the lord chief justice gives the oath as speaker to the house, and not as chancellor" (Petyt 538/7, fol. 264). *The Hastings Journal,* pp. vi–vii.

[76] The "Journal Book of entries" which the subcommittee checked for January and February, 1620/1 must have been Bowyer's draft journal, not his "scribbled book." The "scribbled book" is at the Inner Temple (Petyt 538/7, fols. 193–224). There are no committee marks in the margin similar to those made by the subcommittee on Elsyng's scribbled books. Nevertheless, many questions concerning Bowyer's account were raised by the lords (H.L.R.O., Main Papers, H.L., 13 March, 1621, fols. 149–149ᵛ. See below, pp. 26–27). Bowyer made a note that Bacon, then lord chancellor, recast his draft of the account for January 16 (Petyt 538/7, fol. 193).

[77] British Museum, Julius C. III, fol. 170ᵛ.

[78] H.L.R.O., Braye 13, 29 May, 1624.

[79] *Cf.* L.J., 3: pp. 343–361, 364–370, 371–372, 373–376, 378–379, 380–382.

[80] See above, n. 74; H.L.R.O., Main Papers, H.L., 11 March, 1623/4. *Cf.* L.J., 3: p. 256.

[81] H.L.R.O., Main Papers, H.L., 3, 10, 11 December, 1621.

[82] H.L.R.O., Main Papers, H.L., 10 December, 1621; *cf.* L.J., 3: p. 188.

[83] H.L.R.O., Braye 13, 2 November, 1624. The English version is on a loose sheet and is in Henry Elsyng's hand.

[84] H.L.R.O., Braye 69.

parliament the journal book of entries of the house until the last of February 1620." The subcommittee had worked carefully and with diligence. They suggested a number of corrections. The names of some royal officials they found to be incorrect. In certain places phraseology was inexact; in others the clerk was verbose. The reasons for lords' absences "fills up a great part of the book" and could well be abbreviated. Some gaps should be filled, some questions resolved. Finally the subcommittee asked, "Whether your lordships shall think it fit that the clerk shall set down the reasons conducing to the conclusions of the house, or barely the motion and conclusion and no more." "Motion, and conclusion and no more," was the committee's reply, written beneath in another hand. In the margin of this document Elsyng made his own notes and queries to raise with the subcommittee as he took over the task of correcting his uncle's work for the early days of the session.[85]

Though the lords had carefully checked the "scribbled books" which Elsyng used in drawing up the draft journals, and he had made valiant efforts to secure additional material required, many questions had still to be resolved and corrections had still to be made. For example, as he worked, Elsyng jotted a number of queries in the margins of his draft journals: "*q.* if to be entered."[86] Opposite have been written the changes or decisions reached by the lords.[87] In March, 1621, early in his career as clerk, Elsyng entered names of lords who voted against a motion in the house, adding in his first draft journal, "I desire to be informed by your lordships whether any other lords dissented." Later the whole passage was crossed off and all record of difference obliterated.[88] Elsyng summarized Dorset's report concerning Bacon. Opposite has been written in another hand, "set it down at large." The summary has been scratched through and replaced by the more detailed account now familiar in the Lords *Journal*.[89] Someone has corrected Elsyng's account of the lords' visit with Bacon: "*q. si*" has been written in the margin and a section deleted.[90] Perhaps this was the work of Lord Hunsdon, a member of the group which called on Bacon and also of the committee to view the journal. The order of May 8, 1621, concerning Arundel and Spencer has also been deleted and Elsyng wrote in the margin opposite, "blotted out *per dom. Principi 4 Junii* 1621."[91] Much of the material concerning Sir Henry Yelverton was omitted.[92] On May 15, opposite a memorandum about the mitigation of fines imposed on Yelverton, Elsyng wrote "*q. de hoc* and to move the lords subcommittees etc." His original memorandum has been deleted and rewritten, probably after he had received the advice he sought.[93]

In June, 1621 Elsyng listed a number of "Matters I doubt of, which the lords subcommittees have not yet perused." Among his problems were the king's speeches of April 24 and June 2, Yelverton's speech of April 30 ("*q.* whether I shall omit it because it is unperfect"), the judgment against Yelverton, a speech of the lord treasurer, the prince's advice to the Lords, a report of the Earl of Arundel, and various orders. He reminded the lords that they had not read the entries for three days in December. He inquired what he should enter for March 10, for he found his uncle's "scribbled book" on this his last day in parliament "so unperfect that I cannot draw it up." Finally he asked the lords whether they wished to review all that had been written and corrected at their request, "Or, is it your lordships' pleasure, those things I speak of being amended by your lordships, that I examine this fair written book with the original and then subscribe it with my name (as the ancient manner was) and so bind it up fair, and leave that only for the record of that parliament."[94]

The clerk had fewer queries as the years went on. But his questions did not cease entirely. Corrections in the draft journal continue and probably represent the continued vigilance of the subcommittee.[95] The Earl of Bridgewater made a careful note in 1624 that the entries concerning Cranfield, not perfected when the lords read Elsyng's account, should be reveiwed later.[96] In April, 1628, Elsyng asked "whether I shall speak of the lord chief justice his speech." The query has been crossed off and Whitelocke's speech entered. In the account for May of the same year, a passage has been deleted by order of one of the lords.[97] All of Buckingham's complaint that the men of Banbury

---

[85] H.L.R.O., Main Papers, H.L., 13 March, 1621/2, fols. 149–149ᵛ. The same phrase used by the committee is in a version of "Remembrances for Order and Decency" (Foster, *Proceedings in Parliament 1610* 1: p. xxvi. The date of the memorandum and Elsyng's marginal queries indicate that it refers to Bowyer's work, not Elsyng's, as was incorrectly suggested on p. xxi).

[86] H.L.R.O., Braye 11, fols. 65, 70.

[87] *Ibid.,* fols. 70, 99.

[88] *Ibid.,* 23 March, 1620/1; Foster, "Procedure in the House of Lords," p. 64.

[89] H.L.R.O., Braye 12, 30 April, 1621; L.J., 3: pp. 98–101.

[90] H.L.R.O., Braye 12, 30 April, 1621.

[91] *Ibid.,* 8 May, 1621.

[92] *Ibid.,* 30 April P.M., 1621. *Cf.* Gardiner, *Debates in the House of Lords 1621,* pp. 42–53. Much of it was used in the journal entry for May 14 (L.J., 3: pp. 121–122).

[93] H.L.R.O., Braye 12, 15 May P.M., 1621.

[94] H.L.R.O., Main Papers, H.L., 2 June, 1621, fols. 10–10ᵛ. The king's speech and Yelverton's speech have in fact been entered in the draft journal (H.L.R.O., Braye 12, 24 and 30 April, 1621). The protestation concerning the Floyd case has been omitted from the account for 14 May but included on 12 May (*ibid.,* 14 May, 1621; L.J., 3: p. 119) certainly on advice of the Lords committees.

[95] The names of the Earls of Monmouth and Norwich have been confused and then disentangled (H.L.R.O., Braye 14, 2 April, 1628. *Cf.* L.J., 3: p. 708).

[96] H.L.R.O., Braye 13, 29 May, 1624.

[97] H.L.R.O., Braye 14, 14 April, 1628; Braye 15, 28 May, 1628.

had maligned him has been scratched out.[98] By January, 1629, the lords had checked Elsyng's draft through June 13, 1628.[99] They continued their work after the session was over.[1]

The last stage of Elsyng's journal was the "fair written book" which should, he thought, be compared with his final draft and subscribed with his name as clerk.[2] These books, known as the manuscript Lords journals, are preserved at the House of Lords Record Office, and were printed in the eighteenth century as the *Journal of the House of Lords*.[3] The manuscript journals for which Elsyng was responsible were engrossed on parchment, as the house had ordered.[4] Apparently they were actually checked by the clerk or his deputy, as Elsyng thought they should be. Certain pages in the volume for 1621 are marked "*ex.*" or "*hus usq. ex.*" These marks cease after page 22, but may have been lost when the journal was cropped for binding.[5] Notations are more regular in the next volume for 1624, and one page is initialled "E. K. *et* J. T."[6] Certain corrections have been made: lines or parts of lines have been inserted,[7] "put to the question and expedited" added in connection with bills.[8] Elsyng signed page 388 as clerk of the parliaments. He also signed the first and last pages of the next volume of the manuscript journal for 1625, where some sheets have been marked "*ex.*" as before.[9] The volume for 1626 has not been signed, and there are fewer notes that pages have been examined. But corrections have been made.[10] Elsyng must have checked through the copy himself. He entered a memorandum on page 20, and on page 43 wrote: "L. Willoughby. *Quere plus de hoc* memorandum for my clerk entered it out of a loose paper, wch. he found in my scribbled book without any directions from me to enter the same. *Ideoq.* H. Elsyng." In the volumes for 1628 and 1629, corrections have also been made and some pages marked "*ex.*" Elsyng's signature does not appear, but Throckmorton, as deputy, signed the list of acts at the end of the parliament.[11]

The manuscript journals were copied from the draft journals, probably from those now preserved at the House of Lords Record Office, which, with minor exceptions, they follow closely.[12] As the years went on, there is evidence that Elsyng began to run together the three stages of his account. He was more experienced in preparing his record, and knew what the Lords wanted. The activities of the house proliferated. Demands on his time increased and he probably relied more heavily on assistants. The "scribbled books" became sketchier, and Elsyng increasingly used the archive of parliament to supplement his own account. He expected to copy orders, petitions and reports into the draft journals, or to ask his assistants to do this for him.[13] By 1628, Elsyng did not stop to perfect even the draft journal. In many places he indicated what should be inserted, but the actual entry has not been made in any draft which has survived, and was probably not complete until engrossed copy was prepared.[14]

In one instance of considerable importance to historians who use the journal, an entry Elsyng intended

---

[98] "Some of the town of Banbury have given out that his grace and the L.Bp. of Durham have plotted to carry the whole house. And that his grace is of such an ill disposition that unless he be taken away, the affairs of Christendom will not prosper" (H.L.R.O., Braye 15, 4 June, 1628. *Cf.* Relf, *Debates in the House of Lords 1621*, p. 214).

[99] H.L.R.O., Braye 15, 13 June, 1628. The next draft journal is missing. For other notations of reading by the committee, see H.L.R.O., Braye 12, 24, 30 April; 2 May, 1621; H.L.R.O., Braye 13, 19, 29 May, 1624; H.L.R.O., Braye 14, 21 March, 1627/8; 28 March; 24, 30 April, 1628; H.L.R.O., Braye 15, 1, 9, 19, 23 May; 4 June, 1628.

[1] H.L.R.O., Braye 13, 29 May, 1624; L.J., 3: p. 878 (26 June, 1628).

[2] H.L.R.O., Main Papers, H.L., 2 June, 1621, fol. 10ᵛ.

[3] H.L.R.O., Memorandum No. 13.

[4] L.J., 3: p. 74.

[5] H.L.R.O., Manuscript Journal, Vol. 9; H.L.R.O., Memorandum No. 13, p. 3.

[6] H.L.R.O., Manuscript Journal, Vol. 10, *passim*, and p. 79.

[7] *Ibid.*, pp. 275, 335.

[8] *Ibid.*, p. 336 and elsewhere.

[9] H.L.R.O., Manuscript Journal, Vol. 11.

[10] H.L.R.O., Manuscript Journal, Vol. 12, pp. 51, 77, 84, 92, 135.

[11] H.L.R.O., Manuscript Journal, Vol. 12, pp. 20, 43; Vol. 13, pp. 133, 140, 186, 231; Vol. 14, p. 61.

[12] The manuscript journal for 1628 is not in all respects an exact copy of the surviving draft journal. For example, in the draft journal Elsyng entered "prayers" at the beginning of each day, which does not appear in the manuscript journal. He made a note concerning lords excused, also omitted later (H.L.R.O., Braye 14, *passim*, and 12 and 21 April, 1628). The discrepancies may be explained by the fact that the draft for 1628 is not as finished as others. Elsyng marked each of his draft journals as "the first draft" (H.L.R.O., Braye 11, 12, 13, 14, 15). Possibly he intended to prepare second drafts, but time did not permit. Possibly such drafts were made and have been lost. We know he wrote certain sections of his journal several times; but it seems unlikely that, after the draft journals had been checked by a committee of lords and corrected, he then prepared further drafts of the entire journal. Perhaps Elsyng regarded *his* draft as the first draft, the *corrected* draft as the second.

[13] H.L.R.O., Braye 12, 17 April, 1621; Braye 14, 28 April, 1628; Braye 15, 5, 23, 26, 30 May, 1628. Occasionally he laid in the original documents (H.L.R.O., Braye 13, 20 May, 1624; Braye 15, 5 May, 1628). Sometimes his assistants made mistakes (see above, p. 28. See also H.L.R.O., Braye 15, 6 May, 1628, and L.J., 3: p. 782, where an assistant has done a very poor job of carrying out Elsyng's intent).

[14] H.L.R.O., Braye 15, 10 May, 1628 (L.J., 3: p. 788); 16 May, 1628 (L.J., 3: p. 798); 16 May PM. (L.J., 3: p. 800); 20 May, 1628 (L.J., 3: pp. 804, 806); 22 May, 1628 (L.J., 3: p. 809); 31 May, 1628 (L.J., 3: p. 833); 4 June, 1628 (L.J., 3: p. 837); 9 June, 1628 (L.J., 3: p. 845); 19 June, 1628 (L.J., 3: p. 865); 26 June, 1628 (L.J., 3: pp. 880–881). The note on June 26 is interesting: "Add here in the next leaf a catalogue of all the bills passed with the royal assent this session./*prout* in the printed book." The "printed book" was the book of acts which the king's printer issued at the end of a session. It was also used by the clerk in making entries in the parliament roll (below, p. 30). Possibly Throckmorton was responsible for the manuscript journal for 1628 (see above, n. 11).

was never completed. In the draft journal for June 7, 1628, he laid in a copy of the Petition of Right and made a mark that it was to follow the words, "Then the clerk of the crown read the said Petition of Right." The Petition was not copied into the draft nor into the final manuscript journal.[15] On June 12 the Lords agreed that the Petition and the king's answer to it should be entered in the journal.[16] This was not done. Nor does the Petition appear in the list of bills in the journal, though the Lords ordered that it should be printed (like the statutes) and entered in the parliament roll.[17] Another omission is less significant historically, though no less interesting in revealing the shortcomings of the manuscript journal. On May 22, 1628, the Lords made an order concerning the clerk's fees. Elsyng wrote in his draft journal, "enter it," and left space for this to be done, but the entry was never made.[18]

The final manuscript journal during Elsyng's years as clerk was more nearly complete than the draft journal; but it was not entirely finished. Titles of acts have not been filled in.[19] Names of committees have not been expanded.[20] The name of a county has not been supplied, nor the names of lords excused.[21] It is curious that these imperfections should have remained, for the journal of Elsyng's years as clerk was probably more closely supervised than any one written before. Some entries were made on command of the lord keeper.[22] One was removed by order of the king.[23] At each stage a committee of lords authorized what was to be included and deleted what was inappropriate. Thus the journal for which Elsyng was responsible was a record which the house itself designed and in which he as clerk took pride.

THE PARLIAMENT ROLL

One of the final acts of the clerk in completing his record was to certify the roll of parliament into chancery. Medieval clerks had included in this roll a narrative of proceedings and the text of some of the petitions which had been presented in parliament together with the royal answers. Public acts were enrolled separately in a "statute roll." During the sixteenth century, much of the narrative account was omitted from the parliament roll, which thus came to resemble and was finally merged with the statute roll. Henry Elsyng combined the older and the newer forms. The rolls which he prepared differ markedly from those of his immediate predecessors. They reflect his own personality and interests, illuminate his career as clerk, and illustrate the significance of the parliament roll in the early seventeenth century.

The roll of a parliament was prepared months or even years after the session was prorogued. According to the medieval treatise, *Modus Tenendi Parliamentum,* the principal clerks of the parliament were required to deposit their rolls in the exchequer before the parliament was dismissed. But beginning in the reign of Edward IV, the date of the end of the session was included in the opening paragraph of the roll, which therefore could not have been begun until after parliament was over. Robert Bowyer was working on the roll for the session of February through July, 1610, in the following October; and the Lords, as late as 1626, ordered the clerk to certify in this way judgments made in 1621.[1]

There was apparently little save convention to guide clerks of the fourteenth and fifteenth centuries in their selection of material for the parliament rolls. Though occasionally they were specifically charged to make entries, more often they followed their own ideas. The first three days of a session were usually described in chronological order, including the presentation of the speaker for the Commons. Then might follow declaration of the cause of summons, which led to discussion of affairs of state, the subsidy grant, and the presentation of the Commons petitions with the royal replies.[2] Such

---

[15] H.L.R.O., Braye 15, 7 June, 1628 P.M. The copy is endorsed at the top with the king's answer, *"Soit droit fait come est desiré"* and is without a title. *Cf.* L.J., **3**: pp. 843–844.

[16] L.J., **3**: p. 851.

[17] H.L.R.O., Manuscript Journal, Vol. 13; L.J., **3**: pp. 851, 862–863, 880–881.

[18] H.L.R.O., Braye 15, 22 May, 1628; *cf.* Relf, *Debates in the House of Lords 1621,* p. 194 and L.J., **3**: pp. 810–811. There are other omissions, see above, n. 15.

[19] H.L.R.O., Braye 14, 29 April, 1628 (L.J., **3**: p. 774). H.L.R.O., Braye 15, 3 May, 1628 (L.J., **3**: p. 779); 8 May, 1628 (L.J., **3**: p. 785).

[20] H.L.R.O., Braye 15, 13 May, 1628 (L.J., **3**: p. 793).

[21] H.L.R.O., Braye 15, 11 June, 1628 (L.J., **3**: p. 849); 12 June, 1628 (L.J., **3**: p. 850).

[22] H.L.R.O., Braye 13, 17 June, 1624; L.J., **3**: p. 425.

[23] "Read and approved of generally but not presented to the king, for his matie refused to hear of any and commanded that this be not entered" (Add. 40,090, fol. 129ᵛ).

[1] Richardson and Sayles, "The Early Records of the English Parliament," p. 134; Pollard, "The Clerical Organization of Parliament," p. 47; Petyt 538/12, fol. 358ᵛ; L.J., **3**: p. 676. A member of the House of Commons in 1593 wrote: "It appeared the order of the parliament is the clerk of the parliament should certify a copy of the parliament roll into the chancery that thither men might resort to see the roll, but the private gain of the clerk causeth that he detaineth the copying and certifying of the acts a long time after many parliaments to the end men shall come to him for the search . . ." quoted in Neale, "Proceedings in Parliament relative to . . . Mary Queen of Scots," p. 104, n.

[2] This account is, of course, greatly over-simplified. It is based primarily on Pollard, "The Clerical Organization of Parliament," and the work of Richardson and Sayles: "The Early Records of the English Parliament;" "The Early Statutes," pp. 201–217, 540–570; "The King's Ministers in Parliament, 1272–1377, The Parliaments of Edward I" (*English Historical Review* **46** (1931): pp. 529–550); "The King's Ministers in Parliament, 1272–1377, The Parliaments of Edward II, and The Parliaments of Edwards III" (*English Historical Review* **47** (1932): pp. 194–203, 377–397); *Rotuli Parliamentorum Anglie Hactenus Inediti,* Introduction. Neale, "Proceedings in Parliament relative to . . . Mary Queen of

ordinances or other decisions made in parliament as became statutes, together with royal ordinances made in other ways, were entered on a second roll called the statute roll. The decline of extra-parliamentary legislation and the presentation of bills in substantially their final form brought parliament roll and statute roll closer together. Finally, in the sixteenth century and the early years of James I, the two sets of rolls merged in rolls which recorded little more than legislation, but are today commonly called parliament rolls.[3]

When Robert Bowyer came to draw up the roll for James's first parliament, he studied the form used by his predecessor Sir Thomas Smith and relied upon it.[4] "The public acts," he wrote, "usually are written in a roll in court hand by one of the clerks in the office . . . of the pettybag at the request and appointment of the clerk of the parliament and at his charge." The clerk copied the acts from the book of acts issued by the king's printer at the end of the session "and then the roll so by him written is by the clerk of the parliament examined with the original acts, and by him subscribed, and so transmitted into the chancery. This the clerk of the parliament may write or cause his own clerk or any other to write, but useth one of the underclerks in the pettybag office because they write the chancery hand best."[5] The rolls which were thus prepared for 1 *Jac.*, 3 *Jac.*, 4 *Jac.*, and 7 *Jac.* were essentially statute rolls.[6] They give the full text of all public acts and list all private acts. In 1614, when no bills became law, no roll was made.[7] Bowyer observed one departure from earlier practice. In October, 1610, the attorney general requested him to enroll the general pardon with the other public acts, and the lord chancellor commanded him also to include the subsidies of the temporalty and of the clergy. He followed instructions, but made it clear that "his predecessor . . . did not transfer or enroll, neither the pardon nor the subsidies."[8] It was not a serious break with the immediate past, and Bowyer's rolls are much the same as those prepared by Smith.

Henry Elsyng's rolls, on the other hand, include more than the public acts recorded by Bowyer, and thus give a fuller picture of the parliaments in which he served as clerk. In 1621 only the subsidy bills became statutes. Despite the precedent of 1610, they were not enrolled.[9] Elsyng did, however, prepare an elaborate roll for the parliament, registering other proceedings.[10] His introductory matter in Latin has been badly worn and mutilated.[11] The Commons' charges against Mompesson and Michell follow in English, then the Lords' examination of supporting witnesses on oath.

All which crimes and heinous offences and grievances, being clearly proved against the said Sir Giles Mompesson, the lords spiritual and temporal on Monday the six and twentieth of March in the afternoon sitting in their robes in parliament and meaning to respite their proceedings against the rest of those who were accused until their next sitting after the adjournment

sent word to the Commons that if they with their speaker "would according to their ancient custom of the parliament come to demand of the Lords that judgment may be given . . . they should be heard." The speaker accordingly did demand judgment, and the lord chief justice "(being in place of the lord chancellor) answered." Elsyng paraphrased the chancellor's words, and gave the judgment in full. In the same way he described the proceedings of Lords and Commons in the case of Sir Francis Michell. Again the Lords sent for the Commons, who again came. The speaker at the Bar making "low obeisance" once more demanded judgment, which the lord chief justice pronounced.

Elsyng recorded the charges against the lord chancellor, Francis Bacon, Lord Verulam, at even greater length, giving an account of a conference between the houses, the full text of Bacon's letter to the Lords, further complaints against Bacon, his confession at large and its verification by a committee of lords. "I beseech your lordships," Bacon said to those who came to see him, "be merciful to a broken reed." The serjeant with his mace was sent to fetch Bacon to the parliament house, but found him too ill to attend. The Lords resolved to proceed notwithstanding. They sent a message to the Commons as before, who came to demand judgment, the speaker "making three low obeisances." The lord chief justice pronounced the judgment, which Elsyng included *verbatim*.

Scots," p. 104. *Statutes of the Realm* 1: pp. xxxv, lxv–lxvi. See below, p. 52.

[3] Exceptions are the rolls for 14 and 28 Elizabeth (Neale, "Proceedings in Parliament relative to . . . Mary Queen of Scots," pp. 103–105).

[4] H.L.R.O., Braye 110, #49.

[5] Petyt 538/12, fol. 359.

[6] P.R.O. C65/181, 182, 183, 184. In 1628 the House of Lords ordered the clerk to enter the Petition of Right "in the parliament roll where the statutes are entered" (L.J., 3: p. 862).

[7] "The last intended parliament 10 *Jac.* if you be judged by the journal, it was a large and well occupied parliament, yet because no act passed, nor record is of it, it was resolved by all judges to be no parliament" (Hobart, *Reports*, p. 111). "Note that this was a parliament summoned and assembled, many sittings in both houses, many bills read and passed in either house and some in both and of great importance. . . . The king present the first day and having both houses before him divers times, was yet resolved by the judges to be no parliament in law for no parliament can be without a record of it, and no record can be where no act passes and is consummate" (Cambridge University Library, Mm. 6.62, fol. 70ᵛ).

[8] Petyt 538/12, fol. 358ᵛ. P.R.O. C65/184. *Cf.* the roll for 43 Eliz., where the subsidies and the general pardon are omitted (P.R.O. C65/180). This custom may have stemmed from the earlier practice of indenting the subsidy. (See below, pp. 52, 55, 56–57; H.L.R.O., "Precedents in Parliament," p. 38).

[9] The original acts are not at the H.L.R.O. and apparently have not survived. Spedding, *Letters and Life* 7: p. 333, n.; *Statutes of the Realm* 4, 2: p. 1208.

[10] P.R.O. C65/185.

[11] For this, see *Statutes of the Realm* 4, 2: p. 1208.

The roll also recorded complaints concerning the Bishop of Llandaff, and the fact that he spoke in his own defense. A committee of lords reported on the complaints which had been collected. After the bishop withdrew, "Master Serjeant Crewe came to the clerk's table and read the said collection which followeth. . . ." The Lords, for reasons which Elsyng related, referred the matter to Convocation and the Archbishop of Canterbury.

So likewise the affair of Edward Floyd, who had spoken disparagingly of the Princess Elizabeth, was entered at length in the roll, with the charges against him, and several quotations from his statements during examination. Floyd was brought to the Bar. The "attorney came to the clerk's table" and "prayed the Lords to proceed to judgment against him." Once more the lord chief justice pronounced the judgment, which once more was given in full. Elsyng prefaced his account with a "memorandum" reviewing the precipitous action of the Commons in judging Floyd themselves, an action which the Lords felt "did deeply trench" into their privileges,

for that all judgment do properly and only belong unto them, wherefore they resolved not to suffer anything to pass which might prejudice their right in point of judicature, and yet so to proceed, as the love and good correspondency between their lordships and the Commons might be continued.

After conferences, the houses agreed on a protestation that the judgment against Floyd should not stand as a precedent.

Elsyng wrote the kind of parliament roll he and other antiquarians would have liked to read. In years to come when he was working on his books about parliament, he found the record wanting. The speaker of the Commons was not mentioned, but one could not therefore infer that there was no speaker, Elsyng wrote, "for this is to be noted, that the ancient rolls did record only what acts passed between both houses, and what laws were made, and omitted the forms and ceremonies then used." [12] The record would not tell him who was speaker of the Lords if it were not the chancellor who declared the cause of summons.[13] The medieval rolls "omit the form used in the delivery of bills. . . ." [14] So Elsyng was careful to record that, when Bacon became ill, the Great Seal was delivered to Sir James Ley to supply his place. Elsyng noted that the speaker of the lower house demanded judgment for the Commons in the case of Bacon, the attorney in the case of Floyd. He observed where the Commons stood. He recorded conferences between the houses in 1621; and he must have wished that medieval clerks had been equally explicit when he attempted to prove from laconic records that Lords and Commons also conferred in earlier times.[15]

The parliament roll for 1624 in three parts is Elsyng's most ambitious production. The introductory matter for the first part covers two and a half membranes and includes the proclamation and summons to the parliament in Latin, and the appointment of receivers and triers in French.[16] The presentation of the speaker of the House of Commons is also given in Latin. Then follows a long account of the lord keeper's speech, in English. After this elaborate introduction, Elsyng devoted the whole roll to the narration of the Spanish marriage negotiations and the journey of the prince and Buckingham to Spain. He included letters *verbatim*, and directly quoted remarks made by Charles and Buckingham. The first petition of the Lords to the king is given in full, and the king's reply. Then follows the second petition, with James's reply and explanatory interjections by the prince and duke. The third petition is recorded *verbatim* and the king's reply. "Here for the clearing of something which his majesty spake the last time, his majesty called for the notes of that speech, but the same not being readily to be had, his majesty said, 'I'll tell you by tongue.' " His words follow. Elsyng returned to Latin for the conclusion of the parliament, listed the public acts and the text of the two subsidy acts with the king's reply. Elsyng engrossed the other public acts and the general pardon in a second roll for the parliament with the king's replies and a list of private acts.[17]

His labors were not yet complete, for he produced yet a third roll to tell the story of the impeachment of the lord treasurer, Cranfield.[18] The clerk wrote a full detailed account, transcribing all the relevant documents *verbatim*, the charges of the Commons and Cranfield's answers, the examination of witnesses by the Lords' committees, the second charge against Cranfield by the attorney, the proofs, and Cranfield's answers, then the final call for judgment by the Commons and the judgment itself.

Elsyng prepared one roll for 1625.[19] The introductory matter, in Latin, followed the pattern set in 1624, save that the speeches of king and lord keeper were also given in Latin. Elsyng noted that parliament presented a petition concerning religion to which the king graciously responded. After he recorded the public acts with the king's replies, he entered the full text of the petition with the king's answers to each of its sixteen articles, a precedent of some interest for later times.

For the session of 1626, when no bills became law and the attempt to impeach Buckingham provoked dis-

---

[12] Elsyng, *Manner of Holding Parliaments*, p. 157.
[13] *Ibid.*, p. 144.
[14] Sims, *Expedicio*, p. 15. For other complaints concerning the omission of form and ceremony, see *ibid.*, pp. 33, 38, 40, 99; Selden, *Of Judicature*, p. 120; below, pp. 55, 59.
[15] Sims, *Expedicio*, pp. 38ff.
[16] P.R.O. C65/186. Elsyng did not enter the protestation concerning the form of the subsidy bill as had been ordered (L.J., 3: p. 408).
[17] P.R.O. C65/187.
[18] P.R.O. C65/188.
[19] P.R.O. C65/189.

solution of parliament, Elsyng prepared no roll. The last sample we have of his work is the great roll for 1628 and 1629.[20] It begins with Charles's and Lord Keeper Coventry's opening speeches in English, and the appointment of receivers and triers in French. Elsyng mentioned that the speaker of the lower house made "an elegant oration," and asked for the Commons' ancient privileges, that their persons and goods should be unmolested and that they might enjoy free speech to discuss urgent matters. Then Elsyng recorded the Petition of Right, with the king's response of June 7, in full parliament, *"Soit droit fait come est desiré."* Elsyng listed the Petition as item one, and the Subsidy as item two. The text of other public acts followed with a list of the private acts and the king's replies.

It was an impressive record. Nothing done by Elsyng's predecessors, Smith or Bowyer, provided a pattern for him. Elsyng found in medieval rolls the model which he needed. He constructed accounts of parliament reminiscent of those made in the reign of Edward III whom he so much admired. He returned to the narrative form used by earlier clerks,[21] and added descriptions of procedure often omitted by those who had come before him. With the enrollment of statutes he included speeches of the king's ministers, acts of judicature, and public petitions answered favorably by the crown. He copied relevant documents, letters, judicial examinations, and depositions. He also described "circumstances" and "ceremonies" which he found wanting in the medieval rolls.

Elsyng had not achieved the final form of his rolls easily. Rough drafts of his accounts for 1621 and 1624 show how cautiously he proceeded, seeking the advice of the king's counsel and the Lords' subcommittee for privileges charged with oversight of the journal. The questions he raised, the instructions he received, illustrate how the man proceeded in his work as clerk, and also reveal the importance of the rolls of parliament in the early seventeenth century.

The revival of impeachment which marked the sessions of 1621 and 1624 sent Commons and Lords to the Tower to search out ancient precedents to justify their procedure against Mompesson, Michell, Bacon, and Cranfield.[22] But the difficulties facing the clerk in drawing up the record of these judgments were left largely to Elsyng to solve. In April, 1621, the Lords ordered that "the Acts, *Judgments*, and Standing Orders of the house, be inrolled and kept in parchment." The King's counsel were to draw up the proceedings against Mompesson in consultation with the "Lords subcommittees" and "then inrolled." Somewhat later, Elsyng was ordered by the upper house to certify into chancery the schedule of the fines levied upon all the offenders.[23] In March and early April, 1621, Elsyng drafted an account of the *"processus"* concerning Mompesson. On April 4, he showed it to Serjeant Crewe.[24] He had many doubts how to proceed. Even a more experienced man might have been puzzled; and Elsyng, though long in training, had only succeeded Bowyer as clerk in March.

In his second draft of "The manner how to certify the proceeding of this parliament against Sir G. Mompesson," Elsyng jotted a marginal query,

How to begin, whether after the old precedents or otherwise. The old precedents begin with the declarations themselves and speak not of anything done in the lower house; but this varieth from all, in respect of the commitment by the Commons, the escape [of Mompesson], and the search etc.

Later in the same manuscript, Elsyng observed, "In all former precedents, the declarations of complaints made by the Commons are recited *ad verbum*," specifically those against Lee, Lyons, and Latimer in 50 Edward III, "and generally all other declarations of their grievances were anciently set down in the parliament roll *ad verbum*." Elsyng noted many other questions and talked them over with Serjeant Crewe: "Whether to touch any but Sir Giles," he wondered. Then in another ink he has written, "Mr. Serjeant Crewe, that I certify the effect of all," and noted "This is to follow next the judgment against Mompesson," the position later occupied on the parliament roll.[25] But apparently Elsyng did not finish his work for 1621 at this time. Five years later, in 1626, he was ordered "to draw up the judgments given in the parliament of 18 *Jacobi Regis*," engross them in a roll, and return it (after having been viewed) into the chancery.[26] There was a long gap between Elsyng's first drafts for 1621 and his completed roll.

Normally Elsyng seems to have been a punctual man, not given to delay or procrastination. He had promptly certified the fines levied by the house against Mompesson

---

[20] P.R.O. C65/190.

[21] H. G. Richardson and George Sayles, "The Parliaments of Edward III," *Bulletin of the Institute of Historical Research* 9 (1931–1932): p. 17; "The Early Records of the English Parliaments," pp. 141–142.

[22] Selden, *Of Judicature,* p. 95; H.L.R.O., Main Papers, H.L., 30 March, 1621; L.J., 3: p. 65; C.J., 1: pp. 545–546.

[23] L.J., 3: p. 74 (italics are mine). H.L.R.O., Main Papers, H.L., 28 May, 1621; L.J., 3: pp. 135, 142.

[24] H.L.R.O., Main Papers, H.L., 27 March and 4 April, 1621.

[25] H.L.R.O., Main Papers, H.L., 4 April, 1621. This material is incorrectly calendared in the *Third Report of the Historical Manuscripts Commission* (London, 1872), appendix, p. 21. There are three drafts at the H.L.R.O. of Elsyng's account of the proceedings against Mompesson. The first is a rough draft in his own hand, listed under the date of 27 March, 1621. The cover sheet for that draft is listed under 4 April, 1621. A second draft has been copied out by a clerk (or possibly even by Elsyng himself) and corrected by Elsyng, who endorsed it "My own instructions which I showed Mr. Serjeant Crewe, 4 April, 1621." The third version is a fair copy of the proceedings of the Commons, the king's proclamation concerning Mompesson, and the Commons' accusation as presented to the Lords.

[26] L.J., 3: p. 676.

and the others.[27] He had sketched out the "processes," but was still puzzled about the authority of the record and how it should be drawn.

John Selden, the noted antiquary and lawyer, had some interesting reflections on the problem. Sometime after parliament had been dissolved, Bacon turned to Selden for advice, a natural choice, since Selden had recently been employed by the Lords to search out their privileges.[28] Bacon apparently hoped to set aside the judgment which had been passed against him on the ground that the impeachment proceeding had taken place after the king's assent to the subsidy bills, and thus, Bacon believed, after the parliamentary session had legally terminated. Selden, in his reply of February 14, 1621, dismissed this point. Bacon could, he suggested, make a stronger case: ". . . by reason there is no record of those judgments," Selden wrote, "it may be justly thought that they are of no force." The declarations of the lower house against Bacon were written on paper, Selden recalled, the judgments of the Lords given orally and only noted by the clerk in the journal. "Now the record that in former times was of the judgments and proceedings there, was in this form," the antiquarian asserted.

> The accusation was exhibited in parchment, and being so received and indorsed was the first record, and that remained filed among the bills of parliament, it being of itself as the bills in the king's bench. Then out of this there was a formal judgment with the accusation entered into that roll or second record which the clerk transcribes by ancient use and sends into the chancery. But in this case there are none of these.[29]

There is no record at all and the journal is not a record "of itself." Selden thought the clerk could not enter a record after parliament was concluded. Clerks of other courts made records after the term was ended, but the clerk of the parliament could not do so. If parliament had been dissolved, as in this case it had, the clerk had no relation to it, since it

> is not then at all in being. . . . Besides, there cannot be an example found by which it may appear that ever any record of the first kind (where the transcript is into the chancery) was made in parliament but only sitting the house, and in their view.[30]

No doubt the procedure in impeachment by both Commons and Lords in this parliament of 1621 had been hesitant. Possibly it would not, as Selden suggested, bear close legal scrutiny.[31] But Bacon wisely let the matter drop. Selden's argument would have carried little weight in the political climate of 1621.

Elsyng did not share Selden's assurance about recording impeachment proceedings. Probably for this reason he had not completed his account. In 1624, when he was drafting the judgment against Cranfield, he observed: "Anciently the clerk of the crown did draw up these judgments, and gave them to the clerk of the parliament to be entered." He took his questions to the Lords' committee for the journal.

> If your lordships' pleasure be that I shall certify this judgment against the lord treasurer amongst the acts I desire that it may be penned by the king's counsel, and so given to me signed by the king's attorney. (It is not fit I should do it of myself.) And, that an order be made before the end of this session, that I shall then certify this with the parliament acts in the roll of statutes. Otherwise I may not do it.[32]

Not only legal problems but also matters of form continued to bother Elsyng. He wrote out a careful draft in sixteen folios of the introductory matter for 19–27 February, 1624, with a question whether the lord keeper's speech should be reported in Latin or in English.[33] This, his questions concerning procedure, and the Lords' order of 1626 which mentioned the judgments of 1621 but not that against Cranfield in 1624, all suggest that the roll for 1624 was finished before that for 1621.

When Elsyng completed the other rolls it would be difficult to say. In 1628 both houses urged immediate enrollment of the Petition of Right. Two days after the king's final answer on June 9, 1628, Sir Edward Coke spoke of entering the Petition and answer "into a parliamentary roll" or into the courts, "some of the lords and some of the Commons being appointed to see it truly entered." On June 10, the king agreed to have the Petition printed "or enrolled and entered into all the courts of Westminster." Sir John Eliot returned to the same point on June 18. The printing could be done after the session was over, he said, "but to enter it into the courts that were most fit now the house is sitting." He proposed a conference with the Lords who had shown equal concern for the record. Then John Selden rose and explained to the house how the Petition should be entered: "My lord keeper to send a *certiorari* to the clerk of the parliament to certify it into the chancery, and then by way of *mittimus* to disperse it into the courts." This was, of course, the

---

[27] H.L.R.O., Parchment Coll., H.L., 30 May, 1621.
[28] *The Hastings Journal*, p. vi.
[29] The treatise *Of the Judicature in Parliaments* did not insist that the accusation, the charges, or the judgment should be in parchment (pp. 11–32, 63–66, 176–177), which is perhaps another reason for doubting that it was written by Selden (see below, pp. 42–45). As was characteristic of Elsyng, it described procedure actually followed. Sometimes the accusation was written and engrossed on parchment (as in the case of the Duke of Buckingham, H.L.R.O., Parchment Coll., H.L., 15 May, 1626), sometimes it was not. In the case of Cranfield, the author says that "in the open house, an impeachment by word of mouth had been sufficient" (p. 65).
[30] Spedding, *Letters and Life* 7: pp. 332–333. See p. 29, n. 1, above. Clerks were appointed for particular parliaments in the middle ages. From 1510, the office was continuous (Pollard, "The Clerical Organization of Parliament," p. 34; Bond, "Clerks of the Parliaments," p. 81).
[31] Hale, *The Jurisdiction of the Lords House, or Parliament*, p. xv.
[32] H.L.R.O., Main Papers, H.L., 22 May, 1624.
[33] H.L.R.O., Braye 66.

usual procedure for private bills. It had also been used in 1621 to transmit the schedule of fines against Mompesson, Bacon, and others, and, according to Sir Edward Coke, was customary "for the better observation of any act of parliament enacted for the commonwealth, or of a petition of right, or judgment in parliament." When the conferences of Lords and Commons met in the afternoon, it was "shewn unto the Commons, that the Lords have already ordered the said Petition of Right" and the king's answer

> to be entered into the parliament roll, and to be printed. And also, that Mr. Attorney hath order . . . to prepare writs for the certifying and transmitting of the same said Petition into the courts in Westminster Hall. . . .[34]

In 1629 the Commons sent a committee to see whether the Petition and royal answer had in fact been entered in the parliament roll. Presumably it had, as no protest on this particular point is recorded.[35]

The debate on the Petition of Right reflected the concern for the record characteristic of parliament in the seventeenth century and the significance which it attached to the parliament rolls. This concern was, as we have seen, expressed in both houses by close attention to entries in the journals.[36] The journals had not, however, the legal standing of the statutes themselves or of the statute and parliament roll. Sir Henry Hobart, writing between 1614 and 1621, said,

> Journals are no records but remembrances for forms of proceedings to the record, they are not of necessity, neither have they always been. . . . The Journal is of good use for the observation of the generality and materiality of proceedings and deliberations as to the three readings of any bill, the intercourses between the two houses, and the like, but when the act is passed, the Journal is expired.[37]

The incontrovertible record of any parliament was the legislation passed by both houses and accepted by the crown. To some members of parliament, therefore, it seemed best to incorporate in statutes the actions, policies, or promises they wished to record permanently. Several times in the parliaments of James and Charles, attempts were made to stretch the preamble of the subsidy to include royal promises or declaratory laws. Hakewill thought of recording the king's declaration concerning impositions in this way in 1614.[38] Speakers in 1628, uncertain how to enforce the provisions of the Petition of Right, suggested that the Petition be registered in the same manner.[39] The subsidy, as a general public act, was usually enrolled and always widely publicized in the counties.

"The clerk," wrote Bowyer, "keepeth the original acts passed as well public as private."[40] These documents, preserved since 1497 in the parliament office and for earlier times among the records of the chancery, are the authentic record of legislation for the period which they cover.[41] They were not the only such record of public acts in the early seventeenth century. These the clerk continued to inscribe on a roll, which bore the same legal significance as the acts themselves. "At the end of every session of parliament," Bowyer wrote,

> all the public acts are engrossed into one great roll by Bowyer as clerk of the parliament, and the same roll, being by him subscribed, he delivereth into the Chapel of the Rolls; which is thereupon there received, and placed among the records of chancery, being the highest records of the kingdom, without any other warrant than his hand, which acts or statutes so by him transcribed, do bind his majesty's subjects of all degrees, forever.[42]

Though he was speaking in defense of his own position as keeper of the records and as clerk, there was truth in what Boywer said.

The history of parliament was a subject of keen intellectual interest in the early Stuart period. It also had its uses.[43] Precedents for impeachment, for the privileges of the nobility, were drawn from medieval parliaments. So too were the precedents concerning impositions, arbitrary imprisonment, martial law in time of peace, cited in both houses and in the courts of law.[44] Those who had thus searched out history

---

[34] L.J., 3: pp. 135, 142, 862–863. The diary of Sir William Borlase for June 9, 10, 18, 1628 (British Museum, Stowe 366, transcript at the Yale Center for Parliamentary History). Coke, *Fourth Institute*, p. 43.

[35] *Commons Debates 1629*, pp. 4, 6n.; C.J., 1: p. 920. Elsyng had also arranged to have the Petition and the king's answer printed while parliament was still in session (*ibid.*, p. 921).

[36] See above, pp. 21–29; Foster, "Procedure in the House of Lords," pp. 64–65.

[37] Hobart, *Reports*, pp. 110–111. See also Richardson and Sayles, "The Early Statutes," pp. 201–217, 540–570.

[38] "It was said that it was dangerous to have his [the king's] word for words may be forgotten, and therefore if a subsidy were granted it should be inserted in the act" *Commons Debates 1621* 7: p. 655).

[39] In the debate of May 6, 1628, this suggestion was made by Edward Alford, Sir Edward Coke, Sir Robert Phelips, and Peter Ball. See the diary of Sir Edward Nicholas (P.R.O., SP 16/97, transcript at the Yale Center for Parliamentary History, and Harl. 5324, fols. 25, 27–29.

[40] Petyt 538/11, fol. 317.

[41] Bond, "Acts of Parliament," pp. 202–204, 208.

[42] British Museum, Titus B. V, fol. 281.

[43] Levi Fox, ed., *English Historical Scholarship in the Sixteenth and Seventeenth Centuries* (London, 1956), pp. 53–58, 70–71. The papers in this volume by Philip Styles, "Politics and Historical Research in the Early Seventeenth Century," and by Stuart Pigott, "Antiquarian Thought in the Sixteenth and Seventeenth Centuries," are particularly relevant. See also E. Evans, "Of the Antiquity of Parliaments in England: Some Elizabethan and Early Stuart Opinions," *History* 23 (1938), 91: pp. 206–221.

[44] There are several collections of precedents at the Cambridge University Library which were probably connected with these debates. One, concerning impositions 13–50 E. III, is marked "Mr. Finch." Another, concerning impeachment, is marked "Mr. Whitlock." A few concern the royal prerogative to commit without cause (Mm. 5. 65, fols. 139–141, 143–144; Mm. 6. 68, fols. 15–21). For examples of citations from the parliament rolls made in debate, see my *Proceedings in Parliament 1610* 1: p. 289; *Commons Debates 1621* 1: p. 128;

laboriously in the Tower knew, as Bowyer and Elsyng knew, that in the past many "statutes" had not been enrolled as Bowyer enrolled them, nor "passed" as his parliaments had passed them. They might in fact have been promulgated as ordinances or proclamations.[45] Medieval "law" could be found not only in the statute rolls but in a variety of other records. Chief among them were the petitions and replies registered in the parliament rolls. In 1626, the roll of the fifth year of Henry IV was read aloud in the House of Lords. Littleton, speaking for the Commons at a conference with the Lords in 1628 on the proposed Petition of Right, quoted the roll of 36 Edward III, and said, "This concludes the question, and is of as great force as if were printed, for the parliament roll is the true warrant of an act, and many are omitted out of the books that are extant."[46] Cited in both houses and in the courts, the old parliament rolls, in an age devoted to precedent, shared with the statute rolls the character of legal records.

Much of the significant activity of parliament in the early seventeenth century could not be expressed in legislation. It was not, therefore, recorded in statutes nor certified on the kind of roll which had become common in the late sixteenth century. Parliament and its clerk turned to the older form of the parliament roll because it was a record of greater legal validity than the journal, and also because it was more appropriate than a roll composed of statutes only. Thus circumstances reinforced Elsyng's personal interests, and help to explain the form of his rolls.

Chief among these circumstances was the revival of impeachment. The story of trial and judgment could not be contained in the usual roll of statutes, but required a narrative account like those of Edward III. The debate on foreign affairs and the reasons for breaking with Spain in 1624 also required more discursive presentation. The petitions of 1625 and 1628 recalled petitions of earlier times, recorded with their answers in the parliament roll. So Elsyng's materials dictated the form he finally chose. Statutes he enrolled as statutes. But the major actions of his term as clerk were not legislative actions, suitable for a legislative record. They demanded different treatment.

Neither Elsyng nor the men of his parliaments were satisfied with an account only in the journals. They were looking for a public record, unequivocably recognized in courts of law. Judgments in parliament should be public acts, officially recorded, and made known to all the courts. Petitions answered by the crown should be public promises known to all men.[47] To this end in Elizabeth's reign, Lords and Commons moved to enroll the "process" against Mary, Queen of Scots.[48] To this end, it was decided, and the king agreed, to enroll the Petition of Right with the royal answer, so that it would be known as the declared law of England.

The old form of the parliament roll was more flexible than the form which succeeded it, and which had come to be little more than an enrollment of statutes. By reverting to the medieval pattern and, for a brief period, combining the narrative of the early parliament roll with the medieval statute roll, Elsyng expressed his own interests as clerk and historian. He also satisfied the urgent desire of his contemporaries for a public legal record of those achievements of parliament which could not be embodied in legislation.

The dramatic finale to his efforts was written after Elsyng's death, when Henry Scobell, clerk of the parliaments, enrolled and certified the "process" against Charles I.[49] The form of the roll, the narrative style, the details of procedure faithfully recounted, recalled the charge and judgment against Mompesson, against Bacon, and against Cranfield so painfully drafted in 1621 and 1624. It all looked startlingly familiar. Elsyng had laid the way more surely than he knew. He had provided the form, but he would have been loath to record the trial of a king.

MR. ELSYNG'S *MODUS TENENDI PARLIAMENTUM APUD ANGLOS*

In his own day, Henry Elsyng was best known as keeper of the records and clerk of the parliaments. Today he is remembered as an antiquarian and author of *The Manner of Holding Parliaments in England*. The material for this book he had "collected," he said, "with no intent to publish the same unto any." Book

---

L.J., 3: pp. 558–562, 719, 720, 730, 747. For an example from the Elizabethan period, see Neale, *Elizabeth I and Her Parliaments 1584–1601*, pp. 26–27. For the investigation concerning the privileges of nobility, see *The Hastings Journal*, pp. vi–vii. For other precedents concerning impeachment, see H.L.R.O., Main Papers, H.L., 30 March, 1621.

[45] Elsyng recognized that statutes were drawn after parliament had adjourned and might differ from the petitions and answers recorded in the parliament roll, or even "vacate" them. He spoke approvingly of practice in his own day (Sims, *Expedicio*, pp. 5, 37–38, 56, 62, 64–65). He also understood that not all "acts of parliament" were ultimately drawn into statutes and entered on the statute roll. For this reason, he said, the Commons were "careful" of the parliament roll (*ibid.*, pp. 101, 103; *cf.* p. 120, n. 42). See also the chapter proposed for his third book: "*Ordinationes Actus Parl., Statuta*—their differences" (Cambridge University Library, Mm. 6.62, fol. 59ʳ). See above, p. 7.

[46] L.J., 3: pp. 581, 719.

[47] Sir Edward Coke in the debate of May 6, 1628, on the proposed Petition of Right, said, ". . . must go in a parliamentary way. A general promise no satisfaction to us. . . . The king to speak by himself in a parliamentary way, in a matter of record . . ." (Harl. 5324, fol. 26).

[48] In 1586 the speaker of the House of Commons requested that the petition of the house and the proceedings of parliament concerning Mary be entered on the rolls of parliament. This was done. For the text, see Neale, "Proceedings in Parliament relative to . . . Mary, Queen of Scots," pp. 106–113. For the fate of the roll, see Neale, *Elizabeth I and Her Parliaments 1584–1601*, p. 133. *Cf. Manuscripts of the House of Lords* 11: pp. xvii, 23–25.

[49] H.L.R.O., Parchment Coll., H.L., 3 March, 1650/1.

One was first printed in 1660, long after Elsyng's death. Chapter 5 of Book Two, then recently discovered, was published in 1954,[1] and chapter 6 identified. Nothing more has hitherto been recognized as his.

When Elsyng began the actual writing of his book in 1624, he had already served as clerk for two parliaments of great complexity and major significance. He continued to write during intervals between three more. Thus he brought to his work both knowledge of past parliaments, whose records he had read in the Tower, and practical experience on the floor of the house.

Elsyng started Book One in December, 1624, parliament having been prorogued in November, and apparently finished it in May, 1625.[2] He must have begun his second book promptly, or perhaps was working on it concurrently. Charles's first parliament met from June through August 12, 1625. On August 13, Elsyng made a note that he had loaned to Bishop Williams chapters 4–7 of Book One, and also the first chapter of Book Two, "War and Peace. Of all the kings' times in the Tower" and also "War and Peace of Ed. III only."[3] A draft of chapter 2, "Subsidies," was probably also written in 1625. It refers to Charles's first parliament but not his second (February–June, 1626).[4] The first part of "Judicature," chapter 4, was substantially finished in August, 1627, before Charles's third parliament convened, and emended in 1628, after the first session was over.[5] Chapter 5, *"Expedicio Billarum Antiquitus,"* was finished in 1632. Chapter 6 may be the tractate published in 1685 as "The Manner of Passing Bills in Parliament."[6] Elsyng died in 1635 or 1636.

Elsyng probably thought about his book for a long time. A copy of a preliminary plan has survived among some papers said to have belonged to John Selden, now at the Cambridge University Library. The chapter headings proposed in this plan for Book One correspond to those later written and published, with the exception that "Receivers and Triers of Petitions" is listed as chapter 7, and *"Prolocutor domus Communis"* as chapter 8, rather than the reverse.[7] This, in fact, seems the more logical arrangement and may have been the order which Elsyng himself preferred. The note made in August, 1625, also gives chapter 7 as "Receivers and Triers," as does one of the cross references in his chapter, *"Expedicio Billarum Antiquitus,"* completed in 1632.[8]

In his preliminary plan, Elsyng outlined in some detail the subjects he intended to discuss in each chapter of Book One. He also sketched out five chapters for Book Two: Chapter 1, "Of matters handled in parliament"; Chapter 2, "Proceedings upon Bills"; Chapter 3, Conferences and Committees; Chapter 4, "the officers and their duties"; Chapter 5, "Continuance of Parliament," adjournment, prorogation, and dissolution. He indicated three chapters for a third book—one, a summary of every parliament "from Henry III to this day"; two, "the several great councils of every king . . . the difference between a parliament and a great council"; and three, ordinances, acts of parliaments, statutes, and "their differences."

Book One, when he came to write it, developed basically as he had planned. Most of the topics he thought appropriate have been covered, though some "lists" and "catalogues" were apparently omitted. His ideas for Book Two were not so clearly fixed. An outline, which Elsyng must have been considering later, in May, 1625, expanded "matters handled in parliament," formerly the title for chapter 1, to embrace the subject matter of the entire book. The topics to be discussed, though redistributed, were the same. Two have been added: chapter 10, concerning the rolls of ordinances, acts and statutes, and the journal book; chapter 11, concerning *"Errata in parliamentis,* and by whom committed, my own especially."

In 1625 Elsyng still contemplated a third book. "Include this in the next," he wrote opposite an alternative heading for chapter 10, "Ordinances Acts Statutes," which he crossed through. Possibly other topics, also deleted, were similarly intended for a third book. But *"Coronae dignitas & Praerogativa Regis"* seems to have been set aside. It was not Elsyng's nature to meddle with a topic which the king had reserved for himself.[9]

WAR AND PEACE

The chapter on "War and Peace," which was the first chapter of Book Two, may have been written at several times and in different ways. Among the Petyt papers at the Library of the Inner Temple are a series of precedents in Elsyng's hand, entitled *"Lib. 2, cap.* 1 War and Peace," which probably belong to a preliminary stage of this project. They begin with the parliament of 17 E. III and continue through 50 E. III.[1] After some folios which have been left blank, precedents from 13 E. III and 14 E. III start abruptly.[2] Something is missing and probably the leaves are out of order, though the heading, *"Lib. 2, cap.* 1, War and Peace," continues to identify them as part of the same

---

[1] Sims, *Expedicio,* pp. xviii–xix, xxv.
[2] Elsyng, *Manner of Holding Parliaments,* p. vii, n.
[3] H.L.R.O., Main Papers, H.L., 13 August, 1625.
[4] Below, p. 59.
[5] Below, p. 44.
[6] Sims, *Expedicio,* pp. 143, xxi. See also "The Method of Passing Bills," *Harl. Misc.* 9: pp. 112–122.
[7] Cambridge University Library, Mm. 6.62, fols. 58–59ᵛ. I am greatly indebted to Sheila Lambert for this reference.
[8] H.L.R.O., Main Papers, H.L., 13 August, 1625; Sims, *Expedicio,* pp. xxiv–xxv. In the notes for his chapter, "War and Peace," Elsyng referred to the chapter on "Proxies" as chapter 4 of his first book (below, p. 52).
[9] Sims, *Expedicio,* p. xx, and n. 11. I prefer to think that "N.M.T." signifies *noli me tangere,* rather than *Non Modus Tenendi.*

[1] Below, pp. 50–51. Petyt 538/12, fols. 228–45.
[2] Below, p. 51.

work. On fol. 263ᵛ, Elsyng referred to the chapter about proxies which was part of his first book.[3]

Throughout his notes on "War and Peace," Elsyng made running comments concerning the material he had collected.[4] He twice remarked that he had included too much about the parliament of 13 E. III, having found it particularly instructive: "I have written more than I meant, as I may the better understand how each several business was handled," "I have dwelt too long in this parliament."[5] He made no apology for his lengthy commentary on the parliament of 14 E. III:

> the Lords and Commons so accorded with such dutiful respect to the king, and the king showed himself as loving to them, and all matters are so exactly entered, that it is the first best precedent that shows the proceedings of each house, both in matters which concerned the Commons, and in affairs of state wherewith they meddled not, but I will proceed, to show how the like order was observed in all other parliaments of this king's time. . . .[6]

Elsyng has done just this. He abstracted from each parliament roll in the Tower everything which concerned war and peace, often in great detail and almost *verbatim*.[7] He showed to his own satisfaction how, in meeting after meeting, the monarch—or his officers for him—sought parliament's advice on war in France, the claim to the title to the French crown, the terms of a truce, the defense of Scotland and of Wales. He found what seemed to him evidence that sometimes Lords and Commons resolved together after each had debated separately, or sometimes the Commons declined to offer advice at all.

Elsyng's notes, as we now have them, are not reshaped into a treatise or chapter comparable to his other finished work. Nor do they extend beyond the reign of Edward III whom he so greatly admired. In 1625, when he was writing a chapter on subsidies, Elsyng spoke of "the former chapter concerning War and Peace,"[8] and observed,

> I have elsewhere collected the several precedents of E. III in what manner the king demanded advice of his parliament touching war and peace and defense of the realm, so that I need not write them here again. Yet having lent forth that treatise . . . I have gone briefly over them all again.

It would be interesting to know exactly what Elsyng had loaned to Bishop Williams, and how complete the "treatise" was.[9]

Sometime before September, 1625, Elsyng wrote the puzzling comment: "War and Peace, begun by me, enlarged by Sir Robert Cotton." Cotton's house and library lay between Westminster Palace and the river, close at hand. Both men were antiquarians, both were interested in parliament, and both were working over the same ground. Cotton wrote a tract, "That the Kings of England have been pleased usually to consult with their peers in the Great Council, and Commons in Parliament, of Marriage, Peace, and War." He especially acknowledged his debt to Elsyng: "I have been much assisted by the painful labour of Mr. Elsyng, clerk of the parliament."[10] There can be no doubt that Cotton used Elsyng's material; but it is questionable whether this particular essay is in fact the "enlargement" of Elsyng's treatise on war and peace, as has been suggested.[11] Cotton was writing a tract for the times, addressed to a particular person or persons, and is said to have composed his piece in 1621.[12] If this is the case, it would have been directed to the treaties with Spain, the proposed marriage of Prince Charles with the Infanta, and the problems of England's responsibilities to the Princess Elizabeth and her husband in the Palatinate. Elsyng did not become clerk until March, 1621. He would hardly have started "War and Peace" when the first part of his book, to which "War and Peace" refers, was not begun until December, 1624. If Cotton's tract and Elsyng's chapter are connected, we must move the date of Cotton's piece along to 1624 or 1625, when the Spanish marriage proposal had already failed, the treaties with Spain were soon to be or had already been broken, and possibly (if the date is late enough) Charles, as king, was still concerned with imperial affairs but had taken a French princess for his bride. Possibly Cotton's advice will fit the context, though one would expect some reference to the dramatic events of 1624, when Charles's and Buckingham's relation of their adventures in Spain brought crown and parliament into partnership in the conduct of foreign affairs.

Cotton's tract was primarily political in intent and basically rather slight. Though Elsyng occasionally drew on knowledge of the past to suggest policy for the present or for the future,[13] it seems unlikely that he

---

[3] Below, pp. 51–52; Petyt 538/12, fols. 259ᵛ–64.
[4] Petyt 538/12, fols. 233, 236ᵛ, and below, pp. 50–52.
[5] Below, p. 51.
[6] Below, p. 52.
[7] For a discussion of some of the records of parliament known to Elsyng, see Richardson and Sayles, *Rotuli Parliamentorum Angliae Hactenus Inediti*, pp. xx–xxii. For evidence that Elsyng worked directly from the rolls, see below, p. 38, n. 8.
[8] Below, p. 58; see also Petyt 538/15, fol. 45. Elsyng referred to his chapter *"Expedicio Billarum Antiquitus"* in the section on Subsidies, though it was not finished until later (Petyt 538/12, fol. 319).

[9] Petyt 538/15, fol. 41ᵛ. In the margin is written *"Vᵈ Lib. 1, cap. 1."* This may be an error for *Lib.* 2; or possibly Elsyng originally planned the volume beginning with "War and Peace" as *"Lib.* 1," and is referring to notes loaned to Cotton, not Williams.
[10] Sims, *Expedicio,* p. xx; *Cottoni Posthuma,* p. 34.
[11] Sims, *Expedicio,* p. xx. This suggestion was first made by Tyrwhitt in his introduction to *Manner of Holding Parliaments,* p. viii, n.
[12] *Cottoni Posthuma,* pp. 11, 34, 39.
[13] See Elsyng's memorandum for the Earl of Danby, discussed below, pp. 46–50, and his remarks concerning Charles I (below, p. 59).

would have so focused the first chapter of his second book on parliament. Whether he finished the section, "War and Peace," or not, he must have planned it on a larger scale than Cotton's work, and would surely have written it with a broader purpose in mind. It was in this way that he wrote chapter 5, *"Expedicio Billarum Antiquitus,"* a serious, scholarly study based on painstaking and detailed analysis of available sources. Elsyng's surviving notes for "War and Peace" laid the groundwork for a similar study, more thorough than Cotton's work, more consistent with Part One of his book and the surviving chapters of Book Two.

SUBSIDIES

Notes and drafts of Elsyng's chapter on "Subsidies" are at the Inner Temple.[1] Characteristically, he based the essay on a number of sources. Material collected by Bowyer gave him a running start. "I will not here set down what subsidies have been granted unto the king in parliament, they are collected to my hand by that painful gentleman my Uncle Bowyer."[2] Elsyng used the old *Modus Tenendi Parliamentum,* believing like most of his contemporaries that it and the parliament it described dated at least from the Conquest,[3] but he placed greater reliance on the rolls and records of parliament and was quick to observe differences in practice from those recorded in the old *Modus.*[4] He used Speed's *Chronicle* and possibly others.[5] He made a memorandum to check a precedent with "Mr. Selden."[6] But, like Bowyer, he also had "notes" from the days when he was keeper of the records in the Tower and an "abridgement." On occasion, when these proved inadequate or terse, he made a memorandum *"vide* the record."[7]

The value of Elsyng's work for this chapter as for his others lay in his constant reliance on the rolls and petitions of parliament.[8] He also studied the summons and the statutes.[9] Whatever use he made of Bowyer's notes or his own, Elsyng was never far from the original documents. As student of parliament and clerk, as keeper of the records, he knew them well and used them with care. He spoke of the rolls of Edward III as the best:

The first records (now extant) that mention the proceeding in parliament touching subsidies are those of E. III, with which I will begin, not only for that they are the first, but also for that his times are the best, of the ancient, without exception, both in respect of the king and of the subject, he being the right heir to the crown, beloved of his people, and of ripe years to govern. All which you shall not find in any of his successors (H. V excepted) until H. VIII.[10]

In the reigns of Richard II, Henry IV, Henry V and Henry VI, he said, the records show "somewhat of the form in demanding and granting of subsidies . . . agreeable unto those of E. III. But in those of the next 3 kings, whose times the civil wars had made even barbarous, nothing but the thing granted is recorded. . . ."[11] "We are now come to the precedents of R. II wherein, and in the following ages, I will not spend much time, for that they are not so pleasing as the other."[12]

There are in Elsyng's notes at the Inner Temple two separate drafts of his proposed chapter on "Subsidies." It was characteristic of him to write in this way. Composition did not come easily and he had many facts to digest, several alternatives to try before he found a satisfactory form. An original draft of his fifth chapter, *"Expedicio Billarum Antiquitus,"* at the Inner Temple, shows how he worked.[13] "I have altered this tedious discourse and written another leaving much of it out. H. E.," he wrote opposite a section concerning bills and statutes. Following others he noted, "I have written this all over and much altered it. H. E."[14] "I purpose

---

[1] Petyt 538/12, fols. 265–305ᵛ, 309–309ˣ, 312–323ᵛ, 330–334, 391–397ᵛ. Petyt 538/15, fols. 36–94ᵛ. One long section has been marked "Omit all this" for precedents on war and peace had been collected elsewhere (see above, p. 37, n. 9), which might indicate that he had started his notes on subsidies before he began on war and peace and later deleted what was redundant.

[2] Below, p. 52. I examined a great number of "collections" on subsidies hoping to find the one used by Elsyng, but could not make a positive identification. See, for example, British Museum, Titus B. IV, fols. 89–92; Cleopatra F. IV, fols. 197–199ᵛ, 202–207; Harl. 293; Harl. 738, fols. 231–247; and the notes of grants, aids, and subsidies, Henry I–James I, among the Montagu papers (*H.M.C. Buccleuch* 3, 6: p. 247). Elsyng may also have been referring to the abstracts of parliamentary records made by William and Robert Bowyer, later published as *An Exact Abridgment of the Records in the Tower* (for this and other collections by Robert Bowyer, see above, p. 8, n. 5.

[3] Below, pp. 52, 58. But see below, p. 45.

[4] Below, pp. 58–59.

[5] Petyt 538/12, fols. 285, 294.

[6] Petyt 538/15, fol. 44.

[7] *Ibid.,* fol. 88. Petyt 538/12, fol. 294. The abridgment may have been that made by the Bowyers (see above, n. 2). It may have been Elsyng's own. He called it "my abridgement." In the chapter *"Expedicio Billarum Antiquitus,"* he referred to "the collections of Mr. Hennage my learned predecessor in the records in the Tower (unto whose painful labours I owe much)" (Sims, *Expedicio,* pp. 35–36).

[8] On his use of the petitions, see Petyt 538/15, fol. 294: "Divers chapters in the statutes, I have nothing recorded in the parl. roll to warrant the same. Of these there are many, but it may be they are on the file of the bundle of petitions. *Vde.*" Elsyng's notes make it clear that he used the original rolls, not the abstract. In one place he remarked that he had in effect transcribed the roll (Petyt 538/12, fol. 285); in another, he spoke of the roll being torn (Petyt 538/15, fol. 66). He also used the commission for the levy of subsidies (below, p. 52).

[9] Petyt 538/12, fol. 241ᵛ; below, p. 51. *Cf.* Mrs. Sim's discussion of the sources for Elsyng's fifth chapter (Sims, *Expedicio,* pp. xxvi–xxvii).

[10] Below, p. 53.

[11] Below, p. 54.

[12] Below, p. 59.

[13] For Elsyng's drafts of this and other chapters, see Petyt 538/12, fols. 1–171, 181–212ᵛ; Petyt 538/15, fols. 122–294. There is a copy of *"Expedicio Billarum Antiquitus"* in Petyt 538/4.

[14] Petyt 538/15, fols. 114, 122.

to write this section all over again and put it into a better method when I have perused the rolls of R. II, H. V and H. VI."[15] Similarly, he planned to revise his material on "Subsidies": "leave out all that follows."[16]

A completed chapter on "Subsidies" (or indeed "War and Peace") would have been worth publishing in full; but with only drafts or notes at hand it seemed best to summarize the main argument and include some excerpts in an appendix. The points concerning subsidies which Elsyng planned to cover in his two drafts were basically the same, as his tables of contents show.[17] In what seems to be the earlier piece,[18] Elsyng said his "only purpose is to find out how these subsidies were demanded and granted, and how the parliament anciently proceeded therein."[19] He laid special emphasis on the precedents of Edward III, which he gave at large, and then proceeded to "Observations out of those precedents touching the manner how subsidies were demanded in the time of E. III."[20]

The next important point was how subsidies were granted in parliament. The grant was, Elsyng said, "upon conference between the Lords and Commons." When was it, he inquired, that "the Lords first lost or waived their right to this conference"? The grant was made "by indenture, sometimes sealed," but "by whom, and the occasion thereof. And upon what occasion the same was first without indenture." A third point was "the conditions of the subsidy, the petitions of the Commons, whether the lords of the committee did treat with the Commons thereon or no. And how the king granted the same." The fourth point was "the presentment of the subsidy," and the fifth, "the king's royal assent."[21]

As he had done in "War and Peace," Elsyng went methodically through the parliaments of Edward III, noting in considerable detail how subsidies were demanded and granted.[22] He then drew brief conclusions: that Edward III "demanded no subsidy but for the defense of the land, and to maintain his wars in France." "And if this king had had any other occasion to demand his people's aid, proceeding in the same manner he did, the Commons (no doubt) would have granted it." If the aid was insufficient, they willingly granted more. "And now and then he called a parliament only to congratulate with his people; showed his readiness to redress their wrongs; and demanded no subsidies, *annis* 21, 25, 28 *et* 40."[23] Early parliaments

> stood upon it to have the conditions of their subsidies enrolled, and a charter thereof made and sealed, ... Yet afterwards (a° 25 E. III. H.) the king yielding to the condition demanded (that no other tax nor charge be demanded nor levied); they contented themselves with their repose they had in the king for the performance of their requests, not demanding any charter.

In many parliaments, subsidies were granted with no condition that wars must continue and the money be spent solely for that purpose. In 51 E. III, Elsyng found a suggestion that two earls and two barons be appointed "guardians and treasurers of the subsidy," but parliament was usually content, he thought, to trust the collection to officers appointed by the king.[24]

Thus Elsyng concluded the first main division of his chapter. He later seems to have revised it and indeed to have started all over again. This time he grounded his work on a wider range of precedents. He began, as before, with the old *Modus Tenendi Parliamentum*,[25] he continued to lay great emphasis and praise upon the parliaments of Edward III,[26] but he included a study of how other monarchs demanded subsidies, proceeding from Richard II, Henry IV, Henry V, Richard III, Henry VII, Henry VIII, to Elizabeth, James I and the first parliament of Charles.[27]

Subsidy was, Elsyng thought, inevitably linked with war, for it was demanded, the records seemed to show, "in all the times of E. III, R. II, H. IV, and H. V (one or two parliaments excepted) either for an invasive war, or defense at home."[28] "In those times," he observed,

> if the war were proposed, their counsel and advice were only required, and yet the parliament (with their advice for the war) promised their aid also. But if the war were once begun by their assent, and on foot, then their aid was directly demanded. So likewise for defense of the realm, if the damages were apparent, then their aid, otherwise their counsel was required how to resist the enemy, and defend themselves.

"In the times of H. VI and E. IV," he went on, "these circumstances were not so duly observed." The chancellors, being bishops, took "a text, as if to preach . . . The times of R. III, H. VII and the beginnings of H. VIII much resembled those of H. VI touching the bishops' texts." He had, he said, little information about requests for aid in Elizabeth's reign.

> Her successor, the learnedest of kings, did ever propound the cause of summons himself. And when he intended war for recovery of the Palatinate . . . he briefly propounded

---

[15] *Ibid.*, fol. 154. He also intended to incorporate precedents from these reigns in his discussion of the validity of the public ordinance (*ibid.*, fol. 229). For other comments which suggest rearrangement of material and changes, see fols. 166, 178, 179, 191, 207.
[16] Petyt 538/12, fols. 284ᵛ, 286.
[17] Below, pp. 52, 55, 57–58.
[18] This can be found in Petyt 538/12, fols. 265–305ᵛ, 309–309ˣ, 312–323ᵛ, 330–334, 391–397ᵛ (see below, pp. 52–57).
[19] Below, p. 52.
[20] *Ibid.*
[21] *Ibid.*
[22] Petyt 538/12, fols. 274–305ᵛ.
[23] Below, p. 54. This was a policy which Elsyng felt Charles I might wisely follow (below, pp. 46–50).
[24] Below, p. 55. See also Petyt 538/12, fol. 305.
[25] Below, p. 58.
[26] Petyt 538/15, fols. 46–71.
[27] *Ibid.*, fols 40ᵛ–42, 72–94ᵛ.
[28] Below, p. 59.

the business to the parliament and required their counsel *super totam materiam*. . . . His royal son (our dread sovereign) in his first parliament, remembered them of their counsel given his father, and their aid promised for the war. How well do these agree with the precedents of that famous and victorious king, E. III.[29]

Parliament, Elsyng said in summary, first "treated of matters of state (as in the former chapter)," the chapter on "War and Peace". . . "Their next consultation (and indeed the chiefest) was to provide money to maintain the wars, and to defray the king's other extraordinary charges. . . ." The old *Modus,* he continued, enumerated three occasions when the king might demand aid, *"pro guerra instanti,"* "to make the king's son a knight," and "to marry the king's daughter." The demand, he said, was "in full parliament" and "delivered in writing unto each degree of the peers": to the lords spiritual, lords temporal, the procurators of the clergy, and to the Commons. Of these three occasions for aid,

the demand . . . for the wars continueth, though not given in writing as then. But that touching the king's son and the king's daughter hath been so settled by usual payments thereof, as it is grown due by custom, and so never demanded now, but levied by commission. Which the ancient parliaments feared would happen to that for war also, and not without cause.[30]

Elsyng cited precedents in the reign of Edward III of levies by commission "for the wars and guard of the sea,"[31] which led to protestations by the Lords and Commons under Richard II, Henry IV and Henry V "that they, their heirs and successors, and the realm of England, be as free touching the charge of the said wars etc. as they were before the grant of their aid, the levying thereof only excepted."[32]

Demand for subsidy was, Elsyng believed, linked with war, and so too was the nature of the grant. After Elsyng had presented evidence from the reigns of Edward III, Richard II, Henry IV, and Henry V concerning the "causes for which subsidies were demanded, and the manner thereof," he concluded,

And for the grant, I observe it was of the subsidy of wools etc. and of later times of an impost on merchandise also, if the cause were not great. But if the war were on foot, then a xth and a xvth, and the like were granted also.[33]

Elsyng then proceeded to later parliaments, but unfortunately the account ends at the conclusion of the reign of Edward IV. It breaks off abruptly, suggesting that more was written which has been lost.[34]

After Elsyng finished the first part of his chapter on subsidies, "For what causes subsidies have been demanded, and the manner thereof,"[35] of which we have two drafts, he turned to the second part, how subsidies were granted to the king. But for this part, only one draft has survived—the earlier one, devoted largely as before to the reign of Edward III, with a few precedents from the reign of Richard II.[36]

Grants, he concluded, were made by both Lords and Commons following a conference held between them, usually by committees of the two groups.[37] His earliest precedent is 13 E. III. The Lords, he found, first agreed together how to aid the king, then

a committee was appointed to treat thereof with the Commons. The record (I confess) names not the Commons, but they are necessarily understood. They treated long, the record sayeth upon this business, which cannot be understood to be amongst themselves, they being already agreed on the thing to be granted. Neither doth the record mention any committee to be appointed for this treaty, this age being very sparing to record circumstances; but that it was then the use to appoint committees for the like conferences will appear in the following precedents of this king, and Richard II. . . .[38]

In the next parliament, Elsyng found, the Commons

exhibited in their grant in a writing indented sealed with the seals of prelates and other grands, n. 8, (not of all the prelates and grands), and therefore of necessity a committee of prelates and grands is understood who did treat with the Commons herein.[39]

Elsyng's clinching precedent came from 2 R. II, when the Commons requested that five or six lords "might come to them to treat and commune with them." The Lords took offence at what they regarded as recent innovation.

But they said, and confessed that it hath been accustomed that the Lords should choose of themselves some certain small number of vi or x. And the Commons likewise some like number. And that the same lords and Commons so chosen might treat together in quiet manner without great cry or noise, and so shall they come the sooner to some good end or purpose. . . . This precedent is so plain and direct that I will proceed no further; but rest satisfied that the Lords had such a right in the grant of subsidies (whereunto now they do only assent) as that the Commons never granted the same but upon conference first had with their lordships either in the upper house or at a committee between both houses.[40]

Elsyng's practical experience is evident throughout. Precedents, he admitted, did not always mention the conference nor the committee, yet the indenture, to which he turned later, proved it: "and whosoever shall peruse the rolls and consider the short times of those parliaments will conclude that the Commons could not otherwise dispatch their many businesses but by several committees." Elsyng knew how many men could sit

---

[29] Below, p. 59.
[30] Below, p. 58. On the question of whether the demand was in writing, see below, pp. 58–59.
[31] Below, p. 58.
[32] *Ibid.*
[33] Below, p. 59.
[34] Petyt 538/15, fol. 94ᵛ. "R. 3" has been written at the bottom of a sheet, indicating that these were the first words of a sheet to follow.

[35] Below, p. 57.
[36] Petyt 538/12, fols. 312–323ᵛ.
[37] Below, pp. 52, 55, 57–58.
[38] Below, p. 55.
[39] *Ibid.*
[40] Below, pp. 55–56.

together in certain rooms. "I cannot think," he wrote of a meeting in 29 E. III, "that this parlance was with all the lords in the open house, but with the temporal lords only, or with some of them, apart in that room, *vizt.* the court of requests, which is large enough for that purpose." He always read records with the eye of a parliament man.[41]

Elsyng planned to develop the point concerning conferences more fully in his second draft of the chapter on subsidies. If the text of this later draft was completed, it is not now at the Inner Temple, but a table of contents shows that Elsyng intended to answer "six objections against the conference." The objections were (1) "The Commons did sever from the Lords in the grant a° 13 E. III," (2) "They alone are mentioned in divers other grants," (3) "The Lords' assent is only mentioned in divers kings' times," (4) "The Commons alone granted . . . a° 31 H. VI," (5) "Their speaker presents the grant, and the kings acknowledge it theirs," (6) "The account made to them alone."[42] Some idea of the way Elsyng would have answered the first point may be found in his earlier account. In reply to other objections, Elsyng said he would prove "the conference by many precedents," that the Lords' assent was given at a conference, and that a conference was held "to perfect the Commons' grant." He would show "why the king acknowledged it to be the Commons' grant," and finally, in reply to the last objection, show "why the account is to them, and when the first."[43]

Elsyng then turned to his "second observation" concerning how subsidies were granted. Only one draft is extant. He found, upon examining the records of Edward III, that the grant was by indenture. "I suppose," he wrote,

the grant was indented, not as a deed made between the Lords and Commons as parties, the one to grant, and the other to accept the thing granted (for they both granted unto the king), but it was indented, as nothing might be altered by the Commons, and as the lords of the committee might truly report the same to the house.[44]

At a parliament in 14 E. III, there is no mention that the grant was indented "for that the two houses sitting together, there was no private conference by committee and therefore no indenture."[45] But when conference was by committee, the grant or the schedule of the grant was indented "and so continued even in the time of H. VIII, as shall be declared hereafter."[46] Sometimes the part of the indenture "which the Commons kept and presented" was sealed by the lords of the committee.[47] On one occasion, the indenture was sealed by all the prelates, earls, barons present and also by those who were then absent.[48] In each case, the king was away from parliament, overseas. "I do not yet find," Elsyng wrote after surveying the records of Edward III, "that any were sealed but when the king was absent."[49]

The one surviving draft of Elsyng's "third observation" concerning the subsidy grant is incomplete and covers only the period from 6 E. III through 20 E. III.[50] He intended to discuss the "conditions of the subsidy and the petitions of the Commons. Whether the lords of the committee did treat with the Commons upon the said conditions and petitions or no. And how the king granted the same."[51] In the material which we now have Elsyng has just begun to collect his precedents. The parliament of 6 E. III, he noted, "is of the time when the houses sat together, which fits not our turn. For then of necessity it is understood that they all agreed, both Lords and Commons, to the penning of the grant and the conditions thereof."[52] In 13 E. III (Michaelmas), Lords and Commons could not agree, "therefore I suppose they did not treat together of the conditions thereof, which the Commons delivered in writing (promising a subsidy the next parliament), n. 8, 13."[53] Later in the same year, the Commons

presented their grant under certain conditions contained in indentures thereupon made and sealed under the seals of prelates and other grands, etc., n. 8. The record names not the conditions . . . but for certain, the Lords treated thereon with the Commons, for their seals are to the indentures.[54]

The conditions attached to their grant by the Commons in 18 E. III and in 20 E. III are cited by Elsyng at large[55] and there the notes break off.

The last two sections on the method of granting subsidies were entitled "The presentment of the sub-

---

[41] Petyt 538/12, fol. 318ᵛ. *Cf.* the comment by J. Enoch Powell: "This is one advantage, at any rate, which a working member of such an institution has in investigating its history: he asks - even if the answers are not forthcoming - such practical questions as, who arranges the members, who decides who shall and shall not enter the chamber? who presides over debate? who puts the question, and in what order and so on" (Powell and Wallis, *The House of Lords in the Middle Ages*, p. xiii).

[42] Below, pp. 57–58.

[43] Below, pp. 55, 57–58. Elsyng also discussed conferences in chapter 5 (Sims, *Expedicio*, pp. 35–44), and had planned earlier chapters on the subject (*ibid.*, p. xx; above, p. 36).

[44] Below, p. 56.

[45] Below, p. 57.

[46] *Ibid.* "Note that anciently the subsidy was granted upon a conference and the grant indented and the speaker presented that part which rested with the Commons. H.E." (H.L.R.O., "Precedents in Parliament," 23 Elizabeth).

[47] Below, p. 56.

[48] Below, p. 57.

[49] *Ibid.*

[50] Petyt 538/12, fols. 391–397ᵛ.

[51] *Ibid.*, fol. 391.

[52] *Ibid.*

[53] *Ibid.*, fol. 392.

[54] *Ibid.*

[55] *Ibid.*, fols. 394–397ᵛ.

sidy"[56] and "The king's royal assent"[57] in the first draft of Elsyng's table of contents. Originally he made a memorandum opposite these words, as he did against the titles of the sections on conferences and on conditions: *"deest"* or "wanting." *Deest* has in each case been scratched through, presumably when the section was completed.[58]

When Elsyng drew up the table of contents for his second draft of the chapter on "Subsidies," he divided his material into three parts: "For what causes subsidies have been demanded," "how subsidies were anciently granted to the king" which would cover the question of conferences, and

The third part. How subsidies have been presented to the king. Whether any in the beginning of a parliament. Whether several subsidies at several times in one session. Whether the royal assent to the subsidy grant hath made it a session. The precedents touching the presentment, whereof two by the lord chancellor. The manner thereof at this day.[59]

Perhaps Elsyng completed this draft. It would be interesting and significant reading if it could be found.

JUDICATURE

Elsyng planned to discuss the judicial activities of parliament in chapter 4. During the seventeenth century, judicature in parliament was not only a subject for antiquarians but became, like many other topics which antiquarians studied, a matter of immediate political consequence and constitutional importance. The weapon of impeachment, a little rusty when first revived in 1621, soon became sharp with practice on a lord chancellor and a lord treasurer. By 1626 it was pointed at the lord admiral, Buckingham, and by 1640 at the Archbishop of Canterbury and the king's chief adviser, the Earl of Strafford, though the last two were finally brought down by actions of attainder. After the Restoration, interest in impeachment continued, and the impeachment of the Earl of Danby involved both houses in debate in 1679. In 1681 the Lords refused to consider the impeachment of one Fitz-Harris. Despite the Commons' resolution that this was "a denial of justice and a violation of the constitution of parliaments," Fitz-Harris was left to the common law.[1]

Controversy concerning impeachment centered chiefly on procedure. Debate on other problems of judicature raised more fundamental problems. Before 1640, there is some evidence that lawyers in the lower house encouraged the Lords to extend their judicial activities. But after the Restoration, the whole subject of judicature became a matter of controversy between the houses, and the Commons bitterly attacked judicial power claimed by the Lords. After 1668 the upper house virtually ceased to function as a court of the first instance in civil cases. The Lords' claim to original jurisdiction over crimes without impeachment from the lower house was condemned by the Commons in 1668, and by the judges in 1693. Claims to appellate jurisdiction by the Lords likewise came under fire. For political reasons, the Commons seem to have accepted the right of the upper house to hear cases in equity on petition, but its broader claim to appellate jurisdiction over all courts and causes, to supreme jurisdiction as a court of last resort, raised furious debate.[2] The widespread interest in judicial activity in parliament prompted a number of treatises. Some, not published till later, probably circulated in manuscript.[3] Among them was a study entitled "Of the Judicature in Parliaments," said to have been written by John Selden. Since the first recorded edition is that of 1681, both publication and the attribution to Selden were posthumous.[4] If, as is suggested below, this treatise was written between 1627 and 1629, it reflects the first period of interest in impeachment and judicature of parliament. By 1681, when the essay was probably first published, impeachment and judicature were still being widely discussed.

The essay itself—carefully based on records of parliament—eschews controversy. There is no significant evidence for attributing it to Selden, the great antiquarian. Yet it was the kind of study he might have done. He was known to have been interested in judicature of parliament, and particularly in the privileges of the peers. In 1621 a committee of lords, appointed to consider privilege, consulted Selden and Hakewill and obtained from them a "note of privileges belonging to peers and lords of parliament." Later recopied for the Lords by Selden, these notes were known as "The Book of Collections or Book of Privileges" and were published as Selden's treatise, *The Priviledges of the Baronage of England when they sit in Parliament.*[5] Selden studied the rolls and other records of parliament with care. He left a number of collections concerning the rights of peers and the jurisdiction of the upper

---

[56] For additional material on this point, see "The Exhibiting of the Bill" (Sims, *Expedicio*, pp. 9–12).

[57] There is a section on the royal assent in *"Expedicio Billarum Antiquitus,"* which touches on the acceptance of the subsidy (Sims, *Expedicio*, pp. 49–65).

[58] Below, p. 52. For a slightly different wording of these titles, see p. 55.

[59] Below, p. 58.

[1] Pike, pp. 232–233.

[2] Relf, *Debates in the House of Lords 1621*, pp. xxx–xxxii. Hale, *The Jurisdiction of the Lords House, or Parliament*, pp. xc–clxviii. Pike, pp. 231–234.

[3] For a discussion of the most important of these treatises, see Hale, pp. clxix–clxxvii.

[4] *The Dictionary of National Biography* lists among Selden's works, "*Judicature in Parliament* 1640 4to." The reference is probably not to *Of Judicature* but to *A Briefe Discourse concerning the Power of the Peeres and the Commons in Parliament in Point of Judicature*, a pamphlet, sometimes attributed to John Selden (see Berkowitz, appendix E. Berkowitz believes that *A Briefe Discourse* was written by Sir Robert Cotton).

[5] *The Hastings Journal*, pp. vi–vii. See also Spedding, *Letters and Life* 7: p. 332. Berkowitz, sec. I, pp. 33, 44–48.

house.[6] Perhaps the treatise was attributed to him in all honesty, perhaps use of his name was the scheme of an unscrupulous publisher. In 1674 and again in 1682, there appeared *Johannis Seldeni Angli Liber de Nummis*. This popular book on coins had in fact been written by Alexander Sardis and was first published in 1579. The reprint, carrying Selden's name and a dedicatory epistle to D'Ewes, proved even more popular than the original issue.[7] David Wilkins, when he collected Selden's works for publication in 1726, reluctantly included the treatise on judicature. "It is," said Wilkins, "a very maimed piece, and as such does little deserve to be placed among the works of so great a man, as Selden was." The original manuscript, formerly in the library of Lincoln Cathedral, is, he continued, "now lost and could not be found to correct this imperfect treatise."[8] The treatise, as we have it, is indeed "maimed" or incomplete. Six sections had been planned,[9] but only one "Judgments against Delinquents" has apparently survived. Perhaps this is all that was finished.

The evidence for Selden's authorship is slight.[10] What Wilkins described so disparagingly may not have been Selden's work at all, but an essay by Henry Elsyng, intended for the fourth chapter of his second book of *The Manner of Holding Parliaments in England*. Here the evidence is more substantial. We may turn first to the manuscripts. Among the collections at Crowcombe Court, along with Henry Elsyng's "scribbled books" for the upper house, was a treatise "On Judicature in Parliament, *Lib. 2, Cap. 4, pars prima*, concerning judgments on delinquents." The opening sentence ran, "The execution of all our laws hath long since been distributed by parliament . . . ," the familiar words so long attributed to Selden. The closing section, unlike the printed versions, was "Of levying fines to the king," and at the end was written "23 Aug. 1627 *apud* Cornewall." The commissioners who were so fortunate as to see this manuscript described it as the author's corrected copy, with an autograph "Anglesey, his book." The next document calendared is *"Expedicio Billarum Antiquitus,"* dated "Cornewall 24 April, 1632,"* the treatise now identified by Mrs. Sims as Elsyng's fifth chapter. Unfortunately, when the Crowcombe Court manuscripts were sold in 1903, the material concerning judicature dropped out of sight.[11]

If what may be the key documents are missing, there are other clues. "Of the Judicature" circulated widely in manuscript and many copies have survived—some, like the printed version, without the final section "Of levying fines to the king," others with it.[12]

At the Folger Shakespeare Library in Washington, there is a copy of the fuller version, with the clerk's notation that the last section had been added in Mr. Elsyng's own hand.[13] Across the continent in California, at the Huntington Library among the Ellesmere papers, is yet another copy. The last division of the Ellesmere manuscript, here called "For levying the fines to the king," has been much corrected. The first four sentences were struck out:

At this day in the star chamber, the clerk estreats those fines immediately into the exchequer. And so I believe the clerk of the parliament did anciently. Otherwise this high court which makes laws should not have so great authority as are in inferior court criminal. But judicature having been long out of use in parliament these formal parts thereof are uncertain, but by conjecture.

Then follows a section which could only have been composed by Elsyng.

A° 18 *Jacobi* a writ was sent me out of the chancery (sitting the parliament) to rectify the fines of that parliament into the chancery. The lord treasurer then affirming that the use and manner thereof was so, and that the chancery should transmit the same into the exchequer.

The words which follow have been deleted, but are legible and read:

I obeyed the writ (as in duty I ought) but it then seemed very strange unto me, that any other court should by hearsay (as it were) take notice what is done in parliament. Or that that court which hath the power to impose should not have power to estreat the same fines.

At the end Elsyng has added in his own hand,

---

[6] See, for example, Lincoln's Inn Library, Hale #11, fols. 127–129; #12, fols. 54, 194–195, 254–258ᵛ.

[7] Catalogue 23, Hofman and Freeman, Booksellers, Shoreham, Kent. C. E. Doble, ed., *Remarks and Collections of Thomas Hearne* (Oxford, 1885) 1: p. 24. Similarly, *The Exact Abridgement of the Records in the Tower* was attributed to Sir Robert Cotton by William Prynne, who should have known better (see Richardson and Sayles, *Rotuli Parliamentorum Anglie Hactenus Inediti*, p. xxii).

[8] *Joannis Seldeni Jurisconsulti Opera Omnia Tam Edita Quam Inedita in Tribus Voluminibus* (London, 1726) 3: "To the Reader." It is interesting that the manuscript should have been at Lincoln, Williams's seat. Did he borrow this chapter also? See above, p. 36.

[9] Selden, *Of Judicature*, pp. 8–10.

[10] Berkowitz (sec. V, pp. 37–43) raised questions concerning Selden's authorship of this treatise, and the date of its composition. Also, see above, p. 33.

[11] *H.M.C. Fourth Report*, appendix, pp. 369, 372. Sotheby's sale catalogue, May 6, 1903, item #251. It went to the bookseller, Ridler. The *Modus Tenendi Parliamentum* was item #263. Elsyng's "scribbled books" were items #259–260. Anglesey is probably Arthur Annesley, first Earl of Anglesey (1614–1686), who was deeply involved in the controversy concerning the judicature of the House of Lords. He was a sound lawyer, a member of Lincoln's Inn, a collector of law records, and formed a great library which was sold at his death (Hale, *The Jurisdiction of the Lords House, or Parliament*, pp. xciii–xcviii, civ, cxxvii–cxxviii, cxxx, cxxxiii, clviii; *Dictionary of National Biography*).

[12] A few examples are: fMS Eng 919 (Houghton Library, Harvard University); Clark Library Ms. (Selden-Hale) (University of California, Los Angeles); Petyt 538/14; *H.M.C. Fourth Report*, appendix, p. 252. See also Berkowitz, sec. V, p. 38, note 63.

[13] Folger Shakespeare Library, V.b.130, fol. 44. *Cf.* H.L.R.O., Braye 6.

And 18 *Junii*, 1628 the lord keeper and the Baron Denham affirm this to be the ancient manner of certifying or estreating anything out of the parliament. And the like writ is directed to the clerk of the star chamber to estreat fines out of that court. And thus much touching judgments on delinquents.

Only the clerk of the parliaments would have received such a writ from the chancery, or obeyed it "as in duty I ought," and the clerk who received this writ in 1621 was Henry Elsyng.[14] The final section of the Ellesmere manuscript was apparently corrected by Elsyng himself, sometime after the treatise as a whole had been written. The table of contents concluded with the words *"finis 30 Aug., 1627,"* but Elsyng added the last sentence on or after June 18, 1628. Someone has scrawled on the final folio, "These precedents given me by Mr. Elsyng, clerk of the parliament."[15]

Thus the manuscripts provide a number of clues concerning the writer of "Of the Judicature in Parliaments." The text itself supplies still more since the author referred to himself several times.[16] He was consulted about procedure in the House of Lords: "A question was demanded of me and others in private, the last parliament," touching the order of the Lords that the "Earl of Bristol's cause should be wholly retained in this house."[17] The description could also fit John Selden, but other references are less apt. The author knew the house well and referred to a dissenting vote by the Earl of Dorset 1621. Elsyng, as clerk, did not record this negative vote in the journal of the House of Lords, but has a note of it in his "scribbled book."[18] Twice the writer questioned whether it was right for him to examine the proceedings of the Lords: "If it may be lawful for me to examine the proceedings of the Lords in the complaints against Mompesson," and again, concerning the case of the Earl of Bristol, "if it be lawful for me to speak freely, I believe the Lords thought they were but misdemeanours when they allowed him counsel in parliament."[19] The point was important since the king's charge against Bristol was treason. The use of the term "the Lords," when the writer referred to himself in the first person, suggests that the author, though intimately involved with the Lords, was not himself one of them. All in the house were bound to keep its affairs secret, but the clerk was sworn to do so by oath. To write about proceedings might well be "unlawful."[20]

The author looked at precedents with a practical eye. He wrote that, in the reign of Richard II, the Lords gave judgment against Weston without royal assent. But this, he said, may have been for lack of time to consult the king on the last afternoon of parliament.[21] He seemed to understand what could happen in the rush at the end of a session. The author noted that both king and prince were present in the house in 1624 when an order was voted that counsel should be allowed delinquents "in all cases generally." "I did expect some reply thereunto on the king's behalf," he wrote, "and especially observed whether the prince would any ways dislike of it, either in words or countenance; and he shewed none: which made me verily believe that he had been acquainted therewith beforehand; but he was not, as I shall make it appear."[22]

Not a lord but closely involved with the upper house, a man with knowledge of parliamentary precedents who was consulted on procedural matters of significance, who was bound to keep secret the affairs of parliament, who was present when votes were taken and during debate—the clues point to Henry Elsyng.

The essay on judicature resembles other writing by Elsyng—his first book of *The Manner of Holding Parliaments in England,* his finished fifth chapter for the second book, and the drafts of his first and second chapters. The author made use of the same sources which Elsyng used: chronicles, rolls, and petitions of parliament, close and patent rolls. It is interesting, however, that there is no reference to the old *Modus* in either the section on judicature or the *"Expedicio*

---

[14] The full text of the writ is given in L.J., 3: p. 142. *Cf.* Scobell, pp. 52–53, who has mistaken the date. In a collection of "Precedents in Parliament," Elsyng has made a note concerning fines levied by the House of Commons on members absent without license: *"Quere* how these fines can be levied, for though the Commons had power (as they have not) of judicature, yet their clerk cannot certify these fines. A *certiorari* can be directed to none but to the clerk of the upper house, and to him by the name of *clerico parliamentorum,* without distinction. The clerk of the lower House is *subclericus.* H.E." (H.L.R.O., "Precedents in Parliament").

[15] El. 8392, fol. 122. This manuscript has been annotated in several hands, one of which was that of the second Earl of Bridgewater (1622–1686), who was also noted on the fly leaf its shelf mark in the Ashridge Library. Someone else annotated the manuscript earlier. The most interesting of this annotator's comments is the statement quoted and a marginal note on fol. 75ᵛ: "K. Charles should have had his testimony used against the Earl of Bristol for treason when he was prince." The table of contents is fuller than the table given in printed versions and lists the five sections to come (*cf.* Selden, *Of Judicature,* pp. 8–10), but these are not in the manuscript. El. 8392 was loaned in March, 1795, to Francis Hargrave, whose comments are on the first page and on the table of contents. In many places, this copy is superior to the printed version. There are two other manuscripts of the treatise at the Huntington Library, El. 8393 and El. 8394, which seem to be copies of El. 8392, even to the annotations. I am grateful to Jean Preston, curator of manuscripts, for her assistance and for identifying the hand of the second earl.

[16] Selden, *Of Judicature,* pp. 71, 101, 106.

[17] *Ibid.,* p. 50.

[18] *Ibid.,* p. 131. Relf, *Debates in the House of Lords 1621,* pp. 38–39. L.J., 3: p. 67. It was not considered appropriate to record dissent in the journal (see above, p. 27).

[19] El. 8392, fols. 33ᵛ–34. The printed version in Selden, *Of Judicature,* p. 63, omits the word *if;* Selden, *Of Judicature,* p. 105.

[20] For the oath, see Bond, "Clerks of the Parliaments," p. 79, n. 7.

[21] Selden, *Of Judicature,* pp. 141–142.

[22] *Ibid.,* p. 103.

Billarum Antiquitus." In 1625 Elsyng apparently began his second book. In the notes for "War and Peace" and "Subsidies" probably made during that year, he used the *Modus* as a source for early times "before the Conquest." But sometime around 1626, Elsyng may have come to question the authority of the old *Modus*, just as Selden had done in 1614.[23]

Other minor differences distinguish "Of the Judicature" from the rest of Elsyng's work. Usually, Elsyng referred to himself in the first person, and to the reader as "you"; but once in the essay on judicature a more formal reference, "The Reader," is used.[24] There are none of the references to earlier chapters characteristic of his other writing. Possibly as the essay on judicature developed, it became too long to serve as a chapter for a book. *"Expedicio Billarum Antiquitus"* ran to about 52,000 words, longer than any chapter in Book One. But the first division of "Judicature" ran to 37,000–38,000 words, with five more sections to come. Possibly "Judicature" would stand by itself.

The chief proposition of the treatise was that judicature belonged to parliament in six cases. The first, which was fully discussed, was in judgments against delinquents. The second was "in reversing erroneous judgements."[25] A brief beginning on this topic, written in Elsyng's hand, has survived among his papers at the House of Lords Record Office, together with a paragraph on "Erroneous Judgements in Parliament."[26] These fragments with the other available evidence suggest that what has so long been attributed to John Selden is the work of Henry Elsyng: the notations concerning "Cornewall," his manor in Oxfordshire, which correspond to that on his other manuscripts; the chapter's designation *"Lib. 2, cap. 4," pars prima,*[27] which clearly marks the treatise as part of a larger work and corresponds with the "contents of the second book" in which Elsyng listed his chapters;[28] the emendations in Elsyng's hand;[29] the references in the text to the author; and the style of presentation.

Elsyng did, we know, plan a chapter on judicature, and had indeed already written it by 1632 when he finished chapter 5. To subtract this "poor, maimed piece" from the works of John Selden will not materially lessen the glory of that renowned scholar, but to add it to the writings of Henry Elsyng will round out knowledge of his studies of parliament and appreciation of his "painful labour."[30]

MR. ELSYNG AND THE USES OF ANTIQUITY

The "matters handled in parliament" which Elsyng discussed in his second book were, like judicature, subjects of intense political concern. Parliament's role in war and peace—even the examples from the reign of Edward III—were of more than antiquarian interest. Events of 1624 involved parliament in the conduct of war and later occurrences led to parliamentary investigation of naval affairs. The subject of subsidies to which Elsyng turned in his second chapter was also politically significant. There are many seventeenth-century "collections" on the subject. As early as 1612, Sir Robert Cotton listed "Means to repair the king's estate" for the Earl of Northampton.[1] The crown was hard pressed for money. Parliament was quick to capitalize on its need and, even in the flush of enthusiasm for war with Spain, appointed treasurers to control expenditure of the subsidy. In 1625 and the years following, it neglected to vote Charles the right to collect, for his lifetime, certain customs duties known as tunnage and poundage.

Elsyng did not exploit his studies nor shape his research to political ends. It is a question whether many of his contemporaries knew that he was writing. Copies of his first book, a few corrected in his own hand, indicate that some saw it in manuscript. The chapter on judicature was probably more widely read. But it is interesting that Edward Littleton, who took a major role in the debates of 1628 and later became lord keeper, did not recognize Elsyng's book when he came upon a draft of the table of contents. He made a note to inquire of Selden what it was.[2] Writings of Sir Edward Coke were published triumphantly in 1642 by order of the Long Parliament,[3] but none of Elsyng's book appeared during the heat of controversy. The first part was printed in 1660 when the House of Lords and the monarchy had been reestablished. It is significant and appropriate that it should have been so. Elsyng was primarily concerned with the institution of parliament

---

[23] John Selden, *Titles of Honor* (London, 1614), p. 274. Selden thought the old *Modus* could not date before the time of Edward III (*Titles of Honor,* third edition, London, 1672, p. 611).

[24] Selden, *Of Judicature,* p. 59.

[25] *Ibid.,* p. 8.

[26] H.L.R.O., Main Papers, H.L., [28 May, 1624]. For notes in Elsyng's hand concerning release of lords' servants, a subject to be covered in the sixth case, see Petyt 538/12, fols. 175–177, 179–179ᵛ.

[27] Sims, *Expedicio,* p. 143; H.M.C. *Fourth Report,* app., p. 369.

[28] Sims, *Expedicio,* p. xx.

[29] Folger Shakespeare Library, V. b. 130, fol. 44; El. 8392, fol. 122.

[30] Sims, *Expedicio,* pp. xx–xxi, xxv, 112. For further proof of Elsyng's authorship, see also "The Moderne Forme of the Parliaments of England," which Mrs. Sims believes to have been written by Elsyng (*American Historical Review* 53 (1948): pp. 288–305). A shortened version of "The Moderne Forme" was with other papers of the clerk in the possession of Lord Braye at Stanford Hall. The section concerning judicature was printed in Relf, *Debates in the House of Lords 1621,* pp. ix–x. Both versions of this section follow the same outline as the essay "Of the Judicature in Parliaments" and could serve as a précis of it. Both, like the longer treatise, deal only with "Judgments against Delinquents."

[1] See above, p. 38, n. 2; British Museum, Cleopatra F. VI.

[2] Cambridge University Library, Mm. 6.62, fol. 158. Elsyng is said to have presented a copy of Book One to Sir Thomas Coventry, lord keeper, in 1626 (see the manuscript owned by Mr. David Holland, librarian of the House of Commons).

[3] *Dictionary of National Biography.*

and its development. His historical interests and his practical experience fortified each other. His antiquarian knowledge and tastes served him well as clerk. He drew on contemporary activities in the house to illustrate his essays—the cases of the Earls of Arundel and Bristol, the impeachment of Mompesson and Cranfield.[4] But he did not, like Sir Robert Cotton and the lawyers in the House of Commons, turn history to political account. Once, in 1625, commenting on the king's request for subsidies to carry on war, Elsyng permitted himself to hope that Charles would not, like Edward III, be "overtaken with subtile treatises, nor feigned truces."[5] Five years later, he again compared the two monarchs, and in an unusual private memorandum forsook his wonted objectivity to reveal his political bias.

ADVICE TO THE EARL OF DANBY

On a pleasant afternoon in early March, 1630, Henry Elsyng dined with Henry Danvers, Earl of Danby, a member of the privy council. Though there were probably others present, it must have been an intimate group of trusted friends, for talk fell upon the king's desire to win the affection of his people. This, said Elsyng, could easily be done. When dinner was over, his lordship drew Elsyng aside into the garden and pressed for an explanation. The king, Elsyng explained, could win his people's love by parliament, as Edward III had done in the seventeenth year of his reign. Danby, possibly less familiar with the precedent than his guest, was not to be put off, and in the end Elsyng promised to bring him the story in writing. He set to work on March 6 and finished the first draft of his account on March 8, read it again, revised and recopied it on March 11. He was a careful man and doubtless kept his appointment with the earl on the following day.[1]

It was characteristic that Elsyng should turn to the reign of Edward III for a solution to the problems of Charles I. He gave the earl a straightforward but startlingly simple account of the tangled events of 1341–1343, "this angry, jealous parliament of 15to E. III, and the reconcilement thereof,"[2] and briefly summarized the conclusions to be drawn from his parable.

Elsyng had thought a good deal about the parliaments of 1341 and 1343. He had worked through the records in preparing the chapters of his book which dealt with "War and Peace," "Subsidies," and "Judicature."[3] He was to return to the same parliaments again when he wrote his fifth chapter, "*Expedicio Billarum Antiquitus*," and when he added a section concerning the Earl of Arundel to the first book of his *Modus Tenendi Parliamentum*.[4]

Edward III had, Elsyng wrote in his memorandum for Danby, only one "distraction" with his parliaments, and that was in the fifteenth year of his reign. Yet two years later, "he summoned another parliament where all was reconciled in so loving a manner, that never after any disagreement or jar happened betwixt them."[5] In 1340, the fourteenth year of Edward's reign, Lords and Commons had voted a large subsidy for the French wars, under conditions laid down in the grant. While the king was in France, he was betrayed by his officers who failed to forward the money needed, so that he was forced to abandon the victory which lay within his grasp, make a truce, and return to England. Once home, Edward instituted commissions of inquiry but these, having "ill instructions," dealt unjustly with the people. Nor were the conditions upon which the subsidy had been granted performed according to promise, so that the Commons refused to pay the second year's allotment. "The greatest mischief happened by the clergy, they seemed to be most incensed against the king, and demanded unreasonable things for themselves under pretense of the liberty of the church." The king, knowing that the pope favored his enemies the French, suspected Stratford, Archbishop of Canterbury, of connivance in withholding supplies for the war. "So upon these terms stood that glorious king, when he summoned his parliament of 15to, his honor deeply engaged in a war, and the hearts of his loving subjects stolen from him by the popish clergy." The situation was not promising, nor did events which followed improve matters. The archbishop, who had been summoned to answer charges in the court of exchequer, was refused entrance to parliament. In a dramatic scene, he claimed his right to a seat as *primus par Angliae*, and threatened "excommunication against them all, if he might not come in." The Lords, in turn, forced the king to consent to a declaration that "peers of the land, whether officers or not, be not bound to answer the king's suit but in parliament." At length, the archbishop was admitted. The meeting of parliament continued to be tempestuous. The king promised to redress the wrongs

---

[4] Elsyng, *Manner of Holding Parliaments*, pp. 192–242; Selden, *Of Judicature*, pp. 30–32, 46–47, 49–51, 103–105, 131–132, 179–180. On Elsyng's account of the Arundel case, see below, "Advice to the Earl of Danby," n. 4.

[5] Below, p. 59.

[1] Below, pp. 60, 64.

[2] Below, p. 63.

[3] Petyt 538/12, fols. 228–229, 283–287; Selden, *Of Judicature*, p. 5 (see the comment in Pike, p. 193, n.).

[4] Sims, *Expedicio*, pp. 109–113. Here Elsyng used the story to illustrate the way in which statutes were made; but his presentation and even his words were basically the same as those of his statement for Danby. Elsyng, *Manner of Holding Parliaments*, pp. 198–199; below, p. 61, n. 10. This section of Elsyng's book, entitled "Concerning a commitment of a peer of this realm in time of parliament," is part of the report of the subcommittee appointed by the Lords to search precedents concerning the privilege involved in the Arundel case. It was not included in the manuscript (Harl. 1342) from which Tyrwhitt printed the first part of the 1768 edition of Elsyng's book. Presumably Harl. 1342 was completed before the Arundel case occurred (Elsyng, *Manner of Holding Parliaments*, pp. x–xi, 192).

[5] Below, p. 60.

perpetrated by his commissions of inquiry and to carry out the conditions laid down for the previous subsidy, thus winning a new grant "in lieu of the former, and so all parties satisfied therein." Further difficulties arose. Neither Lords nor Commons were content with the king's answers to their petitions, and appointed a special committee to prepare amendments. The result was a statute, "disorderly penned," which the king let "pass with silence," but commanded to be sealed with the Great Seal.[6] Elsyng paused in his narrative to show, "for the full clearing of the king's honor," how certain sections of the statute were prejudicial to the king and to the laws of the land.[7] "Who can blame the king for repealing of this statute, had it been done in a due manner?"[8] But instead it was repealed at a great council, under pretext that Edward had "assented not, but dissembled."

> This proceeding of the king's could not but be distasteful unto his people having received a subsidy ... for that statute, and then repealing the same by a private act of his great council (which he could not do by law) and in that act to confess his dissimulation ... But this glorious king (E. III) did so handle the next parliament he called (which was a^o 17) that he did not only obtain an absolute repeal of this statute but in the end dismissed them to the full contentment of the Commons.[9]

In this parliament of reconciliation in the seventeenth year of Edward's reign, the climax of Elsyng's story, the king requested no subsidy, but proposed a treaty of peace with France and inquired how justice could be administered equally to rich and poor.[10] He issued a proclamation in answer to a petition against "the unjust provisions and shameless abuses of the pope" presented by the Commons, and thus purchased "their entire affections." Having by these means regained the love of his people, Edward "summoned another parliament and then demanded a subsidy and had it and almost in every year after during his life, he had a parliament and a subsidy if it were demanded, or his wants but made to appear."[11]

So, Elsyng suggested with proper humility, might Charles win the love of his people. First, he should call another parliament, proclaiming that elections would be free and according to the statutes, "which will bring them together with quiet and contented minds." In the initial session, his majesty should ask no subsidy at all, and indeed insist that he expected none. He should "propound some pleasing diversion from complaints as the increase of trade, a commission for musters or the like."[12]

Despite these precautions, three things might prove troublesome in debate and yet could be avoided: "1. Privileges, 2. Impositions, 3. Religion." As for privileges, Elsyng wrote, freedom of speech could be "promised and permitted" the Commons "by his majesty in as large manner as it was confirmed by that act of 2 H. IV which is so much insisted on." "Here is no privilege neither for treason, felony, nor breach of the peace, which three were never privileged in parliament, no not in parliament time." Let the Commons speak freely, and take no notice of what they say until their conclusions are sent to the Lords or the king, Elsyng recommended: "it will give them great content, and much further and expedite all the business of parliament. For they can but commune together and agree upon a petition or complaint."[13] On other points of privilege, the Commons had, Elsyng admitted, extended their power of judicature into two areas "which did anciently belong to the Lords, as for the arrests and assaults on their own members and servants." They had also taken it upon themselves to judge election returns of knights and burgesses. It would, he felt, be wise for the king to grant them these powers, which in fact "they have long enjoyed," especially control of elections, for the "undue and violent courses" of Mary's reign had made the Commons fearful and jealous. "The ancient manner of judicature in parliament for all other matters" might well "be reviewed, agreed on and sealed, that the right of his majesty and

---

[6] Below, pp. 60–62. I have summarized Elsyng's own account. For modern, critical accounts of these events, see Lapsley, pp. 231–272; E. B. Fryde, "Parliament and the French War, 1336–40," in T. A. Sandquist and M. R. Powicke, eds., *Essays in Medieval History presented to Bertie Wilkinson* (Toronto, 1969); Wilkinson, pp. 177–193.

[7] Below, p. 62.

[8] *Ibid.* In his chapter on Subsidies, Elsyng wrote: "In October following [the parliament of 15 E. III], the king summoned a great council and revoked whatsoever was done this parliament *contra prerogativam suam*. Yet read the chronicles before you censure this parliament and the revocation thereof. The pope favored the French, and the king was jealous that the Archbishop of Canterbury did the like, and that he secretly crossed his design for money, without the which the king could not proceed in his wars" (Petyt 538/12, fol. 285).

[9] Below, p. 62.

[10] *Ibid.*

[11] Below, pp. 62–63.

[12] Below, p. 63.

[13] *Ibid.* The statute is probably 7 H. IV, c. 15, concerning the manner of election of knights of the shire for parliament: "they shall proceed to the election freely and indifferently, notwithstanding any request or commandment to the contrary." In his first book of *The Manner of Holding Parliaments,* Elsyng had written: "And, if my poor opinion may be heard, what hurt or prejudice can it be to suffer the Commons to have their consultations free, without check or control? They will use no unseemly terms of any man. They can do nothing of themselves; neither can they propound any thing but by way of bill or petition. If they be suffered to proceed freely, their proposition will the sooner be rejected or agreed on among themselves. If agreed on, it will be related to the Lords or to the king; and when it comes before his majesty, it is in his power (if the Lords stop it not) to make a full stay thereof, if he like it not. Whereas on the contrary side, to be denied liberty of speech seems very harsh unto them, and hath made them so jealous of their privileges, that they have appropriated more unto themselves of late than ever they claimed heretofore; I mean, judicature, which they ever disclaimed; as shall be shown hereafter" (Elsyng, *Manner of Holding Parliaments,* p. 183).

of each house may be known, it cannot but please them all."[14]

A second troublesome point in the lower house might be impositions.

> Let them dispute it freely; therein they can conclude nothing; for nothing of theirs cannot be exemplified as a record, nor given in evidence at any bar. And this late example on some will make them all remember to speak soberly.

If a bill or petition is formulated, then what is prejudicial to the crown "may be qualified or avoided." But the king "may gain more by silence than by interrupting their ordinary freedom of speech by messages or otherwise."[15]

The same policy might well be used concerning religion, the third problem which would inevitably arise in a parliament. Doubtless the Commons "will complain most of the increase of Arminians and papists." Let them "prepare their bill or complaint, wherein the king may proceed as he please."[16]

The first session having thus "knit the hearts of the people unto his majesty," they will surely grant him a large subsidy in the next. "And the best way to compass this (in my opinion)," Elsyng wrote,

> is to demand no subsidy in the first, for therein rests the only strength of the Commons; but to call it at such a time, as the end of the first session may not be precipitated, and yet the subsidy grant serve his majesty's occasions at their next meeting, when all rubs are first removed. Which God grant, [Elsyng concluded] Amen, Amen.[17]

Elsyng had been dining with a peer of the realm, and a member of his majesty's privy council. He must have known or sensed the earl's sympathy with his ideas, or he would probably not have spoken out and set down his views in writing. Possibly Danby took Elsyng's advice deeply to heart. Six years later, in 1636, in a curious sequel to this dinner party, the earl sent a letter to the king. He thought long before he acted and discussed his plan with other powerful lords. The letter, which greatly displeased the monarch, was considered seriously at court, and ultimately discussed by the privy council. Danby warned the king. His subjects were universally discontented. They resented the collection of impositions and extraordinary taxes which they felt had been levied contrary to their fundamental laws and privileges. Men would gladly pay the same sums if they were properly voted. Charles, Danby advised, should call a parliament.[18]

Charles did not, in fact, call parliament again until 1640. Danby would live to see it, but not Elsyng, who died in 1635 or 1636. He had, when he drew up his memorandum for the earl, in effect written his political testament. Like his analysis of the events of 1341–1343, the plan Elsyng suggested was astonishingly simple. Yet it merits attention. It was the program of a man who had studied the history and procedure of parliament. It was the considered advice of an experienced clerk who had recorded debate in the upper house from 1621 through 1629.

The lesson which Elsyng drew for Danby from the years 1341–1343 was plain. Charles could win the love of his people and manage parliament if he followed the example of Edward III. Elsyng did not pursue the subtler implications of his story. The crisis of 1341, as he described it, raised questions of control of royal ministers, the trial of peers, and the right of the archbishop to his seat in parliament.[19] Each of these issues was repeated in Elsyng's years as clerk. The king's ministers were attacked in the impeachment proceedings against Bacon, Cranfield, and others, the drive against

---

[14] Below, p. 63. In the chapter on judicature, which I believe was written by Elsyng, there is a discussion of six "cases" in which judicature belongs to parliament. The sixth is: "In setting at liberty any of the members or servants imprisoned, and in staying the proceedings at the common-law during the privilege of parliament. . . . In certifying the elections and returns of knights and citizens for the parliament. But now the Commons alone determine of this: Wherefore I will only shew that the Commons did heretofore petition to the Lords for redress herein, and what course was then taken. I leave it to the clerk of that house to shew how the Commons proceed herein at this day" (Selden, *Of Judicature*, pp. 8–10). *Cf.* Lord Ellesmere (Foster, *Proceedings in Parliament 1610* **1**: pp. 277–278). Elsyng had his own explanation of how the Commons came to assume control over the elections of their own members. This can be found in a long note in a book of "Precedents in Parliament," under the date 23 Elizabeth. Elsyng wrote: "I do conceive that the lord chancellor can take no notice of the want of a member of the lower house, but by message from the lower house: which was usually signified in writing from the speaker: which was afterward in process of time termed a warrant from the speaker for a new writ. And, thinking it presumption to make a warrant to the lord chancellor, they did direct it to the clerk of the crown. But this is my own conceipt: and my reason is, that if the Commons make their warrant for a writ, then they are judges, and if judges they may judge in all other cases as well as in return of their burgesses. And plainly judicature belongs not to them. See the writ for their elections, which is to warrant all their actions. But they, and none else, may signify the defects of returns, or misdemeanors, and pray redress (as anciently they did) and a new writ being granted of course upon such significance it got the credit and title of a warrant. H. E.

The Commons enjoy this privilege *de gracia* et *non de jure*: anciently they had it not. Compare the precedents before H. VIII (when none of the king's privy council were returned of their house) with those of subsequent times, and it will appear that they have many more privileges of late than ever they had before. H.E."

[15] Below, pp. 63–64. For the arrest and trial of members of the House of Commons in 1629–1630, see *Cobbett's Complete Collection of State Trials* (London, 1809) **3**: pp. 294–310.

[16] Below, p. 64.

[17] *Ibid.*

[18] Correr to the Doge and the Senate, December, 1636 (H. F. Brown and A. B. Hind, eds., *Calendar of State Papers and manuscripts relating to English affairs in the archives and collections of Venice . . . , 1636–39* (London, n.d.), pp. 110–112, 119). Danby was a member of the western circuit in 1631 to inquire into the execution of laws concerning poor relief and other public services (Thomas Garden Barnes, *Somerset 1625–1640* (Cambridge, Mass., 1961), pp. 177–178).

[19] Lapsley, p. 258.

Buckingham, and the threat to Weston. In 1626 the cases of the Earls of Bristol and Arundel involved the trial of peers and the right of a lord to his seat. If events which preceded the angry parliament of 15 E. III forced that king to curtail his wars in France, so the foreign adventures of James and Charles were limited by their resources and the mistrust of their people. The commissions of trailbaston which roused the subjects of Edward III had their counterpart in the compositions for knighthood which had begun in January, 1630.[20] Charles might even be said to have repealed a statute, if indeed he had broken the agreement made in the Petition of Right.[21]

But such political parallelism was not for Elsyng. "It becomes not me to apply it to the present times."[22] He contented himself with a simpler prescription: since the House of Commons has little real power, let it talk freely and "so knit the hearts of the people unto his majesty" that in a subsequent session, parliament, like that which met in 17 E. III, will be ready to vote the subsidies the king desires.[23] "They can but commune together and agree upon a petition or complaint," Elsyng wrote of the Commons.[24] "Touching impositions, let them dispute it freely; therein they can conclude nothing. . . . Afterwards when their bill or complaint comes up . . . then whatsoever shall seem prejudicial to the king may be qualified or avoided." So also in matters of religion, the Commons might "be permitted to prepare their bill or complaint, whereon the king may proceed as he please."[25]

Legally Elsyng was right. There was too a certain wisdom in his advice "to demand no subsidy in the first [session], for therein rests the only strength of the Commons."[26] In all the parliaments of James and Charles, grievances and supply had marched together. But did Elsyng really believe that if Charles proceeded "as he please" with bills, he could retain the love of his subjects and succeed in obtaining subsidies? Did Elsyng so misjudge the temper and perspicacity of the Commons as to think that members would be satisfied with freedom of debate and forego the substance of power?

Elsyng's advice that the king should "propound some pleasing diversion from complaints as the increase of trade, a commission for musters or the like" is even more puzzling than his other suggestions.[27] In 1621 and 1624, parliaments which Elsyng knew well, the Commons' consideration of trade had led directly to an attack on royal patents and monopolies. Discussion of commerce would also, as Elsyng expected, revive the attack on impositions which had troubled the parliaments of 1621, 1624, and 1628. The subject of "increase of trade" would certainly please the Commons but would hardly divert them from complaints. Nor did a commission for musters seem any more promising. One of the grievances in the Petition of Right had been of

> divers other charges . . . laid and levied upon your people in several counties, by lords lieutenants, deputy lieutenants, commissioners for musters, justices of peace and others, by command or direction from your majesty or your privy council, against the laws and free customs of this realm.

Members of the upper house, like Danby, who served as lord lieutenants in the counties were well aware of the difficulty of collecting money to pay their muster masters. An investigation of musters, suspected of being yet another royal scheme to raise money, would be welcome but would not provide an adequate "diversion" from grievances.[28]

There is no ready explanation for what seem to be flaws in Elsyng's memorandum. Perhaps it was politic when writing for an earl to emphasize the position of the Lords and of the crown. Perhaps it was natural that a man whose parliamentary experience had been primarily in the House of Lords should underestimate the growing strength of the House of Commons. Elsyng had never been a Commons man. Robert Bowyer, his uncle and predecessor as clerk of the parliaments, knew the lower house well and had sat there as a member from 1601 through the first three sessions of the reign of James. Elsyng had served only in the House of Lords; but if he looked at the House of Commons from a different perspective from that of his uncle, he was certainly not ignorant of its ways. He shared chambers at the Middle Temple with Bowyer, and had served as his assistant in the Lords as early as 1610. At the Temple and in Westminster, Elsyng must have encountered many of the lawyers and gentlemen who debated impositions, supply, grievances and religion in the House of Commons, and who were effectively cooperating with members of the House of Lords in

---

[20] Bishop Williams also failed to receive a writ of summons in 1626 (John Hacket, *Scrinia Reserata, A Memorial Offer'd to the Great Deservings of John Williams, D.D. . . .* (London, 1693), Part II: p. 68). Gardiner, *History of England*, 7: p. 167.

[21] *Commons Debates 1629*, pp. 4–6.
[22] Below, p. 63.
[23] Below, p. 64.
[24] Below, p. 63.
[25] Below, p. 64.
[26] *Ibid.*
[27] Below, p. 63.

[28] Captain John Prust, muster master of Dorsetshire, complained to the council that he had not been paid for two and a half years. The county alleged, he said, that there was no law for any such taxation (John Bruce, ed., *Calendar of State Papers, Domestic Series, of the Reign of Charles I, 1629–1631* (London, 1864), p. 451). In 1629 the deputy lieutenants of Northamptonshire declined to issue the usual warrants for the collection of money to be expended at the musters or for the entertainment of officers, since these warrants had been "lately publicly impeached" (*ibid.,* pp. 20–21). See also *Acts of the Privy Council of England 1628 July–1629 April* (London, 1958), pp. 31, 219, 240, 379; Barnes, pp. 263–264.

preparing and passing the Petition of Right.[29] Perhaps an antiquarian, looking forward from the long perspective of the records in the Tower, saw king, Lords, and Commons in a different light from those who look back upon them from the present.

To modern eyes, the memorandum had serious flaws. Though Elsyng had searched the parliament rolls with care, he clearly found some precedents more pleasing than others.[30] He was inclined to dwell on what he regarded as the accomplishments of Edward III and overlook his failures. But how strikingly the "Advice" reveals Elsyng's mind and the temper of his times. His research in medieval records led him to observe that the most successful monarchs had conferred with their parliaments. To succeed as king, Charles must do likewise. Danby, by another route, was to come eventually to the same conclusion. In order to secure subsidies, Elsyng wrote, Charles should allow the Commons to speak and act freely. This he could safely do since the lower house had no real power. Members could but commune together and agree upon a petition or complaint. Sovereignty rested ultimately in the crown and was protected by the Lords. The message of Elsyng's "Advice" is clear. In 1630 and the years shortly thereafter, men, experienced and thoughtful men, believed that Charles could still manage parliament and win the love of his people. Indeed, if he would but follow the example of earlier kings, this might easily be done.

CONCLUSION

The whole of Elsyng's working life was devoted to parliament. He preserved its records, searched its records, wrote its records. Though he lived in stirring times and in the center of the political arena, politics were not his real concern. No matter how the men around him might manipulate parliament, his job as clerk was to forward, to execute, and to register its business. In the journals he prepared, in the parliament rolls, in hundreds of notes, orders, and memoranda, Elsyng revealed what parliament, and particularly the upper house, actually did in the years 1621–1629, and how it was done. His picture of the House of Lords in this period is unsurpassed. On vacation in the country at his manor of "Cornewall," he liked to work on his book, *The Manner of Holding Parliaments in England,* and thus to place his labors in Westminster within a wider historical context. In Book One of his treatise, he wrote down all that he had discovered and observed about the "form" of parliament "and all things incident thereunto," "with," he said, "no intent to publish the same unto any."[31] In Book Two, he tackled the more difficult problem of describing "matters handled in parliament," doubtless also for his own instruction. Fundamentally loyal to the crown, he saw some kings as wiser than others, and tended to measure their wisdom by their success with parliament. His writing, like his work as clerk, was cautious and careful. An antiquarian, and searcher of records, he rarely went beyond the evidence he had painstakingly assembled from the documents in the Tower or the proceedings he had himself observed. He looked at the structure of the institution, the way in which it worked, and the business which came before it. He recognized that parliament had changed and would continue to change, that the bill of his own time was more efficient than the ancient petition, that the House of Commons had extended its jurisdiction in recent years.[32] In his study of parliament, Elsyng was neither bemused with mythical origins nor hypothetical powers which could not be thoroughly documented. Writing for his own pleasure and for his own use, he hewed close to the line he had set for himself. He avoided the lawyer's brief and the political pamphlet, and soberly constructed a description of parliament as he understood it to be. Of those parliaments which he served as clerk, he left a solid record in journals, rolls, and notes. Of those which he studied in earlier times, he wrote a careful analysis, linking past and present with the practical experience of a man who was working in the living institution. Searching in the Tower, scribbling in the house or in his office in the old palace of Westminster, Henry Elsyng's "painful labour" was dedicated to a single purpose: to understand, explain and record the manner of holding parliaments in England, whether ancient or modern.

APPENDIX

MR. ELSYNG'S DRAFTS FOR BOOK TWO

[Petyt 538/12]

LIB. 2, CAP. 1. WAR AND PEACE ETC.

[fol. 229, a° 17 E. III]

. . . I admire the noble answer of the Commons. The treaty of peace was only given them in charge, and they assented to it, and to aid the king in his wars, if the treaty succeeded not. I observe, that the articles of treaty were not discussed: but whether a treaty for peace or no.[1]

• • •

[fol. 238ᵛ, a° 27 E. III, Ordinances of the Staple]

. . . *they shall be rehearsed and entered in the parlia-*

---

[29] For the relationship between groups in the two houses, see David Harris Willson, *The Privy Councillors in the House of Commons* (Minneapolis, 1940), pp. 164–167, 172, 179–204; and my "Procedure in the House of Lords during the Early Stuart Period," pp. 71–73.

[30] See above, p. 38.

[31] Sims, p. xix.

[32] *Ibid.,* pp. li, 143; below, p. 63.

[1] *Rot. Parl.* 2: p. 136 (17 E. III, no. 9).

ment roll; and so they were, and by that means we have the acts of one great council and so understand the form thereof.[2] That private petitions were exhibited in great councils *vide a° 21 E. III in dorso rotuli,* n. 65, the petition of John Mautravers, but it cannot appear that the petitions of the Commons were ever exhibited there before now.[3]

• • •

[fol. 241, *a°* 29 E. III]

... Thus you see, the Commons were acquainted with the king's treaties for a peace, and prosecution of the war, and their advice required how the war might be ended, and the king aided. And their aid only recorded.[4]

• • •

[fol. 241*v*, *a°* 36 E. III]

... **In the parliament** *a°* 36 E. III, one of the causes of summons was declared to be the business touching Scotland, which our lord the king will cause to be shown unto the Grands and Commons, to have therein their advice and counsel, n. 1. ... The which Grands, being demanded severally, gave their answer accordingly ... n. 6. And this is all of that matter. The Commons are not named here in this consultation.[5]

• • •

[fol. 252, *a°* 13 E. III]

... I have written more than I meant, as I may the better understand how each several business was handled in parliament. I have omitted here what concerned the subsidy, for that I mean to collect the precedents thereof into a chapter by itself.

• • •

[fol. 260, *a°* 13 E. III]

... I have dwelt too long in this parliament.

Here I observe, that on Monday the cause of summons was declared to the Commons, to be for aid to the king and for the safeguard of the realm and themselves, and, for the safeguard of the sea, of the marches of Scotland, of Gascoigne, and of the Isles. The Commons took respite to give their answer until Saturday, 19 Febr. On which day they granted an aid of 30,000 sacks of wool. And the king's necessity for present money being shown, they did grant (after long debate) 2500 sacks presently. In the mean time, the Lords made these ordinances for the defense of the land, the sea, and the marches of Scotland. That they were made before the subsidy was granted, *vid.* n. 25, 26, 28, and 37. And the Commons are not named in any of those ordinances.

But the Commons assented unto the ordinance, n. 28, that the inhabitants of the Isle of Wight be respited their aid etc. and unto the ordinance, n. 33, for the restitution of the temporalities to the Provost of Wells. They are not named in these 2 ordinances, but understood by these words: *accordez est per comune conseil en plein parlement.* I suppose that those 2 ordinances also were made first by the Lords and then being read before the Commons, they assented, and those words *per comon conseil* etc. added.[6]

• • •

[fol. 263, *a°* 14 E. III]

... My observations of this parliament, *vizt.*

1. The cause of summons was declared first to the Lords. Here may be a question, where the Commons were then.[7] *Vid. a°* 38 E. III. The cause of summons was first delivered unto the Lords and Commons in the Painted Chamber, n. 2. Then the king, leaving the Commons in the Painted Chamber, took with him the Lords into *La Chambre Blanche,* and there declared the causes in especial unto them, n. 7.[8] This order I suppose was observed now. They all met in one room the first day. The Commons were called (as now) and notice taken of the absent lords. The parliament was adjourned, and afterwards the king and Lords met together first in one room, where the cause was declared especially. Then they went into the other room where the Commons expected their coming, and there the same was declared generally to the Lords and Commons.[9]

2. The general cause of summons is only entered, but in the declaration of the particular causes to the Lords alone, no doubt but those matters also which the Lords particularly handled were given in charge, for the writ of summons is, *super arduissimis et urgentibus negociis tam nos et statum, ac defensionem regni nostri Angliae quam expedicionem guerrae nostrae etc.*

3. It is plain that the Commons were not privy nor parties to the treatises touching the force [?] in matters of war and peace, nor touching the defense of the land, nor the musters of soldiers for Scotland. You will ask what the Commons did in the meantime for the matter of the subsidy and their petitions ended, n. 12.[10] And then (sayeth the record) committees were appointed for Flanders, Brussels, etc. and the parliament adjourned till after Easter, and met again, and yet nothing spoken of the Commons, but the value of money, n. 21, and the accounts of them who received the king's money, n. 22, etc. all which is before Easter, the Commons are not named in anything after Easter, when they met again.[11]

---

[2] *Ibid.,* pp. 246–253 (27 E. III, nos. 1–42).
[3] *Ibid.,* p. 173 (21 E. III, no. 65, *dorso,* a petition to the council).
[4] *Ibid.,* pp. 264–265 (29 E. III, nos. 10–11).
[5] *Ibid.,* pp. 268–269 (26 E. III, nos. 1, 6).
[6] *Ibid.,* pp. 107–110 (13 E. III, Part II, nos. 6–9, 25, 26, 28, 33, 37).
[7] *Ibid.,* p. 112 (14 E. III, Part I, no. 4).
[8] *Ibid.,* pp. 283–284 (38 E. III, nos. 1–2, 7).
[9] *Ibid.,* p. 112 (14 E. III, Part I, no. 5).
[10] *Ibid.,* p. 113 (14 E. III, Part I, no. 11).
[11] *Ibid.,* pp. 113–116 (14 E. III, Part I, nos. 13–57).

[fol. 263ᵛ] I answer, it is usual to enter the grant of the aid, and those matters that depend thereon first, and other matters afterwards. It is plain that in this parliament, the aid was first agreed on; then the Commons agreed on their petitions (which we now call bills) which could not suddenly be dispatched, being 21 public bills, as in the printed book, besides the private. And whilst the Commons handled these for the government of the commonwealth, the Lords treated of the other matters for the war, and defense of the land etc.

4. One other objection is, that amongst these committees for Flanders, Brussels, etc., *numeris* 13, 14, 15, 16 and 17, divers are named which were not summoned to the upper House, *vizt.* . . . [names listed] Why may not these be of the House of Commons? Because the record saith not so. For the records do always name the Commons, or express them by some general words, as *comune conseil,* the whole assembly, etc. I suppose rather, they came with proxies for the absent lords, as the use then was to send some of their own, and not to name any of the other lords to be their proctors, *vd. cap.* 4, *lib.* 1. Proxies.¹²

5. Though the Lords did treat touching the articles of peace betwixt the king and France, as may be gathered, n. 34, yet they are not entered in the roll, neither were such treatises handled in the parliament, but in the king's presence, *prout* n. 20.¹³

Here I might *acquiescere,* for at this parliament the Lords and Commons so accorded with such dutiful respect to the king, and the king showed himself as loving to them, and all matters are so exactly entered, that it is the first best precedent that shows the proceedings of each house, both in matters which concerned the Commons, and in affairs of state wherewith they meddled not, but I will proceed, to show how the like order was observed in all other parliaments of this king's time. E. III.

. . .

[Petyt 538/12, fol. 266]

LIBRI 2ᵈⁱ, CAP. 2ᵈᵉᵐ. SUBSIDIES

The contents of this chapter.
How the parliament proceeded herein in the most ancient times.
The parliament rolls of E. III are the ancientest rolls now extant, and the best precedents in respect of the king and his subjects.
That divers parliaments of R. II, H. IV, and H. VI are not to be alleged and the reason.
The precedents of E. III at large.
Observations out of those precedents touching the manner how subsidies were demanded in the time of E. III.

And how they were granted, wherein

1. That the grant was upon conference between the Lords and Commons. The occasion whereupon the Lords first lost or waived their right to this conference.
2. That the grant was by indenture, sometimes sealed, by whom, and the occasion thereof. And upon what occasion the same was first without indenture.
3. The conditions of the subsidy, the petitions of the Commons, whether the lords of the committee did treat with the Commons thereon or no. And how the king granted the same.
4. The presentment of the subsidy.
5. The king's royal assent.

. . .

[fol. 269] The parliament having first treated on matters of state, (as is declared in the former chapter) concerning War and Peace with foreign nations and the defense of the land etc., their next consultation (and indeed their chiefest) was to provide money to maintain those wars, and to defray the king's other charges.

I will not here set down what subsidies have been granted unto the king in parliament, they are collected to my hand by that painful gentleman my uncle Bowyer. My only purpose is to find out how these subsidies were demanded and granted, and how the parliament anciently proceeded therein.

That subsidies were ever demanded and granted in parliament many records do prove, *vizt.* the commissions for levying the same in the times of King John, H. III, E. I and II. But the manner how the parliament proceeded therein I have not found before the 13th of E. III. Somewhat is spoken of it in that ancient manuscript of *Modus Tenendi Parliamentum, capite de auxilliis regis, vizt. debent huiusmodi auxilia peti in pleno parliamento, et in scriptis cuilibet gradui parium parliamenti, liberari et in scriptis responderi. Et sciendum [est] quod ad huiusmodi auxilia concedenda oportet quod omnes pares parliamenti consentiant.*¹⁴ Here I observe, that the cause wherefore the king demanded a subsidy, and the sum required [fol. 269ᵛ] were put in writing, and so delivered unto the prelates, to the lords, the clergy, and the Commons, (the 4 degrees of parliament), to this end that each of them might by themselves discuss whether the said sum, or what other sum, were requisite to be granted; and how the same might be levied.

The parliaments of E. III did observe this order, to deliver unto the Lords and also to the Commons, their charge in writing whereon they were to treat, and they brought back their answer in writing. *vd.* 13 E.

---

¹² Elsyng, *Manner of Holding Parliaments,* pp. 129–131.
¹³ *Ibid.,* pp. 113–114 (14 E. III, Part I, nos. 20, 34).

¹⁴ Clarke, appendix, p. 382.

III, xv^{na} *Michaelmis*, n. 5, 8, 9.[15] I do not say that the same was given in writing unto all the Lords but only to such of their committee as were appointed to treat of the same either by themselves, or with the Commons. *vd. a° 4 R. II, n. 11*, a cedule given to the Commons of the king's demands.[16]

[fol. 270] It is not amiss to observe out of this ancient treatise how the parliament then agreed touching the subsidy, after each degree had reported their several opinions to the house. For then they sat all together, as in divers after ages, but yet had several rooms appointed whether each degree might and usually did resort for their consultations.

This also appears in that manuscript, *capite de casibus et judiciis difficilibus*, which I will but briefly touch, for that it is now altogether out of use. *Et si forte omnes, vel saltim maior pars concordare non valeant, etc.* Then a committee of 24 were chosen, *vizt.* 2 prelates, 2 earls, 2 barons, 3 procurators of the clergy, and 15 of the Commons. If they could not agree, they had power to make a subcommittee of 12, and they of 6, and those 6 of 3, further they could not proceed of themselves, *nisi obtenta licencia a domino rege*. And then, *si dominus rex consentiat*, those 3 (if they could not agree) might subcommit the same unto 2 and those 2 unto one of themselves, who alone (sayeth the treatise) could not disagree with himself.[17]

[fol. 271] The first records (now extant) that mention the proceeding in parliament touching subsidies are those of E. III, with which I will begin, not only for that they are the first, but also for that his times are the best, of the ancient, without exception, both in respect of the king and of the subject, he being the right heir to the crown, beloved of his people, and of ripe years to govern. All which you shall not find in any of his successors (H. V excepted) until H. VIII. R. II was crowned at 11 year old. His youth gave the Commons occasion to allege and demand (before they granted their subsidies) that which they never did of E. III *prout a°*1°, n. 18, 19, 21, 22, 23, 24, 25, 26, touching counsellors to be appointed about the king, and the government of his household, and n. 27, the treasurers of the subsidy were appointed and sworn in open parliament.[18] *A° 2 R. II*, n. 18, 20, 21, etc. touching the counsellors about the king, and an account of the former subsidy.[19] *A° 3 R. II*, n. 12, 13, touching the king's expenses, and touching his counsellors, requiring them to be removed, and a commission to inquire of the king's charges in household and elsewhere.[20] *A° 5 R. II*, n. 17, 18, touching the king's person, his household and his courts of justice, and a commission to redress the same, which commissioners, at the request of the Commons, charged the king's confessor to depart the court, saying they must begin with the head.[21]

[fol. 271^v] 6. *A° 6 R. II*. I find no such demand (the king being of riper years). *A° 7 R*, n. 6, 3. John Plesyngton required a confirmation of the king's pardon in parliament, which the king himself denied, saying he would not that anything which touched his proper grace and regality should be confirmed in parliament or authorized by any other.[22]

8. *A° 8* agrees with that of *a° 6*.

9. *A° 9 R. II*, n. 32, that the king's house be viewed once every year etc. and amended etc. The answer is, *The king will do it when it pleaseth him*. *Et* n. 38, that the Commons may know who shall be the king's principal officers, etc. The answer is, *There be officers sufficient this year, and the king will change them when he please.*[23]

10. *A° 10mo R. II*, n. 18, the Commons annexed this condition to their subsidy, that the king's continual *conseil* there named be not removed. N. 35. The king himself made open protestation for that nothing done this parliament should be in prejudice of him or his crown, but that his prerogative be saved. etc.[24]

These four parliaments (6, 8, 9, and 10 R. II) much resembled E. III. I would that that of *a° 11mo* had never happened (it is not to be remembered), then had not this noble king been so jealous of his prerogative, nor the subjects so careless of their duties, whereby he lost their loves, almost as soon as he had ripe years to govern.[25]

[fol. 272] As R. II came young, so H. IV intruded. He affected the love of his people, yet enjoyed it but feignedly, notwithstanding that to obtain the same, he often waived his prerogative and often claimed it again. *Prout a° 5 H. IV*, n. 9, 10, 16, touching matters of state and revenue and the removing of divers out of the king's house etc. (no such matters being attempted by the Commons in the former parliaments of this king, until now that a rebellion was feared) *et v^d* n. 17 *et* 19, 26 *et* n. 33, the king will to have his house reformed, etc., and that the Lords and Commons should appoint treasurers of the subsidy. *Et* 37, certain privy counsellors appointed by the king at the instance of the Commons.[26] *A° 6 H. IV*, n. 8, the king remembered himself, and charged the Commons to have a special care of his necessity, and to dispatch the subsidy, all other business set apart (it is in other words, but to this effect). Yet in the grant of this subsidy, treasurers are appointed

---

[15] *Rot. Parl.* 2: p. 104 (13 E. III, Part I, nos. 5, 8, 9).
[16] *Ibid.* 3: p. 89 (4 R. II, no. 11).
[17] Clarke, appendix, pp. 380–381.
[18] *Rot. Parl.* 3: pp. 5–7 (1 R. II, nos. 18, 19, 21, 22, 23, 24, 25, 26, 27).
[19] *Ibid.*, pp. 35–38 (2 R. II, nos. 18, 20–26, 29–30).
[20] *Ibid.*, p. 73 (3 R. II, nos. 12, 13).
[21] *Ibid.*, pp. 100–102 (5 R. II, nos. 17–18).
[22] *Ibid.*, pp. 164–165 (7 R. II, no. 63, where the name is Robert de Plesyngton).
[23] *Ibid.*, p. 213 (9 R. II, nos. 32, 38).
[24] *Ibid.*, pp. 220–221, 224 (10 R. II, nos. 18, 35).
[25] *Ibid.*, pp. 228–256 (11 R. II).
[26] *Ibid.*, pp. 523–530 (5 H. IV, nos. 9, 10, 16, 17, 19, 26, 33, 37).

and they to make their account to the Commons at the next parliament and so they did, *a° 7 H. IV, prout* n. 44 *et* 63.²⁷ *A° 7 H. IV*, n. 30, the Commons proceeded fairly with the king for their speaker required he might speak under protestation (as the form then was) *combien q'il avoit riens parlez de prerogatif ou estate roiale nostre seigneur le roy etc.* Which the king granted. This was 15 *Maii*.²⁸ N. 31, 22 *Maii*, the speaker produced a bill for certain persons to be of the king's council, etc., and their authority, etc.²⁹ N. 32, 24 *Maii*, the Commons required to know whether those lords would take upon them to be of the king's council or no, and then recited the danger of Calais, the loss of 96 castles and towns in Guienne, the loss of a great part of Ireland, the rebellion of Wales, and the Scottish borders, etc.³⁰ N. 40, that the prince be sent into Wales with all speed, etc., and speaking of the king's house, he sayeth that the [fol. 272ᵛ] same is more chargeable, and less honourable, than in any times of his progenitors, etc. *vd.* n. 51, *et* n. 56, 59.³¹ N. 66, the king would save the state and prerogative of his crown, etc., touching the requests of the Commons for the oath of the king's councillors, the articles follow, 30 in all, to endure to the next parliament.³² *A° 9 H. IV*, n. 13, 16, 17, 23, a good correspondency between the king and the Commons; and yet his prerogative saved.³³ *A° 11 H. IV*, n. 10, the speaker being presented, the king remembereth the Commons of their duty in fair speeches. Yet they desired to appoint his council in parliament and that they may know them, and that they be sworn, n. 14, 44.³⁴ *A° 13 H. IV*, at the presentment of the speaker, the king said he would have *null nouelrie* in this parliament. N. 25, the king said he would retain his liberty and prerogative in all points as entirely as any of his progenitors etc. and so he did this parliament.³⁵

[fol. 273] The times of H. V are answerable unto those of E. III. He nothing diminished the prerogative of a king, nor debarred his Commons of their privileges.

H. VI came in a very child, was beloved of his people for his father's sake. His youth gave them occasion of fear and boldness. He lost much of the prerogative of a king in that he never had ripe judgement, though years, to govern.

Yet in all these times of R. II, H. IV, V, and VI, you shall find somewhat of the form in demanding and granting of subsidies (as the public and private conferences of both houses etc.) agreeable unto those of E. III. But in those of the next 3 kings, whose times the civil wars had made even barbarous, nothing but the thing granted is recorded. They all came in with the sword.

• • •

[fol. 309] Out of these parliament rolls, I observe that E. III demanded no subsidy but for the defense of the land, and to maintain his wars in France. Before he began those wars in France, he proposed the same to the Lords and Commons in parliament, and had their assent and promise of aid, *a° 11ᵐᵉ*. The roll is lost, but this is alleged, *a°* [blank].³⁶ He also propounded a peace with France *a°* [blank] and the Commons advised it, so it might be honourable; otherwise, they promised their aid to maintain the wars. When the peace, or any truce made with France were broken, he declared the same in parliament, and propounded the wars again, and by their advice proceeded, and had subsidies to maintain the same, *annis* [blank]. And if this king had had any other occasion to demand his people's aid, proceeding in the same manner he did, the Commons (no doubt) would have granted it. For, as he proposed the cause unto them in parliament, and craved their advice and counsels; so he lovingly accepted whatsoever they granted. And if the aid were not sufficient, they did afterwards, when they knew so much, augment their subsidies, *annis* [blank]. And now and then he called a parliament only to congratulate with his people; showed his readiness to redress their wrongs; and demanded no subsidies, *annis* 21, 25, 28, *et* 40.

[fol. 309ᵛ] And in all parliaments he made a fair demonstration of his great love and affection unto his people, seeming unwilling to undertake any enterprise, to put them to charges, without their allowance of the action, and consent. And showed his readiness to hear their complaints and redress their wrongs. One only parliament excepted (*a° 15ᵗᵒ*), the Lords and Commons did in all dutiful manner show their loves to the king, yielded their aid, and contented themselves with such answers as he made to their petitions, though the aid was given conditionally that their petitions should be granted, *annis* [blank].

Although in some of the first parliaments, they stood upon it to have the conditions of their subsidies enrolled, and a charter thereof made and sealed, *prout* [blank]. Yet afterwards (*a° 25 E. III, H.*) the king yielding to the condition demanded (that no other tax nor charge be demanded nor levied); they contented themselves with their repose they had in the king for the performance of their requests, not demanding any charter, *prout* [blank].³⁷

---

²⁷ *Ibid.*, pp. 546–547, 577, 584–585 (6 H. IV, nos. 8, 9; 7 & 8 H. IV, nos. 44, 63).

²⁸ *Ibid.*, p. 572 (7 & 8 H. IV, no. 30).

²⁹ *Ibid.*, pp. 572–573 (7 & 8 H. IV, no. 31).

³⁰ *Ibid.*, pp. 572–573 (7 & 8 H. IV, nos. 32, 33).

³¹ *Ibid.*, pp. 576–579 (7 & 8 H. IV, nos. 39, 40, 51, 52, 56). No. 59 does not seem relevant.

³² *Ibid.*, p. 585 (7 & 8 H. IV, no. 66).

³³ *Ibid.*, pp. 609–611 (9 H. IV, nos. 13, 16, 17, 23).

³⁴ *Ibid.*, pp. 623–624, 634 (11 H. IV, nos. 10, 14, 44).

³⁵ *Ibid.*, pp. 648, 658 (13 H. IV, no. 9, which reads "*nulle manere de Novellerie,*" no. 25).

³⁶ *Ibid.* 2: pp. 103, 136 (13 E. III, Part I, no. 4; 17 E. III, no. 8).

³⁷ *Ibid.*, p. 238 (25 E. III, no. 12). Concerning the date of this parliament, see *Exact Abridgement*, p. 78.

And in many other parliaments they granted their subsidies absolutely without any other condition, save if the wars continue so long; and that the same be spent in the wars only and not elsewhere. And herein also they were contented that such officers as the king had appointed should be trusted therewith, though *annis* 14 E. III, T, n. 11, [fol. 309^a] they strictly provided it should not be otherwise spent.[38] And when, as a^o 51 E. III, they prayed that the king would be pleased to appoint 2 earls, and 2 barons to be guardians and treasurers of the subsidy, upon signification of the great wages of 4 such treasurers, they prayed that the high treasurer might receive the same in manner accustomed.[39]

• • •

[fol. 312] The manner how subsidies were granted unto K. E. III, and how unto his successors.

Wherein these things are chiefly observed, *vizt*.

1. That the grant was upon conference first had between the Lords and Commons.
   And upon what occasion the Lords first waived or lost their right to this conference.
2. That the grant was by indenture, which was sometimes sealed, and by whom, and the occasion thereof.
   And upon what occasion the same is now without indenture.
3. Touching the conditions of the subsidy and the petitions of the Commons, and whether the Lords did treat with the Commons (at the committee) of the said conditions and petitions. And how the king granted the same.
4. The manner how this grant hath been presented to the king.
5. The manner of the king's assent unto the same.

• • •

[fol. 315] . . . As touching the first point, *vizt*. the conference.

Here in this parliament [13 E. III], all the Lords and Commons had some conference together presently after the charge was given, for it follows immediately in the record. (A) The Lords and Commons were of one mind that the king ought to be aided. But this was not usual. And afterwards—before the Lords conferred with the Commons—they treated of this business amongst themselves, and first (B) they agreed that the king should be aided with a covenable aid. Then (a) they searched the manner how he may be best aided. And having found out the means (b) and the same thought to be sufficient for the king's [fol. 315^v] necessities, *vizt*. the tenth sheaf, fleece and lamb for 2 years, etc., a committee was appointed to treat thereof with the Commons. The record (I confess) names not the Commons, but they are necessarily understood (c). They treated long, the record sayeth, upon this business, which cannot be understood to be amongst themselves, they being already agreed on the thing to be granted.

Neither doth the record mention any committee to be appointed for this treaty, this age being very sparing to record circumstances; but that it was then the use to appoint committees for the like conferences will appear in the following precedents both of this king, and Richard II that follows; and after this treaty, the Lords gave their answer in a schedule. (How well this agrees with the report of a committee?). That the Commons were treated with about this business appears by their answer (g) for that the aid is to be granted in this manner, they dare not assent. And yet the record doth not say that they were treated with.[40]

And in the next parliament, *eodem anno xv^{na} Hillarii*, the Commons were willed to agree amongst themselves of the subsidy, n. 8. And they exhibited in their grant in a writing indented sealed with the seals of prelates and other grands, n. 8, (not of all the prelates and grands), and therefore of necessity a committee of prelates and grands is understood who did treat with the Commons herein.[41]

• • •

[fol. 318] . . . And, although divers of the following precedents, both of this king's time and his successors, do neither mention the conference nor the committee, yet the indenture proves the conference and whosoever shall peruse the rolls and consider the short times of those parliaments will conclude that the Commons could not otherwise dispatch their many businesses but by several committees.

• • •

[fol. 322, 2 R. II] The Commons prayed that v or vi lords might come to them to treat and commune with them about the matter given them in charge. Whereunto the Lords answered, that they neither might nor would do so; for that the like manner was never seen in any parliament except in the 3 last past. But they said, and confessed that it hath been accustomed that the Lords should choose of themselves some certain small number of vi or x. And the Commons likewise some like number. And that the same lords and Commons so chosen might treat together in quiet manner without great cry or noise, and so shall they come the sooner to some good end or purpose by the motions made betwixt them, the which end and purpose shall be reported over to their companions of the one and the other part. And thus, in such manner, will the Lords now do and no otherwise. For, they say, that if the Commons will hold themselves entire without

---

[38] *Ibid.*, p. 119 (14 E. III, Part II, no. 11).
[39] *Ibid.*, p. 364 (51 E. III, nos. 20-21).
[40] *Ibid.*, pp. 103-104 (13 E. III, Part I, nos. 4, 5, 8).
[41] *Ibid.*, p. 107 (13 E. III, Part II, nos. 6, 7).

severing (*se vorra tenir entiere sauns eux departir*) even so likewise will their Lordships do (*sans lour departir*) and not sever themselves. And thereupon the Commons assented *de eslire certaines seigneurs et Communes en petit et reasonable number,* in manner as hath been used anciently, n. 23.[42]

This precedent is so plain and direct that I will proceed no further; but rest satisfied that the Lords had such a right in the grant of subsidies (whereunto now they do only assent) as that the Commons never granted [fol. 322^v] the same but upon conference first had with their Lordships either in the upper house or at a committee between both houses.

One objection may be made that it was in the Commons' choice to have a conference with the Lords or no, as may be gathered out of the parliaments of E. III, the words are these (*a° 47 E. III, n. 4. If they, vzt. the Commons, will have the Lords' counsel and advice etc.*) which sound as if it were in the Commons' power to grant without conference, if they be agreed amongst themselves.[43]

But I consider that all parliament matters are entered in a fair language, and not in commanding terms, for so in the declarations of the causes of summons, it is seldom said directly that the king wants or expects money. And in many parliaments, the dangers of the enemy or the like is proposed, and that the king requires the counsel and advice of the Commons how to resist the same, etc. And thereupon, say the records, divers and long treatises were had between the Lords and Commons etc., but what did those produce? a subsidy; and nothing else did they confer of. And so here, the king would not take notice that the Commons ought to confer, nor seem to compel them thereunto; but rather leave it to be required by themselves: which he well knew they would do; for, they might not, nor did not in those days, swerve from any fundamental order of parliament. And in all parliaments, even to the time of [blank], where the roll mentions not the conference, yet the grant is by assent of the Lords spiritual and temporal.

[fol. 323] Yet let us proceed in the parliaments of R. II and H. IV and see how many of them prove this conference.

. . .

[fol. 330] The second observation is
    The indenture
        When it was sealed, and by whom, and the occasions thereof.
        And the occasion that the grant is now without indenture.

$A°$ 13 E. III, xv^{na} Michaelis, the king being then in France, and the parliament held *per Ducem Cornubiae, custodem Angliae.* The Commons gave their answer (touching the aid) in writing, craving time to advise thereof with their country until the next parliament etc., n. 8. Yet they then exhibited their demands, whereupon they would grant a subsidy, requiring to know what assurance the Lords would give them thereof, n. 13. In that next parliament (*a° eodem, octabis Hill.,* the king being yet in France), the Commons offered to grant an aid upon conditions comprised in indentures thereupon made and sealed under the seals of prelates and other grands, n. 8. And, a speedier supply being demanded, the Commons (after long treaty) answered that they would grant the same upon condition etc. as is contained in another indenture thereupon made, n. 9.[44]

As touching the indentures.

I suppose the grant was indented, not as a deed made between the Lords and Commons as parties, the one to grant, and the other to accept the thing granted (for they both granted unto the king), but it was indented, as nothing might be altered by the Commons, and as the lords [fol. 330^v] of the committee might truly report the same to the house, where it was also to be read, as the bill now is; and then, if the house agreed, the Commons heard no more of it; but, if the house did find that the aid was not sufficient for the king's wants, the former grant was not altered but another conference demanded, whereupon the Commons have enlarged the same, *prout hic* n. 9, *et a°* 18 E. III, n. 10.[45]

Hereof more at large in the presentment of the subsidy to the king.

[fol. 331] As touching the seals.

That part of this indenture, which the Commons kept and presented, was sealed by those lords who were of this committee, and not by all the lords of the parliament. For, the record sayeth not *under the seals of the prelates and other grandes*. Neither did the Lords join in this grant with the Commons, but granted a tenth out of their own demesnes by another deed, *eodem* n. 8, so that it did not concern their lordships in general.[46]

The reason why this was sealed, I suppose to be for the Commons' security touching their demands in the former parliament, n. 13,[47] the king being absent in France, (for I do not find that any such indenture was sealed when the king was present), and the same being to be sent unto him; the Commons therefore required the seals of the committee, who were usually the chiefest lords of the king's council, which being recorded gave

---

[42] *Ibid.* 3: p. 36 (2 R. II, no. 23).
[43] *Ibid.* 2: p. 316 (47 E. III, no. 4: "*& q'ils y veinssent lendemain en la dite chambre, issint q'ils feussent pres des grantz qui seroient en la Blanche Chambre, en cas qu'ils vorroient avoir lour avys & conseil*").
[44] *Ibid.,* pp. 104–105, 107–108 (13 E. III, Part I, nos. 8, 13; Part II, nos. 8, 9).
[45] *Ibid.,* pp. 108, 148 (13 E. III, Part I, no. 9; 18 E. III, no. 10).
[46] *Ibid.,* pp. 107–108 (13 E. III, Part II, nos. 7–8).
[47] *Ibid.,* p. 105 (13 E. III, Part I, no. 13).

them satisfaction. And it appears to be sealed for the Commons' security by the words following, *that in case that the conditions be not performed, that they will not be bound to the aid,* n. 8. Their other grant (this year, n. 9) was by indenture also, but not sealed, though upon condition. The reason may be for that neither [fol. 331^v] the grant nor the condition were of any great moment, it being but 2500 sacks of wool, upon condition to be part of their former grant, if the king liked the conditions thereof; if not, yet to be given him.[48]

[The rest of the folio is blank]

[fol. 332] At the parliament a^o 14 E. III in Lent, the Lords and Commons did sit together (although the record doth not directly say so). And the prelates, earls, and barons for them and their tenants, and the knights of the shires for them and for the Commons of the land granted their aid unto the king upon condition that their petitions be granted, n. 6. Here the record mentions neither indenture nor seals. And I suppose that the same was neither indented nor sealed, for that the two houses sitting together, there was no private conference by committee, and therefore no indenture. The seals needed not, the king being present, who satisfied the Commons touching the conditions by appointing a committee of Lords and Commons to sit upon the same and their petitions until they were reduced into the form of a statute, n. 7.[49]

q. Another doubt ariseth, why the grant was made by the knights of the shires, for them and for the Commons? Unto this I answer, that, as all other matters were handled this parliament by committees, so this of the subsidy, and that the knights of the shires were only of the committee for the Commons and none of the citizens nor burgesses. *Quoque tamen.*

[fol. 332^v] In the other parliament that year (a^o 14) held at Christmas (the king being in France) *per ducem Cornubiae custodem Angliae,* a sudden supply of money was agreed upon by the Lords and Commons, n. 10, *vizt.* that 20,000 sacks of wool be taken within the realm and delivered unto the merchants, and the merchants to pay for them at a certain price unto the king. And that the subsidy arising of the second year (granted in the former parliament) be reserved to satisfy them of whom the wools shall be taken, etc. And, it was agreed by the said prelates, earls, barons and others aforesaid, that all the seals of the grands of the realm who were not then present be put unto this assent as well as the seals of them who were present. And that the grands who were absent be thereunto required by the duke. And, that it be put into the form of a patent under the great seal, and delivered unto the knights of the shires to be reported in their countries. And sent to the king, etc., n. 11.[50]

Vd. a^o 7 H. V, n. 9, the Lords promise etc.[51] This shows plainly, that the seals were only to secure them of whom those wools should be taken, the king being absent. The record sayeth not that this grant or agreement was indented; but surely it was, the same being upon conference between the lords and the knights of the shires at a committee. Peruse the record well, n. 10.

[fol. 333] A^o 18 E. III. *Lunae x^t octab. Trinitatis.* The subsidy was granted upon a conference between the Lords and Commons, which appears by the first words of the grant, *vizt. for that the necessity of our lord the king is shown unto his Commons by his council,* etc. which declaration appears not elsewhere in the record. This grant was upon conditions contained in a schedule, but whether indented or no the record sayeth not. But, there being a conference by committee, of necessity it follows that the schedule was indented, for so the use was, and so continued even in the time of H. VIII, as shall be declared hereafter.[52]

A^o 20 E. III, n. 10. The Commons exhibited in parliament a schedule indented containing their grant of subsidy, etc.[53]

[fol. 334] A^o 47 E. III, n. 5, 12. The Commons granted the aid by a schedule indented, without seal, sayeth the record, *quaso diceret,* that usually it was sealed, but I do not yet find that any were sealed but when the king was absent.[54]

No other parliament rolls of E. III mention the indenture, nor the seals. And yet all the grants which were made at a committee were indented. But none sealed but those above mentioned, *vizt. annis* 13 *et* 14 E. III.

* * *

[Petyt 538/15]

LIB. 2, CAP. 2. SUBSIDIES

[fol. 36] This chapter I have divided into these parts following:

1. For what causes subsidies have been demanded, and the manner thereof. The precedents of each king's time.

2. The manner how subsidies were anciently granted to the king. Whether by the Commons alone, or by the Lords and them jointly upon conference.

   Six objections against the conference.
   1. The first. The Commons did sever from the Lords in the grant a^o 13 E. III.[55]
   2. They alone are mentioned in divers other grants.
   3. The Lords' assent is only mentioned in divers kings' times.

---

[48] *Ibid.,* pp. 107–108 (13 E. III, Part II, nos. 7, 9).
[49] *Ibid.,* pp. 112–113 (14 E. III, Part I, nos. 6, 7).
[50] *Ibid.,* pp. 118–119 (14 E. III, Part II, nos 10–11).
[51] *Ibid.* 4: p. 117 (7 H. V, no. 9).
[52] *Ibid.* 2: p. 148 (18 E. III, nos. 9–10).
[53] *Ibid.,* p. 159 (20 E. III, no. 10).
[54] *Ibid.,* pp. 316–317 (47 E. III, nos. 6, 12).
[55] *Ibid.,* p. 107 (13 E. III, no. 7).

4. The Commons alone granted ... *aº* 31 H. VI.⁵⁶
5. Their speaker presents the grant, and the kings acknowledged it theirs.
6. The account made to them alone.

Answer to the first objection.

Answer to the second, proving the conference by many precedents.

To the third, proving the Lords' assent to be given at the conference.

To the fourth, proving a conference to perfect the Commons' grant.

[fol. 36ᵛ] Answer to the fifth objection, showing why the king acknowledged it to be the Commons' grant.

To the sixth, why the account is to them, and when the first.

3. The third part. How subsidies have been presented to the king. Whether any in the beginning of a parliament. Whether several subsidies at several times in one session. Whether the royal assent to the subsidy grant hath made it a session. The precedents touching the presentment, whereof two by the lord chancellor. The manner thereof at this day.

Finis

[fol. 37] LIB. 2 CAP. 2, SUBSIDIES
Pars prima.

1. The parliament having first treated of matters of state (as in the former chapter) concerning War and Peace and other, treatises with foreign princes, and the defense of the land, their next consultation (and indeed the chiefest) was to provide money to maintain the wars, and to defray the king's other extraordinary charges, as shall be here declared.

Wherein I will observe these three points, *vizt.*

1. For what the subsidy was demanded, and the manner thereof.
2. How they were granted: whether by the Commons alone, as now, or by the Lords and Commons upon a conference first had between them.
3. And how they were presented to the king, with the manner of his majesty's royal assent thereunto.

[fol. 37ᵛ] These 3 points are thus set down in that ancient manuscript *Modus tenendi parliamentum, in cap. de auxiliis regi., vizt.*

Rex non solebat petere concilium de regno suo, nisi pro guerra instanti, vel pro filiis suis milit. faciend., vel filiabus suis maritandis. Et tunc debent huiusmodi auxilia peti in pleno parliamento, et in scriptis cuilibet gradui [parium] parliamenti deliberari, et in scriptis responderi. Et sciendum [est], quod ad huiusmodi auxilia concedenda, oportet quod omnes pares parliamenti concordant.

Thus it was before the Norman conquest. The causes here set down are three.

1. *Pro guerra instanti.*
2. To make the king's son a knight.
3. To marry the king's daughter.

The manner of the demand was then in full parliament, and delivered [fol. 38] in writing unto each degree of the peers, that is, unto the lords spiritual, unto the lords temporal, unto the procurators of the clergy, and to the Commons.⁵⁷

The demand of subsidies for the wars continueth, though not given in writing as then. But that touching the king's son and the king's daughter hath been so settled by usual payments thereof, as it is grown due by custom, and so never demanded now, but levied by commission. Which the ancient parliaments feared would happen to that for war also, and not without cause. [fol. 38ᵛ] For in divers years of E. III the Commons complained of levies by commission for the wars and guard of the sea, *prout aº* 20 E. III, n. 11, *et vide aº* 21 E. III, n. 28, *aº* 22 E. III, n. 4, for the levy of men at arms, light horsemen, and archers and for defense of the sea.⁵⁸ *Aº* 25 E. III, n. 9, for often taxes and tallages and their grant of aid was then upon condition that there be not demanded nor levied any tax, tallage, aid nor charges in time to come, *et vide pet.* n. 16 *et* 23. *Aº* 18 E. III *consimile*, n. 10 *et* 12. *Aº* 47 E. III, the Lords and Commons granted an aid for 2 years with this proviso: that no other charge nor imposition be upon the people of England during the said two years, n. 12.⁵⁹

[fol. 39] These and the like levies for the wars (in my opinion) enforced the Lords and Commons to make their protestation *annis* 18 R. II, n. 6, 4 H. IV, n. 28, 6 H. IV, n. 9, 1 H. V, n. 17, *et* 7 H. V, n. 9, that they, their heirs and successors, and the realm of England, be as free touching the charge of the said wars etc. as they were before the grant of their aid, the levying thereof only excepted.⁶⁰

[fol. 40] 1. The first observation.

How subsidies were anciently demanded.

I do not find that either the cause for which the subsidy was demanded, or the sum demanded, were usually given in writing, as that ancient treatise says it ought to be. We may only guess at it, by this, that *aº* 13 E. III xvⁿᵃ *Michaelis,* the Commons delivered their answer in writing, on the top whereof is written: *These are the points whereof treaty is to be had in common*

---

⁵⁶ *Ibid.* **5**: p. 228 (31 H. VI, no. 7).

⁵⁷ *Cf.* Clarke, appendix, p. 382.

⁵⁸ *Rot. Parl.* **2**: pp. 159, 168, 200–201 (20 E. III, no. 11; 21 E. III, no. 28; 22 E. III, no. 4).

⁵⁹ *Ibid.,* pp. 237, 239, 148, 317 (25 E. III, nos. 9, 16, 23; 18 E. III, nos. 10, 12; 47 E. III, no. 12).

⁶⁰ *Ibid.* **3**: pp. 330, 493, 546–547; **4**: pp. 6, 117 (18 R. II, no. 6; 4 H. IV, no. 28; 6 H. IV, no. 9; 1 H. V, no. 17; 7 H. V, no. 9).

this parliament. The points were, the peace of the land, the marches of Scotland, and the defense of the sea.⁶¹ And *a°* 4 R. II, n. 10, the Commons (after one day's consultation upon their charge for an aid) required a fuller declaration of the king's necessities and what sum total he would require. Whereupon was delivered them (by the king's great officers and council) a schedule containing divers particular charges amounting to the sum of 150,000*li.*, n. 11.⁶² [fol. 40ᵛ] By this of 4 R. II, the demand was delivered in writing to the Commons alone for they only required it. By that of 13 E. III, I conceive it was delivered (if at all) to the committee of the Lords and Commons, for in that parliament, and in all other of his time, they conferred together about the aid. But how long this course was observed, it appears not, the records are so sparing in in such circumstances, it being held sufficient once to register the demand itself; which I find to be in all the times of E. III, R. II, H. IV, and H. V (one or two parliaments excepted) either for an invasive war, or defense at home. [fol. 41] In those times, if the war were proposed, their counsel and advice were only required, and yet the parliament (with their advice for the war) promised their aid also. But if the war were once begun by their assent, and on foot, then their aid was directly demanded. So likewise for defense of the realm, if the dangers were apparent, then their aid, otherwise their counsel was required how to resist the enemy, and defend themselves.

In the times of H. VI and E. IV, these circumstances were not so duly observed, for then bishops only (being chancellors) propounded the causes of summons, who took a text, as if to preach, little regarding the good precedents of E. III whose chief justices (being learned lawyers) or some noble lord (though not the chancellor) delivered the king's proposition to the parliament; and they never swerved herein.

[fol. 41ᵛ] The times of R. III, H. VII and the beginnings of H. VIII much resembled those of H. VI touching the bishops' texts. What the succeeding times were, I am merely ignorant, some few only of that noble lady of famous memory, Queen Elizabeth, are extant, somewhat resembling antiquity, as in acquainting the parliament with the dangers threatened to the realm by the enemy, and requiring their aid.

[fol. 42] Her successor, the learnedest of kings, did ever propound the cause of summons himself. And when he intended war for recovery of the Palatinate (for which, and for a marriage of his only son Prince Charles, he had been long abused by 2 treaties with Spain) he briefly propounded the business to the parliament and required their counsel *super totam materiam,* who advised him to break off the 2 treatises, and promised their aid for a war.

His royal son (our dread sovereign) in his first parliament, remembered them of their counsel given his father, and their aid promised for the war.⁶³

How well do these agree with the precedents of that famous and victorious king, E. III. I beseech God to double that king's honour on him, and grant that he be not overtaken with subtle treatises, nor feigned truces after his conquest, as E. III was.

. . .

[fol. 71] By these precedents of E. III, you see that this king desired no subsidy *nisi pro guerra instanti,* otherwise if he were to undertake a war, or did but fear any, he required their advice only, which the parliament accompanied with a subsidy. And during the wars, they very willingly granted large subsidies, *prout annis* 13, 14, 18, 20, 22, 25, 45, 46, 47, and 51 E. III. But when the prosecution of the war was delayed and prolonged by truces and offers of peace, they granted less, as the subsidies of wools etc. to be transported, and ever mentioned their poverty and the great charges they had been at.

We are now come to the precedents of R. II, wherein, and in the following ages, I will not spend much time, for that they are not so pleasing as the other.

. . .

[fol. 86] . . . And thus ended the parliaments of H. V, who died in France, 30 *Augusti,* 1422. Thus have I collected the causes for which subsidies were demanded, and the manner thereof (*annis* E. III, R. II, H. IV, *et* H. V), sometimes mentioning directly the demand of an aid (if the war were in action) and otherwise but their counsel, whether to proceed in the war, or how to provide for defense of the realm; in both which a subsidy was ever granted. And for the grant, I observe it was of the subsidy of wools etc. and of later times of an impost on merchandise also, if the cause were not great. But if the war were on foot, then a xth and xvth, and the like were granted also.

I am afraid to proceed in the parliaments of H. VI and E. IV, the one a child, and the times of the other very barbarous and cruel, yet I will assay them.

. . .

[H.L.R.O., Main Papers, H.L., 28 May 1624]

ERRONEOUS JUDGEMENTS IN PARLIAMENT

[fol. 157] The judgements in parliament have been most commonly upon the accusation of the Commons. The Lords can neither accuse nor add to the accusation (for they are the judges). If they do, the judgement is erroneous; as was the judgement against the Spencers, *a°* 15 E. III, when the Lords and Commons

---

⁶¹ *Ibid.* **2**: p. 104 (13 E. III, Part I, no. 8, *"ceux sont les pointz desqueux len devera treter en commune a cel parlement"*).

⁶² *Ibid.* **3**: p. 89 (4 R. II, nos. 10, 11).

⁶³ For Charles's speech in 1625, see L.J., **3**: pp. 435–436.

accused.⁶⁴ There be other forms also which were anciently observed in judicature. If the crime were not capital, the party (if a peer) answered in his place (*vd.* the Bishop of Norwich's case *a⁰* 7 R. II).⁶⁵ If he were a commoner he had his liberty, and they might have counsel to speak for them. None were committed until judgement. According to that of Magna Charta, *cap.* 26, and other statutes. If in such cases, the party hath been restrained of his liberty, or denied counsel, the proceeding is erroneous. *Quaere,* if then the judgement be so also. And upon the Commons' accusation, the Commons are to know the party's answer, as they may reply, and to know the proofs as they may demand judgement, if they see cause. And anciently judgement was not rendered until they thus demanded it. If otherwise, *q.* if erroneous.

THE REVERSING OF JUDGEMENTS IN PARLIAMENT

[fol. 157ᵛ] The form was anciently by petition to the king in parliament, in which petition the errors are to be assigned *vde* Spencer's petition *a⁰* 15 E. II. The king refers it to the parliament, the Lords appoint a committee to examine the errors, *prout* 2 H. V. for the Earl of Sarum.⁶⁶ The Commons are to be acquainted with it and their opinions known; for the judgement cannot be reversed, but at the petition of the party, by the judgement of the king and Lords with assent of the Commons. *Vd.* 15 E. II and 28 E. III and 2 H. V.⁶⁷

MEMORANDUM FOR THE EARL OF DANBY

[Petyt 538/15, fol. 15]

6 *Martii,* 1629, I began.

The only distraction which E. III had with his parliaments was in that of the 15th year of his reign, which began xvⁿᵃ *Pasche* and ended in May following.¹ And the king to his great dishonor was enforced to repeal the statutes therein made at Michaelmas next, for that he assented not, but dissembled etc.² And yet in the *a⁰* 17ᵐᵒ of his reign, he summoned another parliament where all was reconciled in so loving a manner, that never after any disagreement or jar happened betwixt them. The causes and remedy whereof I will (according to your lordship's command)³ briefly recite and clear that glorious king's honor herein.

The Lords and Commons *a⁰* 14ᵗᵒ granted unto the king a large subsidy for his French wars, to be paid in 2 years, under divers conditions. And the statute thereon was drawn up by a special committee of both houses, who took great care that the king should be duly answered their grant, and they enjoy his majesty's grace in those conditions expressed.⁴ Whereupon his majesty went into France with full confidence to receive this money accordingly. But he was so abused by his officers that that which was paid [fol. 16] of the said subsidy was ill spent and little came to his hands. Wherefore, for want of money, he was enforced to accept of a truce, even then when God offered him a great victory, if not a conquest of that kingdom. Whereupon his majesty returned suddenly, and fell first upon his officers, who excused themselves, and laid the fault upon the collectors. Then his majesty sent out commissions to inquire of them. But they had ill instructions; for they were to enquire also of divers points of eyre in general wherein they most busied themselves, putting the attainted to most grievous fines, not having regard to the quantity of the offence, but of the delinquent's ability, (which was contrary to the law). And they commanded the sheriffs to return all freeholders whatsoever, whether resident or not. And charged the sheriffs to levy the issues of them which came not, to the very value of their lands (which was [fol. 17] also contrary to the law) and commanded their lands to be seized for the same. And in the indictments they proceeded most strangely; for the indictors were of the jury, and their challenge not allowed.

Touching the conditions whereon the said subsidy was granted, they were not performed. For the barons of the exchequer denied to acquit the Commons of old debts. And the other justices also refused to allow their pardons according to the conditions thereof.⁵ Whereupon the Commons refused to pay the subsidy of the second year. But these were not the chief cause of that distraction; for, whatsoever concerned the Commons was remedied in the same parliament upon their usual petition, *I pray do so no more.* The greatest mischief happened by the clergy, they seemed to be most incensed against the king, and demanded unreasonable things for themselves under pretense of the liberty of the church. The occasion whereof was this.

---

⁶⁴ Elsyng is referring to Sir Hugh Despenser and his son of the same name. In 21 R. II, a descendant of Sir Hugh Despenser brought in a bill confirming the revocation of the sentence of exile passed against Sir Hugh in 15 E. II, and also revoking the repeal of the same revocation which had been passed in 1 E. III. *Cf.* Selden, *Of Judicature,* p. 12; *Exact Abridgement,* pp. 372–373; *Rot. Parl.* 2: pp. 3–6 (1 E. III, nos. 1–2); 3: pp. 360–361 (21 R. II, no. 55).

⁶⁵ 7 R. II, nos. 13–23 (*Rot. Parl.* 3: pp. 151–156); *Exact Abridgement,* p. 292.

⁶⁶ The petition of Sir Hugh Despenser is recited in the bill presented in 21 R. II (*Rot. Parl.* 3: pp. 360–361, no. 55). For the Earl of Salisbury's case, see *Exact Abridgement,* p. 539; *Rot. Parl.* 4: pp. 17–19, 35–36 (2 H. V, Part I, no. 12; Part II, no. 13); Selden, *Of Judicature,* pp. 153–154.

⁶⁷ The cases of Sir Hugh Despenser, Roger Mortimer, Earl of March, and the Earl of Salisbury. See above, n. 66; *Exact Abridgement,* p. 85; *Rot. Parl.* 2: pp. 256–257 (28 E. III, no. 13).

¹ See Lapsley, pp. 231–272, and the references there given. Wilkinson, pp. 183–184.

² These are the words of the revocation (15 E. III, stat. 2).

³ Henry Danvers (1573–1644), Earl of Danby (see below, p. 64).

⁴ 14 E. III, stat. 1, c. 20–21; stat. 2, c. 1–4.

⁵ 14 E. III, stat. 2, c. 3.

[fol. 18] The Archbishop of Canterbury [6] was most forward of all others to hasten the king to this French action, willing him to take no care for treasure, because himself would see him abundantly furnished out of the subsidy grant, etc. Which failing and the king knowing that the pope sided with the French,[7] was jealous of the archbishop, and reprehended him for it, supposing this was plotted aforehand, who presently complained of manifest violences against the liberties of the church, and the English nation comprehended in Magna Charta. Whereby he incensed the laity also.

So upon these terms stood that glorious king, when he summoned his parliament of 15to, his honor deeply engaged in a war, and the hearts of his loving subjects stolen from him by the popish clergy. To proceed, in this parliament, his majesty only showed, that the necessity of the French wars continued, that the great aid which was granted (a^o 14to) was withheld, and ill spent by his officers, and required them to consider [fol. 19] how he might come by the arrearages of the first year, and the grant of the second, with the least grievance of his people, and how there might be plenty of money in the land. This was the sum of all their charge.[8]

But as touching the Archbishop of Canterbury, the king had so many causes of suspicion of treason and other matters against him, that he would not once permit him to enter the parliament. Whereupon the archbishop came to the door, claiming his right as *primus par Angliae* and threatening excommunication against them all, if he might not come in.

The Lords, hearing this then fearful thunder of excommunication required first from the king a declaration to be made, that the peers of the land, whether officers or not, be not bound to answer the king's suit but in parliament, which held them in debate a whole week [fol. 20] even from Thursday, when the charge was given, to Thursday following.[9] This being with much importunity obtained, the archbishop was admitted the same day.[10] And then, although in many things the laity and the clergy petitioned the one for the other (which they never did before nor since) and in those petitions which chiefly concerned the clergy, the laity persisted very stiffly. Yet touching the mere grievances of the Commons above named, they were easily satisfied; for upon their petition, the king granted a *supersedeas* to those commissioners that they should inquire of nothing but of his own ministers, that the outlawries against all men except for felony or breach of the peace should stay till the next parliament, that the fines should be mitigated, that the sheriffs should answer the suit of the party for returning any freeholder who was sick or not resident. And that the challenge of the indictors should be admitted. All which the king very readily condescended unto after a communication had with them himself.[11] Touching the conditions of the last subsidy which the whole parliament insisted on, protesting to pay nothing unless they might be observed, they also were granted at the said conference, and a new subsidy given in lieu of the former, and so all parties satisfied therein.[12] But touching their petitions on behalf of the clergy and themselves, the Lords and Commons [fol. 21] were not so soon satisfied but after the king's answers they required a special committee of bishops and lords to consider thereof and to amend the said answers, which the king granted.[13] [fol. 20^v] The statute also upon the said answers was as disorderly penned, not by the king's counsel, who refused to do it, though it belonged unto them, but by others, who penned the same to the great prejudice of the king, adding much more than was in the petition. All which the king and his council observed well enough though for the present he let it pass with silence, and commanded the statute to be sealed with the great seal and delivered to the Lords and Commons.[14]

I have forgotten the proceedings of the clergy with their petitions, which is worth the observing.[15] They (as I said before) petitioned for themselves and the laity also (*quod mirum*) and especially for Magna Charta tacitly threatening the great excommunication, against the infringement thereof, confirmed by the pope.[16] Neither were they satisfied with the king's answers.[17] Whereupon the grands, that is the temporal lords, were appointed to consider thereof, who found their petitions so frivolous and unreasonable that only one of the seven exhibited was admitted into the statute (though made into two chapters, *vizt.* the 5 and 6). And whereas in their second petition, they re-

---

[6] John Stratford, Archbishop of Canterbury, 1334–1348.
[7] Benedict XII, 1334–1342. This was the period when the popes resided at Avignon.
[8] 15 E. III, no. 5 (*Rot. Parl.* 1: pp. 126–127).
[9] 15 E. III, nos. 6–7 (*Rot. Parl.* 1: p. 127).
[10] "The case of archbishop Stratford in the 15 Edw. III is observable here. It appears, that though he were commanded to stay from the parliament until he had answered certain articles in the exchequer, touching an account; yet by a dutiful standing on his right, he did get his place in the house; and so sensible were the lords of that breach of their privilege in that restraint of this archbishop, that they declared, that none of them ought to be questioned in any place but in parliament . . ." (Elsyng, *Manner of Holding Parliaments*, pp. 198–199; see above, p. 46, n. 4). 15 E. III, no. 8 (*Rot. Parl.* 1: pp. 127–128). Wilkinson suggests that the assembly from which Stratford was excluded was not a meeting of parliament in Elsyng's sense of the word, but of the council (Wilkinson, pp. 180–186).

[11] 15 E. III, nos. 62–67 (*Rot. Parl.* 1: pp. 133–134).
[12] 15 E. III, nos. 16–17, 42 (*Rot. Parl.* 1: pp. 128–129, 131); 15 E. III, stat. 3.
[13] 15 E. III, no. 17 (*Rot. Parl.* 1: p. 129). Material written on fol. 20^v has been inserted here, as indicated in the manuscript.
[14] 15 E. III, no. 42 (*Rot. Parl.* 1: p. 131).
[15] For the petitions, see 15 E. III, nos. 18–26; for the king's replies, see nos. 27–33 (*Rot. Parl.* 1: pp. 129–130).
[16] 15 E. III, no. 21 (*Rot. Parl.* 1: p. 129).
[17] 15 E. III, no. 26 (*Rot. Parl.* 1: pp. 129–130).

quired a new oath for Magna Charta, alleging the said excommunication confirmed by the pope, it was absolutely rejected with a check unto them.[18]

Before I proceed any further, it is fit (for the full clearing of the king's honor) to show briefly wherein the said statute of 15to was so prejudicial to the king and the laws of the land. This statute contains 6 chapters. I take no exception to the 1. 3. 5. and 6.

[fol. 21 cont.] *Cap.* 2 limits the trial of peers to be in parliament. Whereas Magna Charta only appoints the triers to be peers. And this could not be available for the lay barons, who are triable *per nobiles pares* out of parliament, as well as in parliament. It would only advance the prelates, who out of parliament are triable by an ordinary jury of freeholders, their honor not being of inheritance. So that it was not only inconvenient to the king to await the parliament for these trials, but contrary to the law, and nothing available to the temporal lords.[19]

Cap. 4 hath 3 clauses. 1. That the king shall place new officers by the accord of the grands which shall be nearest in the country, which is very derogatory to the king, and might prove as inconvenient to the commonwealth if those grands should not be men of worth. 2. That those officers shall be sworn, etc. to which I take no exceptions. [fol. 22] 3. That the third day of every parliament the king shall take all his offices (except the judges) into his own hands, and put them to answer all complaints, and they to be judged by the peers in parliament and the king to cause execution thereof to be pronounced and done accordingly. This is unjust for 2 causes. 1. It is against law to put any man out of his office before conviction and judgment. 2. It is against the king's right to be bound to execute the judgment of the peers in parliament. Whereas in some cases the judgment cannot be pronounced without his assent, and no capital judgment can be executed without his command. And note this was not petitioned for and the whole statute is drawn up more amply than is contained in the petitions.[20]

[fol. 21^v] Who can blame the king for repealing of this statute, had it been done in a due manner? For the repeal whereof may be observed. That first he summoned his great council of bishops and earls and barons in July (the parliament ending in May before) but by reason of the number of the prelates, he could not bring it to pass wherefore his majesty summoned another great council about Michaelmas following, omitting all the bishops and there by the advice and consent of the temporal lords only he repealed the same.

[fol. 22^v] This proceeding of the king's could not but be distasteful unto his people having received a subsidy (as was afterwards objected) for that statute, and then repealing the same by a private act of his great council (which he could not do by law) and in that act to confess his dissimulation: the remembrance whereof could not but grieve his majesty also. All which was drawn upon him by the popish clergy, who did in like sort breed as great disorder or far greater between King E. the First and his people in the parliament about the 25th year of his reign which could not be reconciled but in another parliament, by additions of new liberties unto Magna Charta. But this glorious king (E. III) did so handle the next parliament he called (which was a° 17) that he did not only obtain an absolute repeal of this statute but in the end dismissed them to the full content of the Commons. The manner whereof I will briefly relate unto your lordship.

[fol. 23] In the parliament of 17 E. III, his majesty demanded no subsidy; yet to prepare their hearts against occasion should require their aid, he propounded a treaty of peace with France by mediation of the pope whereunto they consented, so as the pope be not acknowled as a judge but as a friend only. He also propounded unto their consideration how the laws might be more indifferently administered to the poor as well as to the rich. And therein his majesty himself and the Lords treated with the Commons on a commission for the justices of the peace etc. and of means to have plenty of money, which pleased them well.[21] And yet the Commons exhibited their petition against this repeal of the said statute; but such reasons were then given for the same, (they being thus first prepared) that the whole parliament repealed that statute also.[22] One thing more much furthered the king's purpose, *vizt.,* his ready consent to the petition of the Commons against the unjust provisions and shameless abuses of the pope, his majesty referring the redress thereof to be considered of by the temporal lords and Commons, who penned a special act for the same, [fol. 24] how be it the clergy assented not, neither was any statute made thereof, (a bishop being chancellor). Yet these abuses being published by proclamation, it purchased the king their entire affections;[23] what they conceived of the pope and his clergy appears by entertaining the opinions of Wycliff shortly after. When the king had thus regained the hearty loves of his people, he summoned another parliament and then demanded a subsidy and

---

[18] 15 E. III, nos. 20, 28 (*Rot. Parl.* 1: pp. 129–130).

[19] See Lapsley, pp. 255 ff. Elsyng makes substantially the same points in *Expedicio Billarum Antiquitus* (Sims, *Expedicio,* p. 112). For the statute and its revocation by the council, see 15 E. III, stats. 1 and 2.

[20] Cf. Sims, *Expedicio,* p. 113. The material written on fol. 21^v has been inserted here as indicated in the manuscript. On this point and the question of the barons' attitude toward the annulment of the statute, see Wilkinson, pp. 190–192.

[21] 17 E. III, nos. 6–12, 14–18 (*Rot. Parl.* 1: pp. 135–138).

[22] For the petition and the repeal, see 17 E. III, nos. 4, 23 (*Rot. Parl.* 1: pp. 139–140). Cf. Sims, *Expedicio,* pp. 113–114.

[23] 17 E. III, nos. 59–60 (*Rot. Parl.* 1: pp. 143–145). The chancellor was Robert Sadington, knight. John Offord, Dean of Lincoln and Archbishop-elect of Canterbury, became chancellor in October, 1345.

had it and almost in every year after during his life, he had a parliament and a subsidy if it were demanded, or his wants but made to appear. And never had any other jar with his people though he reigned [blank] years.

I fear I have been too tedious in the discourse of this angry, jealous parliament of 15to E. III, and the reconcilement thereof. But it becomes not me to apply it to the present times, yet sith your lordship hath required it I will only show my conceit, humbly submitting the same to your honor. May it please his majesty to summon another parliament and to command by strict proclamations elections of knights and burgesses to be free and according to the statutes, which will bring them together with quiet and contented minds.[24] Then in the first session to demand no subsidy at all but rather to express that his majesty expects none. The cause of summons to be declared, for the etc. And to propound some pleasing diversion from complaints as the increase of trade, a commission for musters or the like.

[fol. 25] There are 3 things notwithstanding may trouble the next parliament; and yet may be avoided.

1. Privileges.
2. Impositions.
3. Religion.[25]

For privileges, in all likelihood they will complain that they enjoyed not freedom of speech. For this (if I may be so bold to speak) it may be freely promised and permitted them by his majesty in as large manner as it was confirmed by that act of 2 H. IV which is so much insisted on, which can be no prejudice at all to his majesty, for the words of that act are [fol. 26] that they have deliberation and advice to commune and treat of all their matters amongst themselves, to bring the same to the better end and conclusion according to their knowledge, for the good and honor of the king and his whole realm, and he will take no notice thereof until it be declared by the assent of them all.[26] Here is no privilege neither for treason, felony, nor breach of the peace, which three were never privileged in parliament, no not in parliament time.[27] Here is only privilege of speech for those things which tend to the good and honor of the king and the realm. And therefore if it would please his majesty to permit this freedom of speech and not to take any notice of what they say or conclude on amongst themselves until it be sent up to the Lords or himself, it will give them great content, and much further and expedite all the business of parliament. For they can but commune together and agree upon a petition or complaint.[28] I know they have accroached unto themselves judicature in these 2 points which did anciently belong to the Lords, as for the arrests and assaults on their own members and servants. And for the elections and returns of their knights and burgesses, yet they have long enjoyed them. Wherefore, may it please his majesty to grant them judicature touching the arrests and assaults and the like, with some limitations.[29] But to permit them freely to certify the elections and returns, for the undue and violent courses used therein $a^o 1^o$ *Mariae* whereby religion was altered hath made them jealous and fearful of the like undue elections if they have not that power fully in themselves.[30] [fol. 27] And if it will please his majesty that the ancient manner of judicature in parliament for all other matters may be reviewed, agreed on and sealed, that the right of his majesty and of each house may be known, it cannot but please them all.

Touching impositions, let them dispute it freely; therein they can conclude nothing; for nothing of theirs cannot be exemplified as a record,[31] nor given in evidence at any bar. And this late example on some will make them all remember to speak soberly.[32] Afterwards when their bill or complaint comes up, or a conference be demanded thereon, then whatsoever shall seem prejudicial to the king may be qualified or avoided.

---

[24] 7 H. IV, c. 15. See above, p. 47, n. 13.

[25] Here a paragraph has been crossed off: "Touching the first, if the cause of summons be declared to consider of the due execution of the laws in general, and of the abuses (if any) of mustermasters, and saltpetremen, and etc. and for an act for the same, it will be a pleasing diversion."

[26] 2 H. IV, no. 11 (*Rot. Parl.* 3: p. 456). Elsyng cites the same precedent in the first volume of his book (*Manner of Holding Parliaments*, p. 181).

[27] This was the accepted view, see Coke, *Fourth Institute*, p. 25.

[28] These additional words have been deleted: "or accusation, they can execute nothing."

[29] The following additional words have been deleted: "reserving the punishment of contempts to the Lords, for the contempt of one house is the contempt of the other."

[30] This conclusion is probably based on the passage in Foxe's *Acts and Monuments* from an oration said to have been delivered to Queen Elizabeth at her accession: "She [Mary], by force and violence taketh from the commons their liberty, that according to the ancient laws and customs of the realm, they could not have their free election of knights and burgesses for the parliament. . . . And therefore in many places divers were chosen by force of her threats meet to serve her malicious affections. . . ." Some duly elected were forcibly put out of the house (*The Acts and Monuments of John Foxe*, fourth edition, edited by the Rev. Josiah Pratt (London, [1877]) **8:** p. 676). Pollard and Neale discredit the idea that Mary attempted to influence elections in her first parliament. Nor does this exaggerated account accurately describe the steps taken before her third parliament. The Venetian ambassador thought the government controlled elections for the second parliament; but the statement lacks substantiation (A. F. Pollard, *The History of England from the Accession of Edward VI to the Death of Elizabeth,* London, 1910, pp. 117, 126; J. E. Neale, *The Elizabethan House of Commons,* New Haven, 1950, pp. 160, 286–288).

[31] Elsyng had originally written "for whatsoever they do cannot." When he deleted the first part of this phrase and substituted "nothing of theirs," he neglected to alter "cannot."

[32] See above, p. 48, n. 15.

Howsoever, the king may gain more by silence than by interrupting their ordinary freedom of speech by messages or otherwise.[33]

Touching religion. It is likely they will complain most of the increase of Arminians and papists.[34] They may be permitted to prepare their bill or complaint, whereon the king may proceed as he please.

[fol. 28] The first session of the parliament being well ended, will so knit the hearts of the people unto his majesty that they will not deny him a very large subsidy in the next session. And the best way to compass this (in my opinion) is to demand no subsidy in the first, for therein rests the only strength of the Commons; but to call it at such a time, as the end of the first session may not be precipitated, and yet the subsidy grant serve his majesty's occasions at their next meeting, when all rubs are first removed.

Which God grant. Amen. Amen. 8 *Martii* 1629, perused again and new written (thus amended) 11 *Martii,* 1629. H. E. *pro Comite* Danby.

Memorandum, that being at dinner with the Earl of Danby, we had some speech of his majesty's desire to gain his people's loves.[35] And I said it might be easily done. After dinner, his lordship called me aside into his garden, and asked me by what means I thought it might be done. I answered by parliament, according to that of 15to E. III and his lordship requiring how that was, I promised to relate it in writing, and bring it to him. Who appointed me the next Friday 12 March. Against which time, I wrote out this discourse fair to carry to his lordship.

---

[33] See above, p. 47, n. 13.

[34] These additional words have been deleted: "which I fear will be tender to his majesty now the queen is with child; whom God bless, and make us happy with a royal issue. If the parliament be not summoned till after her majesty is delivered. And then the Commons may be permitted. . . ."

[35] Apparently in 1628, Charles had a similar desire (Gardiner, *History of England* 7: pp. 28–29).

INDEX

Abbot, George, Archbishop of Canterbury, 25, 31
Alford, Edward, M.P., 34
Almanacs, 13
Anglesey, Earl of, *vide* Arthur Annesley
Annesley, Arthur, first Earl of Anglesey, 43
Antiquarians, 9, 20, 29, 31, 34–35, 37, 42, 50; *vide* Robert Bowyer, William Bowyer, Sir Robert Cotton, John Selden
Apothecaries Company, 16
Archbishops, fees due to clerk from, 10; *vide* George Abbot, William Laud, John Stratford
Arminians, 48, 64
Arundel, Earl of, *vide* Thomas Howard
Attainder, 42, 60
Attorney general, 23; *vide* Sir Thomas Coventry, Sir Henry Hobart, Sir Henry Yelverton

Bacon, Sir Francis, Lord Verulam, Viscount St. Albans, lord chancellor, 5, 8, 13, 16, 18, 22, 25–27, 30–35, 42, 48
Ball, Peter, M.P., 34
Banbury, Oxfordshire, 27–28
Barker, John, printer to the king, 13, 17
Barons, fees due to clerk from, 10
Bedford, Earl of, *vide* Francis Russell
Benbow, —, deputy clerk of the crown, 11, 12
Benedict XII, pope, 46, 47, 61, 62
Bennett, Sir John, M.P., **8, 18, 23, 25**
Bertie, Robert, Lord Willoughby de Ersby, 15, 16, 20, 22, 24, 28
Bible, 13
Bird, Sir William, serjeant-at-law, 23
Bishops, as lord chancellors, 39, 59; fees due to clerk from, 10; list of, 13–14; precedence of, 13–14; *vide* Theophilus Field, Samuel Harsnett, Roger Mainwaring, John Williams
Books of computation, 13
Bounty, Book of, 13
Borlase, Sir William, M.P., 34
Bourchier, Sir John, 26
Bowyer, Robert, clerk of the parliaments, 5, 7, 9, 11, 13–17, 22, 32, 34, 35, 49; abridgement, 7–8, 38, 43; biographical information, 5–6; books and manuscripts of, 6; draft journal, 23, 26, 27; half-brother, *vide* Thomas Knyvett; journal of the House of Lords, 21; keeper of the records, 6, 7–8, 35, 43; M.P., 5, 49; niece, *vide* Blanche Elsyng; notes concerning subsidy, 38, 52; notes and "scribbled books" of the House of Lords, 5, 21–27; parliament rolls prepared by, 29, 30, 32, 34, 35; parliamentary diary, 5; transcript of Lords Journal 1558, 24–25
Bowyer, William, keeper of the records in the Tower, 6, 7, 38; *An Exact Abridgement of the Records*, 7–8, 38, **43**

Bridgewater, Earl of, *vide* John Egerton
Bristol, Earl of, *vide* John Digby
Brooke, Lord, *vide* Fulke Greville
Browne, Anthony, second Viscount Montagu, 10
Browne, John, clerk of the parliaments, 6; fees, 10
Buckingham, Duke of, *vide* George Villiers
Bunbury, John, clerk of the Grocers Company, 16
Burghley, Lord, *vide* William Cecil
Buttrice, George, 15

Caesar, Sir Charles, 16
Cambridge University, 5
Carey, Henry, first Earl of Dover, 10, 27
Carey, Robert, first Earl of Monmouth, 27
Carlisle, Earl of, *vide* John Hay
Catholics, Roman, 48, 64; *vide* Recusants
Cavendish, William, second Earl of Devonshire, 8, 21
Cecil, Sir Robert, first Earl of Salisbury, lord treasurer, 14
Cecil, William, first Baron Burghley, lord treasurer, 13, 16, 23
Chancery, court of, 7, 20, 29, 32–34, 43, 44
Charles I, King of England, 5, 6, 9, 23, 29, 31–37, 39, 40, 45–50, 59, 63; advice to, 46–50, 61–64; as prince, 8, 14, 22, 27, 31, 37, 44, 59
Charles II, King of England, 6, 45
Chief justices, 59; *vide* Sir Nicholas Hyde, Sir James Ley
Church, English, liberties of, 60–61
Clare, Earl of, *vide* John Holles
Clement VI, pope, 62
Clerk of the crown, 10, 11, 17, 29, 33, 48; *vide* Sir George Coppin, Sir Thomas Edmondes; deputy, 18, 20, 22, *vide* Benbow
Clerk of the House of Commons, *vide* House of Commons
Clerk of the parliaments,
  assistants to, 11, 12, 14–17, 19, 21, 22, 24, 25, 28; fees, 11, 12, 14, 17, 25; notes of, 14, 21, 24, 25; oath, 11–12; *vide* Richard Crane, Henry Elsyng, Henry Elsyng Jr., Will Harrison, Thomas Knyvett, Owen Reynolds, John Throckmorton
  authorized to dispose of petitions, 20
  duties and functions of, 6, 10–35, 43–44, 50
  fees and salary, 10–11, 29
  influence on legislation, 16
  oath, 9, 10, 44
  office, 13, 19, 50
  reversion of, 6, 9, 10
  vide Robert Bowyer, John Browne, Henry Elsyng, Anthony Mason, Henry Scobell, Sir Thomas Smith
Clifford, Henry, Baron Clifford, 14; precedence of, 20–21
Clinton, Theophilus, Earl of Lincoln, 17
Coke, Sir **Edward, 33, 34, 45**

Commissions, for levy of subsidy, 38, 58; for musters, 47, 49, 63; of inquiry, E. III and R. II, 46, 47, 53, 60–62; of trailbaston, 49
Common Prayer, Book of, 13
Commons, *vide* House of Commons
Coningsby, Sir Francis, 21
Convocation, 31
Coppin, Sir George, clerk of the crown, 11
"Cornewall," Oxfordshire, 9, 43, 45, 50
Cotton, Sir Robert, 5, 7, 9–10, 16, 26, 37–38, 42, 43, 45, 46; treatise by, 37–38
Council, great, 36, 47, 51, 61, 62; privy, 7, 19, 46, 48, 49
Councillors, royal, control of, 48, 53, 54, 62; *vide* Impeachment
Coventry, Sir Thomas, first Lord Coventry, attorney general, 23, 24, 25, 31, 33, 34; lord keeper, 9, 14–16, 31, 32, 44, 45
Cowell, Dr. John, 9
Crane, Richard, assistant to the clerk of the parliaments, 12
Cranfield, Lionel, first Earl of Middlesex, lord treasurer, 8, 20, 26, 27, 31–33, 35, 42, 46, 48
Crawley, Richard, 23
Crewe, Sir Randolph, serjeant-at-law, 24, 31, 32
Crewe, Sir Thomas, speaker of the House of Commons, 31
Crowcombe Court, papers at, 43
Cunningham, Sir James, 19

Danby, Earl of, *vide* Henry Danvers, Sir Thomas Osborne
Danvers, Henry, Earl of Danby, 37, 46, 48, 50, 60, 63, 64
Davenport, —, serjeant-at-law, 21
Denham, John, Baron of the Exchequer, 44
Denny, Edward, Earl of Norwich, 27
Despenser, Sir Hugh, *vide* Index Precedents, cases
Devonshire, Duke of, *vide* William Cavendish
Dewe, Benjamin, 19
D'Ewes, Sir Simonds, 8, 25, 43
Digby, John, first Earl of Bristol, 8, 15, 44, 46
Dike, Richard, 18
Dorset, Earl of, *vide* Richard Sackville, Robert Sackville, Thomas Sackville
Dover, Earl of, *vide* Henry Carey

Earl marshal, 14, 23
Earls, fees due to clerk from, 10
Edmondes, Sir Thomas, clerk of the crown, 10, 11
Edward I, King of England, 52, 62
Edward II, King of England, 52; *vide* Index Precedents, cases
Edward III, King of England, 7, 32, 35–41, 46–63; *vide* Parliaments, Edward III; Index Precedents, cases and rolls of parliament

65

Edward IV, King of England, 7, 29, 38, 40, 54, 59
Edward V, King of England, 38, 54
Egerton, John, first Earl of Bridgewater, 10, 19, 20, 22, 27
Egerton, John, second Earl of Bridgewater, 44
Egerton, Sir Thomas, Baron Ellesmere, lord chancellor, 7, 14, 16, 30
Eliot, Sir John, M.P., 33
Elizabeth I, Queen of England, 11, 35, 39, 59, 63
Elizabeth, Princess, daughter of James I, 31, 37
Elsyng, Blanche, 6
Elsyng, Henry, clerk of the parliaments, 5, 7, 9–36, 38, 40–41, 43–44, 46, 48, 50; abridgement, 38; antiquarian, 20, 35, 45–46, 50; as assistant to clerk of the parliaments, 6, 7, 9, 14, 22, 25; as keeper of the records, 5–9, 35, 36, 38, 50; biographical information, 5–7; children, vide Mary Elsyng, Henry Elsyng Jr., Robert Elsyng; family, 5–6; houses, 7, 10, vide "Cornewall"; intervenes for petitioner, 19–20; method of writing, 38–39, 42; notes, 38; oath, 9–10; office, 13, 19, 50; parliament rolls prepared by, 5, 18, 23, 29–35, 50; political opinions, 6, 35, 36, 48–50, 63–64, vide House of Commons, Elsyng's view of; preparation of draft journal, 25–28; preparation of the journal, 21–29; salary and fees, 10; "scribbled books," 7, 8, 10, 12, 14, 21–28, 43–44, 50; treatises, 45–50, vide Modus Tenendi Parliamentum, Elsyng
Elsyng, Henry, Jr., 6, 7, 12; as assistant to the clerk of the parliaments, 6, 22, 24
Elsyng, Mary, 7
Elsyng, Robert, 7
Exchequer, court of, 29, 43, 46, 60
Expedicio Billarum Antiquitus, vide *Modus Tenendi Parliamentum*, Elsyng, Book Two, chapter 5

Fenton, George, 19
Field, Theophilus, Bishop of Llandaff, 31
Fiennes, William, first Viscount Saye and Sele, 9, 21, 22
Finch, Heneage, M.P., 34
Finch, Sir John, speaker of the House of Commons, 32
Fitz-Harris, —, 42
Fleet, prison, 15, 18; warden of, 23
Floyd, Edward, 27, 31
Foxe, John, Book of Martyrs, 13, 63
France,
 treaties with, 47, 54, 59, 62
 wars with, 37, 46, 49, 54–57, 59–61
Frederick V, Elector Palatine, 37

Gardiner, George, 15, 20
Garter, roll of peers, 13
Gillett, George, 15
Grants, royal, 8, 18, 49
Greenland, fishing rights off, 19
Greville, Fulke, first Baron Brooke, 24
Grievances, 8, 18, 30, 32, 39, 46–49, 50, 54
Grocers Company, 16
Gunpowder plot, 13

Hakewill, William, M.P., 12, 34, 42
Hamersly, Alderman, 19
Hargrave, Francis, 44
Harrison, Will, assistant to clerk of the parliaments, 12, 19
Harsnett, Samuel, Bishop of Norwich, 22, 25
Hastings, Henry, fifth Earl of Huntingdon, 12, 15, 17, 26
Hatton, Sir Christopher, lord chancellor, 16
Haughton, Lord, vide John Holles
Hay, John, Viscount Doncaster, Earl of Carlisle, 24
Heneage, Michael, keeper of the records in the Tower, 7, 38
Henrietta Maria, Queen of England, 37, 64
Henry III, King of England, 36, 52
Henry IV, King of England, 38–40, 52–54, 56, 59; vide Index Precedents, rolls of parliament
Henry V, King of England, 39–40, 52–54, 59; vide Index Precedents, cases and rolls of parliament
Henry VI, King of England, 38, 54, 59; vide Index Precedents, rolls of parliament
Henry VII, King of England, 39, 59
Henry VIII, King of England, 38, 39, 41, 53, 59; vide Parliaments, Henry VIII
Herbert, Philip, first Earl of Montgomery, 8
Herbert, William, Earl of Pembroke, 22
Hertford, Earl of, vide Edward Seymour
Hobart, Sir Henry, attorney general, 30, 34
Holinshed, Raphael, *Chronicle*, 13
Holles, John, Lord Haughton, first Earl of Clare, 22, 24
Hooker, John, alias Vowell, 10, 11
House of Commons,
 attendance, 24
 clerk, 16, 44, 48
 Commons, medieval, 37, 39–41, 46–48, 50–63; advise with and report to constituents, 56, 57; bill, 48; committees, 40, 41, 53, 55–57, 59, 60; conference with Lords, 39–41, 52–59
 elections to, 47, 48, 63
 Elsyng's view of, 47–50, 63–64
 judicature, 44, 47–48, 50, 63
 petitions to the crown, 9, 47, 48, 50, 63, 64; vide Parliament, petitions
 power to levy fines, 44
 privileges, 32, 47–49, 54, 63
 proposed conference with House of Lords, 63
 role in judicature of parliament, 59–60; vide Impeachment
 speaker, 29, 31, 41, 48, 54, 58; vide *Modus Tenendi Parliamentum*, Elsyng, Book One, chapter 8; Sir Thomas Crewe; Sir John Finch; Sir John Puckering; Sir Thomas Richardson
House of Commons, 1621–1629, 5, 15, 25, 31–35, 42, 48, 49, vide Impeachment; arrest of members, 48, 63; conferences with House of Lords, 8, 15, 16, 25, 30, 31, 33–35; records, journal, 34; search for precedents, 32
House of Commons, 1660–1668, attack on judicial activities of the Lords, 42
House of Commons, 1681, 42
House of Lords,
 administration of oath to members of, 14, 26
 attendance, 14, 24, 28
 bills, private, fees due for, 10, 11, 17, 23
 chamber, 7, 12–13, 21–22
 judicature, 33, 35, 42–45, 47, 48, 59–63; vide Impeachment
 list of members, 13–14
 Lords, medieval, committees, 39–41, 47, 51–53, 55–57, 59–61; conferences with Commons, 39–41, 52–59
 orders, 11, 14
 power to levy fines, 43–44
 precedence in, 13–14, 20–21
 precedents, 9, 32
 presiding officer, 14–17, 26, 31; vide Lord chancellor, Lord keeper, Sir Francis Bacon, Sir Thomas Coventry, Sir Thomas Egerton, Sir Christopher Hatton, Sir James Ley
 privileges, 5, 8, 12, 15, 18, 20, 21, 31, 33, 34, 42, 45, 46, 48
 procedure, 6, 8, 14, 16–18, 22, 23, 25, 26, 30, 44
 proposed conference with House of Commons, 63
 records, journal, 6, 12, 13, 16, 21–25, 33–35; vide House of Lords, 1621–1629
 writs of summons, 13–14, 22, 38, 51
House of Lords, 1621–1629, 5, 8, 9, 18, 29, 32, 49, 50
 agenda for, 14–16
 attendance lists, 24, 28
 committees, 12, 15–18, 22
 committee of privileges, 12, 17; subcommittee for journal, 23–28, 32–33, 42, 46
 committee of petitions, 15, 19, 21, 22
 conference with House of Commons, 8, 15, 16, 25, 30, 31, 33–35
 hearings, 15, 18–23, 30; vide Impeachment
 imprisonment delinquents, 18
 judicature, 5, 26, 31, 42; vide Edward Floyd, Impeachment
 legal assistants, 21; vide Judges
 lords' fees, 10–11, 23
 orders, 8, 10–12, 14, 19–22, 28, 29, 33, 50
 petitions to, 12, 18–20, 22, 26, 28
 petitions to the king, 9, 31; vide Parliament, petitions
 records, bills, catalogues and lists of, 12, 15, 17, 19, 28; books of petitions, 12; committee books, 12, 16–17; draft journal, 12, 21, 23, 25–29; journal, 7, 9, 10, 12–14, 21, 23–29, 44; judgments, 18; vide Robert Bowyer and Henry Elsyng, parliament roll; Robert Bowyer and Henry Elsyng, "scribbled books"; Clerk of the parliaments, assistants
 serjeant, 30
 standing orders, 5, 6, 16, 23, 32

votes, 17, 22, 27, 44
witnesses, 18, 19, 21, 23, 30, 31
House of Lords, 1660–1693, 45; judicial power of, 42–43
Howard, Charles, Earl of Nottingham, 15, 16
Howard, Henry, Earl of Northampton, 45
Howard, Thomas, second Earl of Arundel, 8, 9, 22, 23, 25, 27, 46, 49
Hunsdon, Lord, *vide* Henry Carey, Earl of Dover
Huntingdon, Earl of, *vide* Henry Hastings
Hyde, Sir Nicholas, chief justice King's Bench, 27
Hyett, Blanche, *vide* Blanche Elsyng

Impeachment, 5, 8, 9, 18, 20–23, 25, 26, 30–35, 42, 44, 46, 48–49
Impositions, 9, 34, 40, 48, 49, 58, 59, 63
Imprisonment, arbitrary, 34; *vide* Petition of Right, 1628
Infanta Maria, 37
Inns of Court, Inner Temple, 5; Middle Temple, 5, 6, 49
Ireland, 13, 54

James I, King of England, 9, 13, 17, 22, 25, 27, 30, 31, 33, 34, 39–40, 44, 45, 49
John, King of England, 52
Judges 20, 42, 59; assistants in House of Lords, 15, 17, 22, 23
Judicature in Parliaments, vide Modus Tenendi Parliamentum, Elsyng, Book Two, chapter 4

Keeper of the records in the Tower, *vide* Robert Bowyer, Henry Elsyng, Michael Heneage
King's Bench, court of, 33
Knighthood, composition for, 49
Knyvett, Thomas, 6, 9, 11

Latimer, William Lord, *vide* Index Precedents, cases
Laud, William, Archbishop of Canterbury, 6, 42
Lee, John de la, *vide* Index Precedents, cases
Leigh, Humfrey, 11
Ley, Sir James, chief justice King's Bench, 10, 16, 18, 22, 23, 26, 30, 31
Lincoln cathedral, library of, 43
Lincoln, Earl of, *vide* Theophilus Clinton
Littleton, Sir Edward, 35, 45
Llandaff, Bishop of, *vide* Theophilus Field
Lord chamberlain, 12, 14, 15; *vide* Henry de Vere
Lord chancellor, as presiding officer House of Lords, 8, 11, 14–17, 22, 31, 39, 42, 48, 58, 59, 62; *vide* Sir Francis Bacon, Sir Christopher Hatton, Sir Thomas Egerton
Lord keeper, as presiding officer House of Lords, 14–16; *vide* Sir Thomas Coventry, Sir Edward Littleton, John Williams
Lords lieutenant, 49
Lord treasurer, *vide* Robert Cecil, William Cecil, Lionel Cranfield, James Ley, Henry Montagu, Thomas Sackville
Lords, *vide* House of Lords, Peers
Lyons, Richard, *vide* Index Precedents, cases

Maddox, Robert, 15
Magna Carta, 60–62
Mainwaring, Roger, chaplain to Charles I, Bishop of St. Davids, 8, 9, 18
Mandeville, Viscount, *vide* Henry Montagu
"Manner of Passing Bills in Parliament," *vide Modus Tenendi Parliamentum,* Elsyng, chapter 6
Mansfield, Viscount, 24
Marquis, fees due to clerk from, 10
Mary I, Queen of England, 25, 47, 63
Mary, Queen of Scots, 35
Mason, Anthony, clerk of the parliaments, 16
Master of the Rolls, 20
Mautravers, John, *vide* Index Precedents, cases
Maxwell, James, 11
Mayne, John, 20
Merchant Taylors Company, 5
Michell, Sir Francis, J.P., 8, 18, 23, 30, 32
"Moderne Forme of Parliaments of England," 45
Modus Tenendi Parliamentum, medieval treatise, 6, 29, 38–40, 44–45, 52, 53, 58
Modus Tenendi Parliamentum, treatise by Henry Elsyng, 5–9, 31, 35–36, 50
Book One, 36–38, 44–46, 50, 52, 63
Book Two, 5, 36, 50; chapter 1, 5, 36–40, 44, 46, 50–52; chapter 2, 5, 36–42, 44, 46, 52–59; chapter 3, 36; chapter 4, 5, 36, 42–46, 59–60; chapter 5, 35, 36, 38–39, 43–46; chapter 6, 36; chapter 10, 36; chapter 11, 36
Book Three, 35, 36, 39
sources, 38–39, 44–45, 47, 50
Mompesson, Sir Giles, M.P., 8, 18, 22, 23, 30, 32, 34, 35, 44, 46
Monmouth, Earl of, *vide* Robert Carey
Monopolies, statute of, 8, 26
Montagu, Henry, Viscount Mandeville, lord treasurer, 22, 25, 27, 43–44
Montagu, Viscount, *vide* Anthony Browne
Montgomery, Earl of, *vide* Philip Herbert
Mortimer, Roger, *vide* Index Precedents, cases
Munson, Sir Thomas, 20
Muscovy Company, 19, 21
Musters, 47, 49, 51, 63

Nevill, Matthew, 19–20
Nicholas, Sir Edward, M.P., 34
North, Dudley, third Baron North, 10
Northampton, Earl of, *vide* Henry Howard
Northumberland, Earl of, *vide* Henry Percy
Norwich, Bishop of, *vide* Samuel Harsnett; Index Precedents, cases
Norwich, Earl of, *vide* Edward Denny
Nottingham, Earl of, *vide* Charles Howard

Oath, assistant to the clerks of the parliaments, 11; clerk of the parliaments, 9, 44; of Allegiance, 12, 14; of Supremacy, 12; to observe Magna Carta, 62; witnesses, House of Lords, 18, 23
Offord, John, lord chancellor, 62
Ordinances, 7, 30, 35, 39, 51
Osborne, Sir Thomas, Earl of Danby, 42
Oxford, Earl of, *vide* Henry de Vere, Robert de Vere
Oxford, earldom of, 5, 20, 22
Oxford University, 6

Paget, William, fourth Baron Paget, 21
Palatinate, 39, 59
Pardon, general, 30, 31
Parliament, 5, 6, 34, 45–46, 50
acts of, *vide* Statutes
aid to crown, 52–59, *vide* Subsidy
archive, 5, 8, 12, 18, 20, 21, 23, 25, 28, 33, 34, 50
bills, history of, 50, 52; *vide Modus Tenendi Parliamentum,* Elsyng, chapters 5 and 6
bills, royal answer to, 11, 17, 58
cause of summons, 29, 31, 39–40, 51, 52, 56, 58, 59, 61, 63
clerks of, *vide* Clerks of the parliaments; House of Commons, clerk; Clerk of the crown
committees, *vide Modus Tenendi Parliamentum,* Elsyng, Book Two, chapter 3; House of Commons; House of Lords
conferences, *vide Modus Tenendi Parliamentum,* Elsyng, Book Two, chapter 3; House of Commons, House of Lords
foreign affairs and defense, 8, 40, 45, 52, 58, 59; *vide Modus Tenendi Parliamentum,* Elsyng, Book Two, chapter 1; Sir Robert Cotton, treatise by
grievances, 18, 47–49, 54, 61–64; *vide* Parliament, petitions
history, 36, 39, 40, 45–46, 48, 50–60; *vide Modus Tenendi Parliamentum,* Elsyng
judicature, *vide* House of Commons; House of Lords; Impeachment; *Modus Tenendi Parliamentum,* Elsyng, Book Two, chapter 4
office, 7, 8, 11, 12
petitions to, 60; receivers and triers of, 20, 31, 32; *vide Modus Tenendi Parliamentum,* Elsyng, chapter 7
petitions to the crown, 29, 31, 35, 38, 41, 47–55, 57, 58, 60–63; royal replies to, 29, 31, 35, 47, 53, 54, 60, 61; *vide* Petition of Right, 1628
prayers for, 13
procedure, 11, 31–34, 42–44, 48, 51–60, 62; *vide* House of Commons; House of Lords; Impeachment; *Modus Tenendi Parliamentum,* Elsyng
records, 7, 8, 12, 13, 33–35, 38, 42; *vide* Parliament, rolls; House of Commons; House of Lords; Statutes
rolls, 7–10, 12, 18, 23, 28–35, 38, 39, 42, 44, 50–57, 59; significance of, 34–35; *vide* Robert Bowyer, Henry Elsyng, Sir Thomas Smith, parliament rolls

prepared by; Index Precedents, rolls of parliament
speeches, copies, 10, 12, 25
supplies for, 13
Parliament, 1621-1629, 8, 12, 18, 29-37, 39, 40, 43-45, 48, 59; *vide* House of Commons; House of Lords; Petition of Right, 1628
Parliament, 1640, 45
Parliament, 1660, 6
Parliaments, Edward III, 36-37, 46, 50-54, 59; Parliament 1341, 36-37, 46-49, 54, 60-63; Parliament 1343, 46-49, 60, 62, 64; *vide* Index Precedents, cases and rolls of parliament
  Richard II, 53, 56, 59
  Henry IV, 56, 59
  Henry V, 54
  Henry VI, 54, 59
  Edward IV, 59
  Richard III, 59
  Henry VII, 59
  Henry VIII, 57, 59
  Mary I, 63
  Elizabeth I, 35, 59
  James I, 30, 59; *vide* Parliament, 1621-1629
  Charles I, 46-48, 59, 63-64; *vide* Parliament, 1621-1629
Paulet, John, Baron St. John of Basingstoke, 24
Peers, privileges of, 34, 42-43, 46, 48-49, 61, 62; roll of, 13; trial of, 16, 48, 61-62, *vide* Sir Francis Bacon, Lionel Cranfield, John Digby, John Stratford, George Villiers
Pembroke, Earl of, *vide* William Herbert
Percy, Henry, ninth Earl of Northumberland, 14
Petition of right, 34
Petition of Right, 1628, 5, 8, 9, 16, 17, 29, 30, 32-35, 49, 50; royal answers to, 17, 29, 32-35
Pettybag, office of, 11, 13, 20, 30
Phelips, Sir Robert, M.P., 34
Plesyngton, Robert de, *vide* Index Precedents, cases
Pope, *vide* Benedict XII, Clement VI
Precedents, 9, 11, 32-35, 38, 41, 42, 44-46, 48, 50-60; *vide* Index of Precedents
Prerogative, royal, 34, 36, 53, 54
Prior, St. Johns Jerusalem, precedency of, 24
Proclamations, 7, 13, 32, 35, 47, 62, 63
Proxies, 14, 24, 36, 37, 52; books and lists of, 12, 14; fees for, 10, 11
Prust, Captain John, muster master, 49
Prynne, William, 43
Puckering, Sir John, speaker of the House of Commons, 35

Pulton, Ferdinando, *Abridgement*, 13; edition of statutes, 7
Purbeck, Lady, *vide* Frances Villiers

Rastell, John, *Abridgement*, 13
Ravenscroft, William, clerk of the pettybag office, 20
Reading, importance of in parliament, 16
Records in the Tower, *vide* Tower of London, Keeper of the records in the Tower
Recusants, 9, 13
Religion, complaints concerning, 47-49, 63-64
Reynolds, Owen, assistant to clerk of the parliaments, 11, 17
Rich, Robert, second Earl of Warwick, 19, 22, 24, 25
Richard II, King of England, 38-40, 44, 52-56, 59
Richard III, King of England, 38-40, 54, 59
Richardson, Sir Thomas, speaker of the House of Commons, 30
Russell, Francis, fourth Earl of Bedford, 14

Sackville, Sir Edward, M.P., 25
Sackville, Richard, third Earl of Dorset, 27, 44
Sackville, Robert, second Earl of Dorset, 6
Sackville, Thomas, Lord Buckhurst, first Earl of Dorset, lord treasurer, 6
Sadington, Robert, lord chancellor, 62
St. Albans School, 5
St. Dunstan's in the West, 5
St. John, Lord, *vide* John Paulet
Salisbury, Earl of, *vide* Sir Robert Cecil; Index Precedents, cases
Sardis, Alexander, 43
Saye and Sele, Lord, *vide* William Fiennes
Scobell, Henry, clerk of the parliaments, 35
Scotland, 37, 51, 54, 59
Selden, John, 5, 12, 23, 33, 36, 38, 42, 44, 45; treatises by, 42, 43
Seymour, Edward, Earl of Hertford, 11
Silk-throwsters, bill for, 15-16
Smith, Sir Thomas, clerk of the parliaments, 11, 13; assistant to, 11; parliament rolls prepared by, 30, 32
Soldiers, 21, 51, 58
Spain, proposed marriage alliance, 1624, 8, 31, 37; treaties with, 9, 35, 37, 59; war with, 45
Speed, John, *History*, 13, 38
Spencer, Robert, Baron Spencer of Wormleighton, 23, 27
Star Chamber, court of, 44

Starkey, H., 23
Statutes, 7, 11, 12, 17-18, 29, 30-35, 38, 47, 57, 61-63; enrollment, *vide* Parliament, rolls; "printed book" and other editions, 7, 11, 13, 17, 28-30, 35, 52; royal repeal of, 47, 49, 60, 62
Stratford, John, Archbishop of Canterbury, 46, 47, 61
Subsidy, 18, 30, 34, 38-42, 45-49, 51-59, 61-64, *vide Modus Tenendi Parliamentum*, Elsyng, Book Two, chapter 2; conditions for, 53-56, 60-61; history, 38-42, 52-59; Lords' participation in grant of, 55-58; procedure, 11, 16, 31, 55-59; treasurers, 39, 45, 53-55
Subsidy, 1621-1629, 8, 16, 31-34, 45

Throckmorton, John, deputy clerk of the parliaments, 6, 12, 28
Tower of London, 7, 10; records in, 7, 22, 32, 34-36, 38; *vide* Keeper of the records in the Tower
Trade, increase of, 47, 49, 63
Tyrwhitt, Thomas, 37, 46

Vere, Henry de, eighteenth Earl of Oxford, lord chamberlain, 9-10, 14
Vere, Robert de, nineteenth Earl of Oxford, 9, 15, 20, 22, 24
Villiers, Frances, Lady Purbeck, 15
Villiers, George, first Duke of Buckingham, 5, 8, 9, 15, 22, 24, 27-28, 31, 33, 37, 42, 49
Viscounts, fees due to clerk from, 10

Wales, 37, 54
"War and Peace," *vide Modus Tenendi Parliamentum*, Elsyng, Book Two, chapter 1
Warwick, Earl of, *vide* Robert Rich
Watts, Abraham, 15
Wentworth, Sir Thomas, first Earl of Strafford, 42
Westminster, Palace of, 7, 8, 12-13, 19, 21, 37, 50
Weston, Sir Richard, lord chief baron of the Exchequer, 20, 49
Weston, William, *vide* Index Precedents, cases
Whitelocke, Sir James, M.P., and justice King's Bench, 27, 34
Whittam, Essex, 21
Wilkins, David, 43
Williams, John, Bishop of Lincoln, lord keeper, 9, 14-16, 29, 31, 33, 36, 37, 43
Willoughby, Lord, *vide* Robert Bertie
Wycliff, John, 62

Yelverton, Sir Henry, attorney general, 8, 18, 22, 27
York, dean and chapter of, 21

INDEX OF PRECEDENTS

CASES

Despenser, Sir Hugh, 15 E. II, 1 E. III, 59-60
Latimer, William, Lord, 50 E. III, 32
Lee, John de la, 42 E. III, 32

Lyons, Richard, 50 E. III, 32
Mautravers, John, 21 E. III, 51
Mortimer, Roger, Earl of March, 28 E. III, 60

Norwich, Bishop of, 7 R. II, 60
Plesyngton, Robert de, 7 R. II, 53
Salisbury, Earl of, 2 H. V, 60
Weston, William, 1 R. II, 44

ROLLS OF PARLIAMENT

1 E. III, 59–60
6 E. III, **41**
11 E. III, *vide Rot. Parl.,* 13 E. III, 54
13 E. III, 40, **41**, 51–59
14 E. III, **41**, 50, 51, 55, 57, 59, 60
15 E. III, 61–62
17–50 E. III, 36
18 E. III, **41**, 56–59
20 E. III, **41**, 58, 59
21 E. III, 58
22 E. III, 58, 59
25 E. III, 39, 54, 58, 59
27 E. III, 50–51
29 E. III, 51
36 E. III, **35**, 51
45 E. III, 59
46 E. III, 59
47 E. III, 56–59
51 E. III, 39, 55, 59
1–11 R. II, 53
2 R. II, 40, 53, 55
18 R. II, 58
21 R. II, 59–60
2 H. IV, 63
4 H. IV, 58
5 H. IV, 35, 53
6 H. IV, 53–54, 58
7 H. IV, 54
9 H. IV, 54
11 H. IV, 54
13 H. IV, 54
1 H. V, 58
7 H. V, 57, 58
31 H. VI, 41, 58

TRANSACTIONS

OF THE

AMERICAN PHILOSOPHICAL SOCIETY

HELD AT PHILADELPHIA
FOR PROMOTING USEFUL KNOWLEDGE

NEW SERIES—VOLUME 62
1972

THE AMERICAN PHILOSOPHICAL SOCIETY
INDEPENDENCE SQUARE
PHILADELPHIA

1972

CONTENTS OF VOLUME 62

PART 1. Maurus of Salerno. Twelfth-century "Optimus Physicus" with His Commentary on the Prognostics of Hippocrates. Now first transcribed from manuscript and translated into English by MORRIS HAROLD SAFFRON.

PART 2. Joseph Eötvös and the Modernization of Hungary, 1840–1870. PAUL BÖDY.

PART 3. Respiration and the Lavoisier Tradition: Theory and Modification, 1777–1850. CHARLES A. CULOTTA.

PART 4. Prehistoric Research in Afghanistan (1959–1966). LOUIS DUPREE, in collaboration with J. LAWRENCE ANGEL, ROBERT H. BRILL, EARLE R. CALEY, RICHARD S. DAVIS, CHARLES C. KOLB, ALEXANDER MARSHACK, DEXTER PERKINS, JR., and ALAN SOLEM.

PART 5. The Major Political Issues of the Jacksonian Period and the Development of Party Loyalty in Congress, 1830–1840. DAVID J. RUSSO.

PART 6. The Scientific Papers of James Logan. Edited by ROY N. LOKKEN.

PART 7. Burmese Earthworms: An Introduction to the Systematics and Biology of Megadrile Oligochaetes with Special Reference to Southeast Asia. G. E. GATES.

PART 8. The Painful Labour of Mr. Elsyng. ELIZABETH READ FOSTER.